AUTHORIZING EXPERIENCE

AUTHORIZING EXPERIENCE

REFIGURATIONS OF THE
BODY POLITIC IN
SEVENTEENTH-CENTURY
NEW ENGLAND WRITING

JIM EGAN

PRINCETON UNIVERSITY PRESS

PRINCETON, NEW JERSEY

Library of Congress Cataloging-in-Publication Data

Egan, Jim, 1961–
Authorizing experience : refigurations of the body politic in seventeenth-century
New England writing / Jim Egan.
p.   cm.
Includes bibliographical references and index.
ISBN 0-691-05949-7 (acid-free paper)
1. American literature—Colonial period, ca. 1600–1775—History and criticism.
2. Rhetoric—Political aspects—New England—History—17th century. 3. Politics and
literature—New England—History—17th century. 4. Literature and society—New
England—History—17th century. 5. American literature—New England—History
and criticism. 6. New England—Intellectual life—17th century. 7. Authority in literature.
8. Colonies in literature. I. Title.

PS191.E37 1999
810.9′358—dc21   98-30653 CIP

This book has been composed in Galliard

The paper used in this publication meets the minimum requirements
of ANSI/NISO Z39.48-1992 (R1997) (*Permanence of Paper*)

http://pup.princeton.edu

Printed in the United States of America

10 9 8 7 6 5 4 3 2 1

To Lisa

CONTENTS

ACKNOWLEDGMENTS

THIS PROJECT was supported by a fellowship from the John Nicholas Brown Center for the Study of American Civilization. I am especially grateful to the two directors of the Center during my fellowship, Robert Emlen and Joyce Botelho, as well as to the support of the Center's staff, Jane Hennedy and Denise Bastien. I was also fortunate to have the invaluable assistance of the librarians at both the John Hay Library and the John Carter Brown Library. I owe Daniel Slive and Susan Danforth special thanks for their help and support on this project.

I owe a debt of gratitude to those colleagues and friends who read parts of the manuscript at various stages and who helped make it say what I wanted it to say: Sharon Block, Joyce Chaplin, Stephen Foley, Mary Fuller, William Keach, Carla Mulford, and Ann Plane. I am especially grateful to the anonymous readers for Princeton University Press. And I want to thank my editor, A. Deborah Malmud, for her unflagging encouragement and support throughout the process. I thank her for all her efforts on behalf of this project. Chapter 2 appeared in a slightly different form in *Genre* 28 (1995): 445–64 as "'Hee That Hath Experience . . . to Subject the Salvages': British Colonialism and Modern Experiential Authority." I am indebted to Ronald Schleifer for his patience and suggestions. His comments helped me dramatically improve the essay that ultimately appeared, but they also helped me conceptualize my larger project at a crucial stage in its development.

The staff of the English department at Brown University has provided assistance and support above and beyond the call of duty. The help and encouragement they offered were of invaluable assistance. I would like to thank Heidi Ahmed, Margaret Lippka, Lorraine Mazza, Marilyn Netter, Bonny Tangui, and Ellen Viola. I extend my gratitude to Faye Halpern and Sarah Aldrich, the students who served as my assistants during this project. They provided not only assistance on the mundane tasks that had to be done but also important intellectual stimulation. Lloyd Pratt provided copyediting of the first-order. I offer him my thanks and appreciation for the diligence and care with which he read my prose. The Department of American Civilization at Brown provided air-conditioned office space during the summer when I was revising the manuscript. More than that, Robert Emlen, Robert Lee, and Susan Smulyan offered their encouragement, support, and comradeship during those months. I cannot thank them enough for so generously welcoming me into their community. The book would not be the same without their support.

I owe a special debt to the faculty at the University of California at Santa Barbara. They provided an intellectually stimulating and challenging environment that has proven invaluable in my professional development. What I have accomplished simply would not have been possible without Giles Gunn, Alan Liu, and Paul Hernadi. Zelda Bronstein helped me learn how to interrogate a text and an issue, and she generously gave her time, energy, and support.

At Brown, Leonard Tennenhouse offered support, encouragement, intellectual stimulation, and diversion over the years, the value of which I cannot measure. And no amount of thanks would be enough to express my gratitude to Nancy Armstrong for her support throughout this project. I owe her an incalculable debt.

I owe another kind of debt to the members of my family. My brother, Gordon Egan, and his family—Sylvia, Benjamin, and David—and my sister, Marie Wesenfeld and her family—Gordon, Carl, Susanna, and Gregory—for supporting me through the various upheavals in my life, for providing humor and perspective, and for being patient. Russell Egan, my father, has managed to put up with and even support me in ways that make me feel quite fortunate. Dorothy Egan, my mother, remains an inspiration to me. She exerts a profound influence and maintains a powerful presence in my life long after her death.

I am indebted to Garrett Sullivan and Tamar Katz in ways too numerous to mention. Their humor, patience, and support have helped me through some difficult moments, and they have helped make the joys even more pleasurable. They believed in me when I did not, and they knew precisely how to let me know this. I am honored to call them friends.

I am most indebted to Lisa. Without her, this book would not exist. Indeed, I cannot imagine my life without her.

AUTHORIZING EXPERIENCE

Introduction

INVERTING AMERICAN EXPERIENCE

AMERICA reveres few terms as passionately as it does "experience." No concept plays a more crucial role in the stories told about the nation's founding or in the reasons given for America's distinctive cultural features. That it was not ideology or theory that made America but experience is a story first told at least as far back as the Revolution. As Jack Greene has pointed out, the delegates to the Constitutional Convention in 1787 used the "concurring testimony of experience," "unequivocal experience," or "indubitable experience" to authorize their revolutionary actions and constitutional principles.[1] The frequency of the link made between "America" and "experience" in the more than two hundred years since Madison, Hamilton, and Franklin invoked it in order to form a more perfect union suggests that "America" is unthinkable without "experience."

While few today share such unqualified faith in the clarity of experiential knowledge, twentieth-century scholars of American culture continue to tell the story of America's founding as a struggle between experience and ideology. America begins, or so one line of thinking goes, when its first European colonists were unable to successfully map their "Old World" ideologies onto the experiences of a New World, Virgin Land, Unknown Coast, or Frontier.[2] Try as they might, the colonists couldn't keep things the same because experience simply would not allow it. No less an authority than Perry Miller, who has been credited with providing the foundation for the study of early American culture after World War II, argues that the "process of Americanization" must be understood as a product of the "irresistible" effects of the "American experience."[3] The New England Puritan plan, Miller wrote, was "defeat[ed]" because "life set up conflicts with ideology" that exposed unforeseen flaws in the original blueprint.[4] It was only after the colonists were able to forge a plan that was "phrased out of their own experience" that they achieved success.[5]

Subsequent scholars have given experience a more complicated role in the story of America's beginning even while they continue the tradition of regarding experience as a way of knowing exempt from historicization.[6] Sacvan Bercovitch, Miller's most influential successor in early

American studies, made it impossible for those studying American culture ever again to regard experience as a source of pure knowledge.[7] Bercovitch argues in *The American Jeremiad* that in America "virtually all thought and behavior," including experience, is intertwined with the "ideological hegemony" that he claims came to dominate American cultural life.[8] Thus, in Bercovitch's story of America's founding, ideology and experience are so closely tied to one another that they can never be entirely distinguished. It is a testament to the power of American experiential rhetoric rather than any failure on his part that the lure of experience proves too strong for even so cogent a critic as Bercovitch to resist.[9] In arguing that the jeremiad was successful in providing "a source of social cohesion and continuity" only insofar as it was able to explain "away the gap between fact and ideal," Bercovitch takes "experience" to be the "facts" for which ideology must provide an explanation.[10] Thus, even when he holds rhetoric responsible for America's distinctive ideological features, he still regards experience as the ultimate causal force against which ideology is constantly judged.[11] In this way Bercovitch casts experience as an existential problem from which we cannot escape rather than as a historical one that our forebears have in some way helped produce in the very writings early Americanists study.[12]

Some scholars dissent, pointing out that the story told by Miller, Bercovitch, and a host of others restricts the range of experience that counts as "American." Rather than propose a single experiential starting point for American culture, advocates of a multicultural approach to American literary studies such as Paul Lauter suggest we think of America beginning with the "particular experiences of" the many different groups of "people" representing the various ethnic, gender, and class categories that ultimately produced the patchwork quilt that now constitutes American life.[13] Indeed, this specifically experiential diversity serves as the conceptual glue holding together early American studies at a time when the very assumptions that have constituted the field have come under attack.[14] Frank Shuffelton claims in his introduction to *A Mixed Race* that what links the contributors to this volume is their shared belief "that ethnic variety was a positive fact, an enrichment, of American experience."[15] He hopes, in fact, that this volume will encourage scholars of early American literature to pay more attention to how "ethnic experience" plays a significant role in the development of the "so-called American experience."[16] But while this valuation of multicultural experience expands the range of what qualifies as "genuinely American" experience, it does so by extending the logic of experiential origins that served as the foundation for previous studies of American literature. After all, if experience produces culture, and if America is the result of many cultures coming together, then multiculturalism simply provides a theoretical justification for investigating the various points of experiential origin.[17]

Even those scholars who insist that we can only understand America's development into a multicultural society if we examine how cultural diversity results from colonization and imperialism both inside and outside the United States rely on experience to make their case. Amy Kaplan argues that the traditional "conceptual borders" that determine what does and does not count as American have led scholars to "disavow" the "multiple histories of continental and overseas expansion, conquest, conflict, and resistance which have shaped the cultures of the United States and the cultures of those it has dominated within and beyond its geopolitical boundaries."[18] And what missing piece does Kaplan hope to reclaim with her new method? She argues that by treating American culture as postcolonial we will no longer be blinded to "the historical experience of imperialism."[19]

But perhaps the most compelling revision of the origins of American culture among scholars of early American literature has come from those who have suggested that we pay more attention to the British-American colonies outside New England. Philip Gura, for instance, argues that in order to locate "the archetypal formulations of American selfhood" early American literature scholars must shift their attention "from New England to the Chesapeake (or to the middle colonies)."[20] But those like Gura who advocate a move south rely as much on experience to found their critique as Miller—among others—did to establish the preeminence of New England in America's story. For these critics of the field's myopic focus on New England use the work of social historian Jack Greene to make their case, and Greene bases his critique of the New England focus in early American studies on what he argues are the "atypicality of the experience of orthodox puritan New England and the normative character of that of the Chesapeake."[21] So while we will no doubt learn a great deal from investigating the long-neglected texts of the Southern colonies, the category of experience will continue to be the gold for which American literature scholars mine early modern writing.

Despite signs of its secure position as the foundational category in American literary studies, the very fact that Bercovitch would like to replace experience with ideology has proved sufficiently threatening to make some scholars develop theoretical justifications for the study of experience in what they call an age of ideology. Indeed, the opening sentences of the most widely praised book in this movement, Andrew Delbanco's *The Puritan Ordeal*, announce its commitment to the study of experience.[22] Delbanco proclaims that his book "is about the experience of becoming American in the seventeenth century" and distinguishes it from Bercovitch's on the grounds that his will study "those aspects of human experience which remain at least partly free from ideological co-ercion."[23] Though Delbanco positions himself against Bercovitch, I would suggest that their attempts to explain the origins of a distinctly American culture share certain basic assumptions: both posit experience and ideology as opposing categories and see experience as the underly-ing cause for the creation of a national identity. Like the multicultural-ists' critique of the exclusionary practices of American literary studies, the dispute between Delbanco and Bercovitch is one of degree rather than kind. They establish certain truths to be self-evident in agreeing to disagree over others.

The fact that scholars from so many different critical camps regard experience as a category whose value has always already been acknowl-edged in American writing should be enough to make us pause. How, we might wonder, did this particular category come to be so highly re-garded that it could escape our scrutiny for so long? Indeed, the very idea that the American nation could have emerged from the "facts" of American experience raises some disturbing questions none of these scholars has taken up. I think it is safe to say that all the scholars I have mentioned would agree that experience was not granted such a place of honor in the discursive systems brought across the Atlantic by the first American colonists. Indeed, scholars have long acknowledged the im-portant role European ways of thinking played in colonial American writing. As Howard Mumford Jones argued long ago, "[s]eventeenth-century New England writing . . . began in the Renaissance."[24] How, then, do we explain how experience suddenly came to be valued in Eu-rope and the colonies in an unprecedented way in the late seventeenth and early eighteenth centuries? If people on both sides of the Atlantic understood experiential knowledge to be inferior to the knowledge ob-tained from the ancients or various holy books, then experience itself would not have transformed anyone's cultural practices. Something else must have caused those changes. If one argues that the colonists' Ameri-can experience proved uniquely able to overcome such prejudices, then why had experience failed to do so before? Are we to believe that people had been able to denigrate the category throughout human history until America was colonized by English men and women? Was the experience of a group of English immigrants huddled along an unfamiliar coast so uniquely powerful that it was the first experience able to demonstrate to the world the power of experience to overcome ideology and work di-rectly on the individual's consciousness? Virtually none of these issues have been satisfactorily explained.

Once we recognize that experience emerges from a historical change that experience itself could not have brought about, we must, I believe, turn our attention elsewhere in order to explain the features of American national culture. We must turn to writing. I am not the first to suggest the crucial role of writing in early American culture. Myra Jehlen has argued in *The Cambridge History of American Literature* that "'America' was conceived under the sign of the printing press."[25] She contends that colonial writing helped bring about "a redefinition of writing" which held that "writing could wield material power in shaping history."[26] It is one of the ways in which New English colonial writing shaped history that I will be investigating in this book. I will demonstrate that writing is what makes geographic separation count. As historians such as Peter Dear and Steven Shapin have shown, the seventeenth and eighteenth centuries witnessed a transformation concerning the definition and use of experience and its relationship to authority. So, according to Shapin and Dear, early modern English writers who used experience to claim authority for their position first had to endow that category with a rhetorical authority it had lacked up until the seventeenth century.[27]

What I am suggesting is that the colonial British-American writers had to argue for the very authority of experience that Miller, Bercovitch, and American literary scholarship in general now take as given. Their colonial experience was not something the seventeenth-century writers I will be discussing could invoke to support their view of the colonies' relation to England and thus how they should be governed. Both the colonists and their English counterparts understood "experience" to be an upstart newcomer that potentially challenged the traditional positions of power established by rank and proximity to the king. Thus men such as John Smith, William Wood, and John Winthrop who served at the pleasure of the king in New England had to find a way of neutralizing the offense of contradicting the traditional terms of authority the king embodied as they established another grounding for rhetoric that strengthened their position as colonial subjects. They would not, I contend, have felt so compelled to defend their turn to experience had experience been generally understood as the best source of knowledge. In marked contrast to their early modern predecessors, Miller and Bercovitch never find it necessary to defend experiential evidence. Since it seems only common sense to twentieth-century American scholars that experience provides the most reliable form of knowledge, we tend to quickly pass over seventeenth-century references to experience. But this word we dismiss as mere rhetoric is important for precisely that reason: it identifies experience as a rhetorical category in need of legitimation. It is the history of the term's passage from an upstart form of self-legitimation to a descriptive theory and set of rhetorical tropes virtually identical to New World geography and the cultural rules governing those who inhabited it that I want to trace in this book.

In order to examine the way in which early American writers authorized experience and produced a rhetorical system distinctive to the colonies, I have inverted the interpretive model used by previous scholars of colonial American writing. Whereas they consider how the colonial experience changed established European belief systems to create a uniquely American culture, I will examine many of the very same writers to see how they use the category of experience to reimagine the possibilities for social authority in a specifically colonial setting. Sensitive to the threat experiential authority posed to established social hierarchies, writers such as John Smith, William Wood, John Winthrop, Anne Bradstreet, Benjamin Tompson, and William Hubbard use experience, I argue, to authorize a supplementary status system that would at once enhance England's economic, political, and spiritual status and provide a new basis for regulating both English and native populations. The arguments advanced by these writers in support of English colonialism, as I hope to demonstrate, ultimately helped produce an alternative model of nationalism and individual subject formation.

My first chapter explores the question of what happens to the figure of the monarch's body, a figure used to link the well-being of the nation to that of the monarch in a rather straightforward iconographic equation, when that body is supplanted by a body representing colonial experience. When colonial writers sought to allay fears of what foreign climates would do to English bodies, they were also—and more importantly—assuaging concerns over how such exposure to alien environments threatened both the bodily terms in which English monarchy was imagined and the social order that such an imaginary body sustained. The rhetorical problem confronting colonial writers was to represent England in such a way that Englishmen remained English even when they were no longer living in England. At the same time, they had to make it absolutely clear that in adding to the monarch's body they were in no way impeaching its autonomy, authority, or well-being. In this effort to counter the age-old argument that the "strange and alien" conditions in the colonies adversely affected English bodies, eroding their Englishness, these same writers inadvertently revised early modern theories of the body politic. Moreover, they did so in a way that would eventually endow what I call the English common body with an authority very much resembling that to which Locke would lay claim later in the century. By making each Englishman the head of his own "little commonwealth," this way of figuring the nation displaced the double body of the monarch legitimating early modern political authority with terms we have come to identify as distinctly modern.

My second chapter examines a crucial first step in establishing the rhetorical authority of experience: the disassociation to a form of knowledge specific to life in the colonies from knowledge based on rank and the privileges of a noble education. I read the promotional tracts of Captain John Smith (1580–1631), a sometimes colonial governor and a longtime advocate of English colonization in North America, as arguing that administrative authority should be vested in what he calls "men of experience" rather than granted a priority to men of rank. In his attempt to authorize the "man of experience," Smith provides him with the sanction of God, traces his history to Roman colonial policies, and casts him as integral to the exploitation of colonial commodities. Having done so, however, Smith confronts the other side of the coin of inherited power: what is to prevent anyone from claiming authority over their social superiors were experience to become the source of status? To neutralize the threat his model poses to the very principle of social hierarchies, Smith limits the man of experience's authority to the colonies and restricts the kinds of experience that constitute the basis for authority even there.

But this solution leads to an even thornier problem: if colonial experience were to replace rank as the source of authority for colonial administrators and if experience of place actually did determine national character, as was commonly believed, what is to ensure the very Englishness of those in charge? Chapter 3 explores this question in the promotional tract *New Englands Prospect* (1634) by William Wood, a resident of New England in its initial years.[28] In order to demonstrate that "English bodies" would not be adversely affected by the "strange and alien" world of the colonies, Wood insinuates that colonial experience makes Englishmen more English than they were back in England. The working body he attributes to colonial Englishmen is, he contends, closer to the original English body than the one sported by his relatively idle counterparts back in Europe. Wood uses this figure of the colonial body as the ultimate ground for national community, supplanting though not out and out rejecting the image of the monarch's body as the figure of English unity and permanence. In doing so, I will argue, Wood slides gender hierarchies in place of those based on rank. His notion of administrative authority rests on that of the colonial woman in implicit submission to the masculine body of the monarch. For Wood, experience is both masculinizing and conveniently feminine as he moves rhetorically back and forth, on the one side asserting an alternative authority to that of the king while on the other subordinating his authority to that of the king's, all the while attempting to negotiate this apparent contradiction.

New England writers adapt the figure of the colonial body to establish hierarchies *within* colonial society and to regulate behavior accordingly. In chapter 4, I examine how the gendered logic implied in the colonial body politic plays out in the Antinomian controversy (1636–38), one of the earliest and most influential of seventeenth-century New England's political and religious disputes. In telling the story of the controversy to an English audience, Massachusetts Bay's supporters cast a group of colonists—whom they call "Antinomians"—as a "Plague" attacking the colonial body. To calculate the effects of the figure of the plague on the body politic, I focus on the work considered not only the "first and most authoritative history of the Controversy" but also a book that "set the conceptual terms for recounting the crisis" used by later chroniclers—John Winthrop's *A Short Story of the Rise, reign, and ruine of the Antinomians, Familists, & Libertines* (1644).[29] Winthrop argues that the Antinomian "infection" is spread through the doctrine of experience. The only way to save the imaginary colonial body from "diseased opinions" regarding experience, Winthrop contends, is through recourse to an elaborate bureaucracy established by Massachusetts Bay's magistrates and church elders. For such a bureaucratic system to work, according to Winthrop, a subtle but terribly significant shift in the national self-image is required. This new bureaucracy must treat the national body as if it were made up of many different households rather than simply twin figures wherein the common body must subordinate itself to the aristocratic. This emphasis on the household as the fundamental component of the social body brings with it another alteration in the traditional figure of the national body. Winthrop's rhetoric suggests that the elevation of the common body to the status of national self-image must be accompanied by an increased emphasis on sexual hierarchies in order to ensure that this common body does not become an unruly one.

While the writings of those who were victorious in the Antinomian controversy succeed in making gender the officially sanctioned rationale for the regulation of the body politic, these writings do not entirely purge from colonial discourse the earlier sexless model of the corporate body I have associated with Hutchinson. By looking at Anne Bradstreet's poetry (1630–68), I will argue that Bradstreet held out for an earlier, sexless model of the body of the spiritual community—much as Hutchinson had—throughout her career, and that the persistence of her position throughout her writing demonstrates the existence of a alternative model of the body politic that implied an alternative view of experience within New England discourse.[30] Bradstreet did not share Preparationism's commitment to a "conversion experience" that was best represented as a progressive narrative whereby experience on earth—in clearly identifiable stages—prepared the unregenerate body for translation into the form it would assume through salvation.[31] On the contrary, her poetry rejects the view being advanced by Hutchinson's opponents, the view that experience determines one's individual and communal identity. Instead of positing an opposition between male and female bodily experience, from which individual and communal identities can be said to grow, Bradstreet renounces the experience of the body altogether. Earthly experience, she contends, does nothing to prepare the natural body for its translation into the spiritual one to be had in heaven by those fortunate enough to be saved.

In the second half of the seventeenth century, as New English Puritanism loses its monopoly on political and cultural authority and English political authorities threaten to revoke colonial charters, New English writers turn away from the corporate spiritual body that had served as the figure linking colonial subjects to the ideal English social body. Writers in the final decades of the century use the rhetoric of experience to show how colonial political self-government derives from a body politic that grows out of the colonial ground itself and, as such, is separate from the English communal body. Experience, I argue, fills in for religious ideology as the source of communal identity. My final chapter examines how this process of substitution works in William Hubbard's *A Narrative of the Troubles with the Indians* (1677) and Benjamin Tompson's *New Englands Crisis* (1676). Rejecting the religious interpretation of King Philip's war offered by Increase Mather in his *A Brief History of the War with the Indians* (1676), Hubbard, a New England minister, and Tompson, the son of a minister, nonetheless adopt Mather's representation of the war as a collective experience for New Englanders. It is their experience of native savagery that binds the colonists together, they suggest, not the spiritual covenant that Mather cum Winthrop continues to invoke. Hubbard and Tompson suggest that the colonies as a territory are becoming English as English lives and labor mix with its soil. On the one hand, community identity depends on sharing an imagined experience of native violence, but on the other, the very need to imagine experience as collective sets the colonial community apart from that of European Englishmen. I conclude by showing how Hubbard's and Tompson's use of experience inscribes colonial subjects with distinctively individual and protomodern political identities as well.

My decision to focus on writings from New England may seem counterprogressive given that these colonies are no longer seen as the birthplace of American culture.[32] Whereas once early American literary scholarship seemed "synonymous with 'Puritan'" studies, Puritanism is now seen as only one of the many factors that contributed to the development of a distinctly American culture.[33] David Shields, for instance, states flatly that "New England did not originate the British American self."[34] I have no quarrel with the removal of New England from its position as father of all that is truly American, nor am I in sympathy with those who have wondered if the literature of the other colonies will prove "equal" to that produced by the Puritans.[35] On the contrary, it seems to me that we will learn at least as much about both seventeenth-century culture and the development of a distinctly American society from the writings produced in colonies that have hitherto been neglected in our obsessive return to all things New England.

I have chosen to focus exclusively on writings from New England so that I might analyze the rhetoric of experience within a single colonial discursive community.[36] New England provides an excellent opportunity for such a study since, as Shields argues, it stands out among early modern British-American colonies precisely "in its sense of aggregate identity."[37] I hope to show that the rhetoric of experience played an indispensable part in the production of a New England identity that simultaneously linked and distinguished New English subjects from those in England as well as all those living in England's other colonies across the globe. How the rhetoric of experience was put to use in other English colonial writing or, for that matter, how it bears on the constitution of "experience" in other seventeenth-century discursive fields in which it appears in the seventeenth century, requires further investigation. My focus on the way that New English representations of the experienced colonial body refigured English power prevents me from following the transformation of political authority the rhetoric of experience helped effect across all of eighteenth-century Europe. Indeed, I make no claims that my account represents a comprehensive history of the rhetoric of experience. I do hope, however, that my analysis of the use of this rhetoric in New England writing will be suggestive for other scholars who wish to understand the emergence of what we like to think of as the distinctly modern ways of imagining our relations with ourselves, each other, and the world of objects, especially what we consider to be modern forms of subjectivity and nationalism.[38]

By examining some of the major writings of New England Puritanism, this book will provide some new insight into the American doctrine of experience. Rather than offer yet another argument in which experience (or experiences) constitute(s) the starting point(s) for American culture, I will argue that in order to understand how experience came to be valued at all, one must examine the writing that made experience an important category and a source of rhetorical as well as political authority. I have no interest in uncovering yet another, perhaps truer or more central experience that lies behind the written word. If such moments of revelation do exist, I have no idea of how to sift through the language used to describe them and determine which accurately represents the unmediated experience the writer was struggling mightily to convey. I am confident, however, that we can interrogate the discursive systems that help lend authority to certain ways of understanding our interaction with each other and the rest of the material world. My project is simply to reexamine one of the foundational categories of our analysis of literature and culture, on the assumption that other constructs such as nation, gender, race, and individual have all come to depend in one way or another on this foundation we call "experience." By understanding the experienced body as a rhetorical construct as well as a fact of life, I want to suggest that these and other seemingly ahistorical and purely descriptive categories are bound up in a system of representation in which we, as scholars of early American literature, are the inheritors. We have to use it to think with, but whether we do so as self-consciously as our colonial forebears did remains to be seen.

Chapter One

HOW THE ENGLISH BODY BECOMES THAT OF THE ENGLISH NATION

AMONG seventeenth-century arguments against the English colonization of North America, none were more powerful than those based on climate. To be sure, native inhabitants were thought to pose a danger to the colonists. And, as if the threat of native violence were not enough to deter prospective colonists, opponents of colonization could offer a laundry list of other reasons why colonization efforts should be abandoned. Their reasons included but were not limited to problems such as the logistics of transporting sufficient numbers of people to various parts of the globe, the economics of financing those expeditions and the colonies themselves, and the ethics of taking land that rightfully belonged to another. For their part, promoters of colonization developed ready responses to each of these objections. The Native American threat, for example, was countered by claims that the technologically and culturally inferior peoples of the New World would gladly adopt English ways once they recognized the superiority of those ways.

Climate proved a uniquely daunting obstacle to expansionist policy, mainly because the early modern English believed that the English body was especially suited to the English climate.[1] Consequently, colonization's opponents could effectively argue that colonization would fail, no matter how much money, time, and effort were expended, and that, despite the fact these efforts might temporarily enrich the monarch, in the long run English bodies could not survive in temperatures foreign to their native England. Drawing their data from Classical authors, early modern English intellectuals held that the world was divided into five zones, and those born in one zone would die if they attempted to live in another. As Richard Eden explained in 1561, "[a]ll the inhabitants of the worlde are fourmed and disposed of suche complexion and strength of body, that every [one] of them are proportionate to the Climate assigned unto them."[2] Given this belief that English bodies were naturally equipped to survive only in England, colonial promotion writers had to show the limitations of this theory bonding the body to place, even if they could not entirely disprove it.

George Best, for one, devotes his entire tract, *Experiences and reasons of the Sphere, to proove all partes of the worlde habitable* (1578), to countering the claim that English subjects could not survive in other climates. Since "blacke Moores [and] Aethiopians . . . can well endure the colde of our Countrey," Best concluded, "why should not we as well abide the heate of their Country?"[3] The "experience of . . . thousands . . . to the East and West Indies" disproves climatological theories, he suggests, since English bodies are at least as strong as the bodies of those peoples whose survival in alien habitats cannot be explained by the five-zone theory of climatology.[4] But, during the initial years of colonization, such appeals to experience alone made little headway against "age-old ideas of environmental influence."[5]

Nor did attempts to appropriate the theory of climate in support of colonial expansion. Such appropriation maintained that English colonists adapted so rapidly to local conditions that their bodies could withstand the alien weather. This line of argument failed, however, because it was believed that adjusting to a foreign climate would mean sacrificing whatever it was that made Englishmen English. As Clarence J. Glacken has pointed out, English writers during the first hundred years of colonization understood the relationship between "environment and national character" as a causal one.[6] Nathaniel Carpenter claims in *Geography Delineated Forth in Two Bookes* (1625) that "[c]olonies transplanted from one region into another, farre remote, retaine a long time their first disposition, though by litle and litle they decline and suffer alteration."[7] Climate, terrain, flora, and fauna were thought to determine the character of different cultures, which in turn determined the kind of people who lived there. Such a view of identity meant that, as Karen Ordahl Kupperman has written, "[p]eople considering or promoting emigration feared . . . the possibility that in leaving England they might be leaving their Englishness also."[8] Attempting to defend against this very fear, Richard Eburne suggests in *A Plain Pathway to Plantations* (1624) that those who are concerned about losing their Englishness in the colonies should "imagine all that to be England where Englishmen . . . do dwell."[9] Thus Eburne sought to reverse the established principle which said that place defined people: "it be people that makes the land English, not the land the people."[10]

The English belief that their own rather dreadful climate was what made them who they were has long been noted.[11] Kupperman has used the dogged persistence of English "preconceptions" about the relation of climate to identity as a way to assess "the interaction between perception and reality" in the colonies,[12] while John Canup takes the colonists' arguments over climate to show that colonial Englishmen "became, despite themselves, American."[13] Finally, Joyce Chaplin traces modern racial classification rooted in the body to the debates over how the English body would fare in foreign climates.[14] Each of these arguments has a great deal to tell us about the relationship between colonial debates over the climate and our own epistemological, national, and racial assumptions. None, however, attends to the crucial role that bodily images played in legitimizing early modern political authority.

In fact, the English fear that an alien climate would adversely affect English bodies was overdetermined by what Michel Foucault calls "the political investment of the body" in early modern discourse.[15] When colonial writers sought to allay fears of foreign climates and these climates' effects on English bodies, they were also (even if inadvertently) assuaging concerns that exposure to alien environments threatened both the English monarchy—imagined, as it was, in bodily terms—and the social order that such an imaginary body sustained. So while it is tempting to dismiss climatological objections as the rantings of narrow-minded naysayers who might similarly demonize anything new, these objections are, in fact, symptomatic of a pervasive and systematic way of understanding the world. This understanding may now appear alien to us, but this is precisely because later colonial writings made it so. When opponents to colonialization sought to elicit fear of foreign climates and their effect on the social body, their appeal gained its legitimacy from a premodern discursive system, a system replaced by the kind of thinking or discourse of experience this book will investigate. In what follows in this chapter, though, I want to link this fear of foreign climates to a historically specific model of national identity and show how the "colonial experience" was used quite literally to rewrite that national model in terms we now think of as distinctly modern.

Michel Foucault's description of a "Classical episteme" offers us a way to understand just how the anticolonialists could believe in and base their objections to colonization on an indissoluble bond between place and person. For Foucault contends that in the Classical episteme, which includes fifteenth- and sixteenth-century English and Anglo-American writing, "adjacency is not an exterior relation between things, but the sign of the relationship."[16] "Proximity" indicates a "similutude" between things "upon which is superimposed a resemblance that is the visible effect of that proximity."[17] The anticolonialists could believe that because bodies were literally *placed* by nature in a particular environment, it was no coincidence that Englishmen lived in England. This placement became, under the Classical episteme, a sign of an affinity between bodies and their native soil. Englishmen were put in England, it was thought, precisely because of a similarity between body and place that might be "obscure" or "hidden" but which nonetheless existed. Such bonds in Classical taxonomic systems were fixed, immutable. "The same remains the same," Foucault argues, "riveted onto itself."[18] Thus, to take a body born on English soil out of England was to break the tie between place and person. Losing your place meant, quite literally, losing your identity.

While the belief in the bond between person and place helps explain how geographical displacement, then, could elicit fear, the climatological argument depended as well on the fact that early modern discourses represented the material bodies within a region as together constituting a single idealized body. According to R. H. Tawney in *Religion and the Rise of Capitalism* (1926), European writers prior to the Renaissance imagined society to be an "organism . . . like the human body."[19] This way of imagining society was so pervasive, Tawney contends, that "[f]rom the twelfth century to the sixteenth" the image of the social body was "[i]nvoked in every economic crisis to rebuke . . . dissension with a . . . doctrine of social solidarity."[20] In order for the social body to survive, "a system of mutual, though varying, obligations" must exist among the members of society.[21] The image of a social body whose component parts had clearly defined roles authorized European monarchies by portraying the monarch as necessary to his subjects, in the same way that the head was necessary to the other parts of the body. The survival of the nation, like that of the body, depended on the hierarchical subordination of lower stratum to the rule of the head. This theory of early modern culture—nation as body—has been a scholarly commonplace for many years.

More recent studies have suggested that earlier scholarship was hindered by the assumption that "the body" could provide the model for earlier forms of political power without itself being part of the system of signs that displayed and, in the act of display, helped sustain monarchical rule. Critical of this fundamentally ahistorical use of "the body," recent scholarship insists that there is no such thing as a natural body, or body itself.[22] As Peter Stallybrass and Allon White have argued, "the body is neither a purely natural given nor is it merely a textual metaphor," but a relationship between the social environment one actually experiences and the available ways of textualization: "thinking the body is thinking social topography and vice versa."[23] The physical impact of power relations on members of a population is always, by definition, a symbolic inscription that represents and enforces itself in a single blow. In early modern culture, these inscriptions always rectified the hierarchical relation of head to body.

From his study of the rituals accompanying early modern executions, Foucault concluded that the criminal behavior that allegedly prompted the executions was, in fact, thought to challenge the monarch, the head who rules with "discretionary power" over the bodies of his subjects:

"according to the law of the classical age," criminal behavior "attacks the sovereign physically" since the monarch is the figurative "head of justice."[24] Such acts threaten the social order because they attack the very figure responsible for maintaining that order. Since the figure for political order is the same as that for the social order, an attack on the head of justice, the monarch, constitutes "an injury done to . . . [the] kingdom."[25] All crimes were thus seen as political crimes because they threatened the figurative body politic; all crimes required as well "that the king take revenge for an affront to his very person."[26] The elaborate punishments performed on prisoners laid out on the scaffold, which Foucault describes in *Discipline and Punish,* thus restore the monarch to his rightful position as the "head." They display the "physical strength of the sovereign beating down the body of his adversary and mastering it," and in so doing affirm the relation between the monarch's body and those of the onlookers.[27]

Foucault's reading of torture illustrates that while all bodies within a realm were invested with political significance, the sovereign's body was exponentially more important. Scholars investigating a wide range of early modern discourses from this perspective have demonstrated that images of the monarch's natural body had to adapt to changing historical conditions. Leonard Tennenhouse shows that in Renaissance drama "aesthetic performances centered in the figure of the queen were entirely political, as they aimed at identifying the monarch's body with English power in all its manifestations."[28] But the precise forms and effects of these bodily displays were not static. As Tennenhouse argues, "the politics of the body is susceptible to historical change."[29] Richard Helgerson's investigation of sixteenth- and early-seventeenth-century maps has shown how early modern English maps "strengthened the sense of both local and national identity at the expense of an identity" derived from the image of "Elizabeth herself."[30] Cartographic images quite literally pushed one "system of authority," the body of the queen, off the page in order to make room for a new "source of legitimacy" that we would come to see as "the land itself."[31] Working the other side of the channel, Roger Chartier goes so far as to "hypothesize" that the French Revolution itself was made possible by a "crisis" in printed representations of the "political body of the realm."[32] What he calls "a new way of looking at the king," which began under Louis XIV, "undermined the absolute authority" that the *ancien régime* had placed in the "sacramental body of the king."[33]

While all representations of the body can be called political, not all representations of the body can be said to demonstrate the principle that society was like a body with the monarch as its head. Mikhail Bakhtin's analysis of various early modern symbolic practices argues that Renaissance regimes maintained their positions of dominance by the careful rhetorical use of a binary opposition between a "classical body" and a "popular body."[34] Bakhtin identified the "classical body" as a body that figured as a permanent, closed system that manages to avoid all signs of porousness or lack. This body consequently could "not merge with other bodies" but had to present itself as "a strictly completed, finished product . . . fenced off from all other bodies."[35] Such a body inhabited the "palaces, churches, institutions, and private homes"; in short, this was the body of the "ruling classes."[36] The popular body was ideally subordinated to the classical body and, in this subordinated state, could even be contained within it, as in the frontispiece to Hobbes' *Leviathan*, where the body of the monarch is "composed of a multitude of obedient subjects turned to face their sovereign head."[37]

Thus the idealized, hierarchical representation of the social body politic always implies a second or "other" body that is the enemy of hierarchy and Classical closure. Such a body is supplied by the popular body in its carnivalesque phase, or what Bakhtin calls the "grotesque body." The grotesque body possesses the chaotic, ever-changing, and material qualities associated with the populace in general. Because it is "unfinished, outgrows itself, [and] transgresses its own limits," this body cannot be "separated from the world by clearly defined boundaries."[38] Whenever it does thus get out of place, the popular body enters into its grotesque phase and turns order into its opposite, disorder. Representation helps the state retain its coherence through time; it subordinates the common body to the aristocratic body so as to insist that the welfare of the aristocracy is virtually identical to that of the nation.

In *The Politics and Poetics of Transgression*, Stallybrass and White have famously used Bakhtin's binary model to study what they call "class society" using "a political anthropology of binary extremism."[39] Their study of "the formation of the cultural Imaginary of the middle class in post-Renaissance Europe" takes Bakhtin's bifurcation of the social body as "fundamental . . . to mechanisms of ordering and sense-making in European cultures." From this they extrapolate the principle that "the classifactory body of a culture is always double, always structured in relation to its negation, its inverse."[40] Modern identity is formed, they contend, in "*the very struggle to exclude the . . . grotesque*" from the imaginary body of bourgeois democracy.[41] In making their case, Stallybrass and White represent modern collective identity as an inevitable process of exclusion and repulsion between discrete social bodies. But their binary model provides a convincing method of interpretation from the sixteenth century straight through to Freud's late-nineteenth-century hermeneutic only because they exclude the colonies from consideration. In colonial writing, a new image of the social body emerged, one that shared certain characteristics with but was still distinct from either the grotesque or Classical bodies.

It is in relation to this problematic of the monarch's two bodies that the issue of climate becomes so important. In order to overcome the argument that a colonial climate necessarily robbed Englishmen of their Englishness, colonial writers had to articulate a new rhetoric of the body that would allow Englishmen to remain English even when they were no longer living in England. In arguing over their claim to Englishness, the colonists necessarily involved themselves in ongoing debates over what it meant to be English in the first place.[42] In order to make their claim to Englishness—whatever it might be—stick, these authors had to revise the theory of the social body on which early modern political identity depended, and they had to do so without sounding as if climate had already led them to think and write like disloyal English subjects. It is to this refiguring of social power that I would now like to turn.

Before they could even begin to persuade readers back in England that establishing subjects in a different climate could benefit the body politic, colonial authors had to demonstrate that living in a different climate did nothing to compromise one's political identity. They did so by transforming the very basis of English identity, reimagining the body politic as dependent for its stability and perpetuity on the body's ability to grow, rather than on the head's ability to contain and subordinate that body. It is this refiguring of the social body in colonial New England writing that I would like to sketch out as the foundation for my analysis of how the rhetoric of experience authorized alternative conceptions of personal and political power.

Leonard Barkan pointed out long ago that "Renaissance England represents . . . the heyday of the anthropomorphic image of the commonwealth."[43] Any number of scholars of the English Renaissance have since described the rhetorical use to which images of the body were put during the first years of English colonization.[44] These studies argue that political authority in England was more specifically invested in the monarch's body while in continental European monarchies "the sovereignty of the state [was located] specifically in the crown."[45] For the monarch's body to serve as a figure for perpetual state power required a rhetorical sleight of hand, however, since even though any given monarch's body invariably died, the monarchy itself was meant to continue. Ernst Kantorowicz contends that political theorists in mid-sixteenth-century England resolved this conceptual dilemma by adapting early Christian ecclesiological thought, which said that Jesus could be both man and God, both human and divine. Just as Jesus was said to possess "Two Natures" in one body, the English monarch was said to occupy two bodies at once, a body natural and a body politic.[46] So, Marie Axton argues in relation to Elizabeth, the monarch's "natural body was subject to infancy, infirmity, error, and old age; her body politic, created out of a combination of faith, ingenuity and practical expediency was held to be unerring and immortal."[47] This "physiological" way of authorizing monarchical rule became, according to Kantorowicz, "the ordinary and conventional" way of thinking about royal power in early modern England.[48]

But the monarchy's political authority required a step that ecclesiological logic did not provide, namely, succession. The power of Jesus' dual nature lay precisely in its uniqueness, in the fact that such a dual nature would and could never be duplicated in human history. By contrast, for the state to retain its authority in perpetuity some explanation would have to be offered for the transferal of the body politic from one natural body to another. The solution lay in the idea of a corporate body that could be distinguished from other natural bodies. Since succession was already determined by descent within the aristocracy, it was argued that the body politic was transferred through blood. The authority of the monarchy, like its perpetuity, thus depended on the careful monitoring of aristocratic blood or, in short, on its purity.

By the end of the seventeenth century, however, we can observe certain changes in the way that English political authority was legitimized. Indeed, one of the most influential philosophers of the late seventeenth century used a common body rather than the aristocratic body as the image of the body politic. According to John Locke, England's strength as a nation did not rest on the well-being of the aristocratic body. Locke linked the strength of the nation to an individuated and self-regulating body whose labor made the land productive.[49] Locke forged this link by showing how the familial analogy used to justify absolute monarchy instead should lead us to conclude that individuals have dominion over their own bodies. According to Locke, familial authority ultimately "leave[s] a Man at his own free disposal."[50] We can see this, he contends, if we remember that children become free of their parents' authority when they reach twenty-one, the age when "Reason" allows an individual to know how "to regulate his [own] Actions."[51] In claiming that every individual can regulate his own body, Locke significantly revises the popular body. It is no longer an unindividuated male body composed of the individual members of the nation's households. What these households produce, Locke contends, are self-regulating individuals whose identity derives not from their relation to the monarch's body but rather from their own bodies' labor. What an individual's body produces by "mixing" its labor with the land, thereby "joyning" the individual to that land, rightfully belongs to that body, not to the monarch.[52] In thus presenting a positive image of the common body that implicitly contests aristocratic vision of the unruly populace, Locke revises the Classical bond between person and place. No longer does the place determine the person, but rather the person makes the place.[53]

The significance of this change in the grounds of political authority cannot be overstated. This revision of state iconography endorses individuated identity and representative government. Christopher Hill remarks on the impact of this reimagining of the nation when he marvels that in defiance of traditions as old as recorded history itself, "successful war was levied against the King; bishops and the House of Lords were abolished; and Charles I was executed in the name of his people," all within a decade.[54] By the eighteenth century, "politics had become a rational inquiry, discussed in terms of utility, experience, common sense, no longer in terms of Divine Right, texts, and antiquarian research."[55] Commentators tend to attribute this shift in the basis of political authority to either the English civil war or the epistemological revolution introduced by Enlightenment intellectuals. But, I would argue, the rhetorical currency a new, ontologically hostile social body acquires by the time Locke writes also contributes to this, the onset of modernity. Moreover, when Locke identifies the English action with the common body, he uses a figuration of the political body that was first formulated by colonial writers.

As I have suggested, colonial promotion writers claimed that person makes place, not vice versa, nearly a century before Locke. They did so, though, in their work to overcome objections to the colonial climate. The English bodies that colonial promoters described thrived in North America for much the same reason Locke declares in *Two Treatises of Government* (1698): "in the beginning, all the World was *America*."[56] In order to refute the claim that bodies could survive only in their native climate, colonial promotion writers insisted that English bodies had proven to be well suited to the climates in the "New World" of New England.[57] John Brereton in *A Breife and True Relation of the Discoverie of the North Part of Virginia* (1602) contends that the New England "Climat" suits English bodies so well that those bodies are "renew[ed]" by the weather even though their "diet and lodging [are] none the best" while there.[58] In his *A briefe Relation of the Discovery and Plantation of New England* (1622), Ferdinando Gorges says that "the temperature of the Climate" allows the colonists to "enjoy their life and health much more happily, than in other places."[59] And Edward Winslow in *Good Newes from New England* (1624) claims that the weather in Massachusetts Bay is such that "one can scarce distinguish New England from Old."[60]

Colonial writers did not, of course, set out to untangle the national self-image. They merely sought to demonstrate the flaws in the conventional geographies of English cultural survival, without simultaneously challenging accepted theories of the body politic. They sought, in other words, to show where these theories went wrong in describing the impact of climate on various body types. Rather than challenge the division and hierarchical arrangement of humanity into various body types, they went after the part of the five-zone theory that fixed those body types to geographical places. But in tinkering with the theory of place they ultimately undermined the regime of the fixed and immutable Classical body itself, which, in turn, supported the iconography of English monarchy.

According to colonial writers, Classical theory rightly held that all bodies were adaptable. According to the Ancients, as the colonial promotion writers understood them, bodies were a "mixture" of the "foure Elements" that composed all objects in the world, Earth, Water, Aire, and Fire.[61] The "mixture" differed according to the climate in which a body was born. Previous commentators on the Ancients had taken this to mean that if a body of a certain mixture were to move to a climate where a different mixture was rewarded, that body would die. Life in New England violated this long-standing theory, requiring a revision that effectively reversed the priority of place over person. According to colonial promoters, life in New England demonstrated that since all bodies shared these four basic elements, any body could survive anywhere.[62] Colonization demonstrated, in other words, that English bodies adapted better to alien environments than did any other body type.

So, for instance, Francis Higginson in *New Englands Plantation* (1630) attempts to convince his readers that the foundation of Classical theory holds true in the colonies by using the four elements to structure his narrative. He contends that "the life and wel-fare of every Creature here below . . . depend . . . upon the temperature and disposition of the foure Elements, Earth, Water, Aire, and Fire."[63] To prove that the colonies operate under the very same natural laws as England, Higginson turns to the Classical authors, who taught that the "wholesome temper and convenient use of these [elements], consisteth the onely well-being both of Man and Beast in a more or less comfortable measure in *all* Countreys under the Heavens"[64] (emphasis added). But rather than continue in this traditional view and draw examples from Classical literature, Higginson turns to the contemporary situation and restates his principle in terms of what he calls "experience": "[e]xperience doth manifest that there is hardly a more healthfull place to be found in the World that agreeth better with our English Bodyes."[65] Far from threat-

ening their survival, in other words, a harsher climate improves the
health of English men and women. For proof, Higginson offers the
cases of "[m]any that have been weake and sickly in old England," including himself. The "healing nature" of New England "Aire" is so
powerful it can literally transform his body so that his "Stomacke" can
now digest food that he could not digest back in England. The English
body improved in New England.

And the improved English body was no less English than before. In
order to retain its national identity, though, that body must become English in an entirely new way. Colonial New English rhetoric seized on
the Native Americans for purposes of preserving Englishness. According
to this rhetoric, the English body remained English by virtue of its difference from the Indian body. Native bodies were unruly, out-of-
control—in short, much like the grotesque body in need of regulation.
Indeed, it would be easy to see this strategy as a reproduction of the
iconography by which European monarchy, according to Stallybrass and
White, opposed itself to the popular as the "head" and principle of regulation. To understand the significance of this opposition in colonial writing, we must remember that these authors were not only expressing English authority but were also subject to it, as the natives were to them.
Thus as colonial Englishmen, they had to represent themselves as nonaristocratic but nonetheless superior by race. The way Europe understood its relation to Native Americans is strikingly different from the way
Englishmen represented that same relationship once they began to live
in the colonies. The engravings by Theodore de Bry that accompanied
the 1590 edition of Thomas Hariot's *Briefe and True Report* portray
those natives as premature versions of the British aristocracy. According
to Mary Campbell, De Bry makes the bodies of Native American lords
"European," even presenting those bodies so that they conform to European codes of manners.[66] Indeed, the possibility of representing non-
European bodies as what Bakhtin called "Classical" remains possible up
through *Oroonoko*, where in Anita Pacheco's analysis, the Europeanized
bodily features of the African prince are an implicit endorsement of "the
mysteries of blood" used to support "the claims of birth and rank."[67] In
contrast, New English colonial writing presented the Indians in terms
that correspond to the grotesque body and the basis of modern racial
stereotype. This second, grotesque version of Native American bodies
was clearly favored by later colonial writers, who used it to elevate the
common English body over the unruly savage body. It was understood
to be true that English bodies were by birth disposed to depend on intel-
ligence and self-control, but this disposition came not from noble line-
age. On the contrary, New English writing contended that any English
body was aristocratic and by nature more balanced than the Indian

body. In *A True Relation of The late Battell* (1638), P. Vincent contends that while "[w]e have in us a mixture of all the elements," fire was the most "conspicuous element" in the "Pequet" Indians.[68] This lopsided composition explained their "barbarous and cruel natures," including the penchant for violence that led them to choose war over agriculture.[69]

In casting the Indian body as grotesque, the colonists could question the logic of the five zones and insist that they, rather than the Native Americans, were best suited to inhabit the New World. Colonial writers could argue that birth in the New World did not guarantee one's superiority in withstanding the calamities peculiar to New England. The plagues that had recently devastated native populations but left the English unscathed were said to prove that nature had not equipped native bodies to withstand the local climate.[70] Native susceptibility to disease was seen, Chaplin argues, as an "innate weakness" "natural to [the Indian's] body constitution."[71] In *The Planters Plea* (1630), John White defends English claims to the land by reminding his readers that a plague that "raged above twenty or thirty miles up into the Land" struck only "the Natives, the English in the heate of the Sicknesse commercing with them without hurt or danger."[72] In *New English Canaan* (1637), Thomas Morton carries this argument further, identifying the various plagues as "the means" by which New England was "made so much the more fitt for the English Nation to inhabit."[73] Even those who credited the plagues solely to divine intervention invariably included an argument for English superiority by suggesting that the plagues visited upon the Indians made their land available to a people who could use it more efficiently. Through the plagues, Edward Johnson claims, "Christ . . . made roome for his people to plant."[74] So, no matter who or what they held responsible for these catastrophes, colonial promoters used the plagues to support their contention that English bodies would not only survive in the colonies but were in fact better suited to the climate than those for whom it seemed a "natural" environment.

While such testimony may have convinced some that climatological theories needed to be revised, evidence of the suitability of the English body for colonial life was not sufficient to invert the logic which said that place determined character. Nor, then, could such testimony to English colonial health eradicate the fear that expanding the realm might have baleful effects on the body politic. Colonialism continued to be seen as a threat to the integrity of the body politic, because colonialism put the most vulnerable parts of that body—its margins—in jeopardy. Bodily margins, as Mary Douglas has pointed out, are "specifically invested with power and danger," because they are the entry points that open the imaginary social body to external pollutants.[75] Expanding the body politic beyond its traditional limits required that the unchanging, limited, and closed aristocratic body expand. As the author of *Mourts Relation* (1622) puts it, colonization meant "enlarging the bounds of [the] soverign Lord King James."[76] This enlargement of the body politic was complicated by the fact that bodies buried in England provided the basis of English monarchical rule. The body politic thus had to expand while remaining firmly rooted in England, for its ties to the aristocratic body were what authorized England to "send many thousands of . . . subjects" to the colonies for the purposes of expansion. As Sir William Alexander noted in 1624, the king was only king because he had "Ancestors" whose bodies were "buried" in the "Ancient Kingdom" of England.[77]

This perception that colonial expansion threatened the body politic was widespread enough to prompt New England promotion tract writers to defend against it, and to color the debate over Puritan control of New England. Critics of Puritan dominance cast their arguments in terms of the New England colonies' impact on the body politic, thus forcing those who supported Puritan control also to use the monarchical body cum body politic as a rhetorical figure. The Puritan supporter John White, for example, argued that when forming a new colony, a "State" should think of itself as a mother and the colony as its daughter—but as a daughter whose "new formed body" remains "a part and member of [the mother's] owne body."[78] There were, White conceded, two other options open to the state. The first would be to conceive colonial expansion as a simple extension of the body politic, an extension that did not, as in the maternal figuring, entail a concomitant (if only partial) separation. But to conceive such an expansion would be, White argues, to conceive an expansion that might eventually threaten the body politic from within, an expansion that might "poison" the mother's "humours" by forcing the original, finitely extended body politic to house an ever-expanding, eventually unsustainable population. The ever-expanding population Morton imagines begins to resemble Bakhtin's description of the popular body grown too large and unruly to be contained within the king's body.

The second option would be to conceive colonial expansion as the production of a *completely* separate body, one not tied in any substantial way to the original body politic. But doing so, White claims, would leave the colonies vulnerable to maternal neglect; although the colonies would still be the child of a British political body, they would have no claim to the care that any child requires.

Opponents of Puritan control of New England accepted the position in which the colony, like the populace, was part of the king's body politic. They disagreed only when it came to the question of how the colony could best contribute to the health of the body politic. Morton agreed that the spiritual and financial "riches" available in New England might well help the whole commonwealth "flourish," were it not for the fact that Separatist rule threatened to pollute the body politic before such riches could be put to use.[79] Morton blamed pollution on the unwarranted "translation" of social rank in the colonies, whereby Separatists degraded the established system of social rank by bestowing on one another the "title of . . . gentleman."[80] Morton's use of demeaning names such as Captaine Shrimpe for the Separatists implies their arrogance in assuming positions to which they were not entitled. In so mocking the Separatists, Morton demonstrates his allegiance to English monarchy, and this allegiance makes him the superior colonizer. Although the Separatists claim that Morton has fallen prey to the charms of native life, Morton represents himself as the one who can actually subdue the threat posed by Native Americans. He can, Morton claims, incorporate them into the English body politic, thereby extending monarchical authority to the colonies. It is the Separatists who threaten the English body with pollution. However much Morton and his Puritan critics disagree over who would be better able to govern the colony, by casting their arguments in terms of the health of the body politic, both work toward the same rhetorical end: to transform colonial expansion from a threat to the English body into a project necessary to that body's survival. The logic supporting colonization led its promoters to argue that this idealized popular body was not some separate entity, which must in turn be kept outside the aristocratic body, but part of an internal system of circulation that would keep the aristocracy alive.

These authors placed the idealized popular body—or what I call the common English body—in opposition to the Indian. On this issue, they insisted, English colonists could rule the native on behalf of the king. In other words, the popular body had to be transformed into one that was inherently orderly and productive—not opposed to but necessary to the aristocratic body. England's "wealth and honor," in Hakluyt's words, depended on sending English men and women to various parts of the globe so that they might engage in trade. Writers such as John Smith argued that the potentially corrupting colonial figures could only be isolated from the aristocratic body at that body's peril. The colonists had been placed in such a vulnerable position for the sole purpose of enhancing England's position in the emerging world system, a system in which not only goods but people were circulated back and forth from Europe as well.

In allaying the fear that "English bodies" would be adversely affected by the "strange and alien" conditions in the colonies, colonial promotion writers inadvertently revised early modern theories of the body politic, and they did so in ways that would eventually endow the English common body with rhetorical authority, an authority to which Locke would lay claim later in the century. This authority implicitly challenged the hierarchical body image that legitimated monarchical rule. Thus colonial writers were extremely careful to avoid the kind of confrontational language that could be read as treason and, therefore, expressed criticism using the language of metaphor. As scholars such as Marie Axton and David Lee Miller have demonstrated in relation to other Renaissance writing, however, such criticism was no less challenging for its being metaphorical.[81]

Colonial writers seized on the theory of the body politic as a way to insist on their Englishness. Indeed, to erase any doubt as to the Englishness of the colonial body, these writers equated that body with the very essence of Englishness. They did this by setting English bodies in opposition to other European ones as well as to the Indian bodies that eventually became the basis for difference. As a result, colonialism came to be understood as, in purpose and in effect, the reproduction of Englishness. The colonial desire to remain English combined with the colonial conviction that English bodies were superior to Native American bodies; this combination produced a new nationalism. Colonial culture was, in relation to other European cultures, simply English but in relation to Native Americans, it was superior. So, for instance, in John Underhill's narrative of the Pequot War, *Newes from America* (1638), Indian attacks on the common body are said to represent a threat to bodily distinctions in general. While Underhill begins his narrative of the war with an account of the murder of John Oldham, an assault on the English body politic, he is careful not to make this physical violation the ultimate cause of the war.[82] Underhill lays that blame on the Indians' claim that they "distinguish not between the Dutch and the English."[83] Thus it is the Indians' heresy in threatening to "know no difference between the Dutch and the English" that demands retaliation. The Indians had to be lying, we are told in *Newes from America*, because they have "had sufficient experience of both nations" to allow them to make distinctions between the different European bodies.[84] In other words, so stark are the differences among European bodies that no one—even Indians— could mistake them, proving at once the Englishness of the colonists and the necessity of their leadership over the Indians. For this definition of the body, colonists are willing to die.[85]

But even if a body retains its appearance of Englishness in North America, it might be asked, what is to prevent that body from going native over time? Indeed, what is to say that the colonists do not come to resemble the Indians as they engage in battle after vicious battle with them? Underhill as much as asks the question himself when he puts it in the mouths of his English readers: "Why should [the colonists] be so furious (as some have said)" so as to kill almost four hundred natives, including women and children, in a manner "barbarous" enough to leave the battleground "so thick" with corpses "that you could hardly pass along?"[86] Underhill wards off the predictable answer—namely, that the colonists have themselves become barbarous—by claiming that the colonists' lack of "pity" or "compassion" at the sufferings inflicted on the natives has been misinterpreted in England. What appears to be decidedly savage behavior is actually a sign of the colonists' instinct to defend the English community. Such violent actions are, he contends, the only possible response to foreign encroachments that a true subject of the king can take. The Indians so lack respect for the English body that they degrade that body by using it to clothe themselves. The Indians "cut off . . . [the] fingers and toes" of their victims in order to make "hatbands of them."[87] "Would not this," he asks, "have moved the hearts of men" to engage in such heinous acts of violence as he describes?[88] Whereas before violence impeached Englishness, it now preserves it, thanks to Underhill's subtle but noteworthy transformation. The English community in America no longer represents the porous margins of the English body but has come to represent Englishness itself and its most rigorous defense. Although Underhill certainly imagines the monarch as its head, the English body so represented is no longer an aristocratic body. Rather, it is a body whose well-being depends on the strength of the common body and its integrity under that head.

This vision of the common body as the source of Englishness incorporates the Puritan insistence that the saved be figured into the communal body in order to ensure the survival of the monarchy. Just as "Christ and his church make one body," argues John Winthrop, Massachusetts Bay must imagine itself as "one man" if it hopes to succeed.[89] The men of Massachusetts will know they have consolidated themselves as one magic body when other colonies take them as the models, when, in Winthrop's words, "men shall say of succeeding plantations, 'the lord make us like that of NEW ENGLAND.' "[90] By attributing this request to future colonies, Winthrop implies that only Massachusetts can provide a model that is at once English and Christian. To explain why this is so, Underhill offers the account of the rape of two English "maids" captured by the Indians. Their captivity exposes the pair to "uncleanness." Far from unique, such violation is in "the usual course of God's dealings" to "all . . . his poor captivated children."[91] Indeed, according to this allegory of the English trial in the wilderness, it is during such bodily suffering that "God's presence" becomes "clear[est]."[92] If Puritan identity is to be seen as nothing more than an analogue of English identity, it follows that what is true for religion holds true for politics as well.

It is during times of great peril that English identity makes itself known. Thus Underhill rests his definition of English identity on the paradox that such an identity can be produced only by putting it at risk. To become truly English, England must subject itself to the threat of colonial expansion.

The threat that this elevation of the common body posed to the traditional figure of the monarch's body becomes apparent during the political crisis in 1640s England. Once it had been demonstrated that the English could survive and even remain English in foreign climates, we might expect fear of colonial expansion to become a moot point. During the civil war, however, English tracts continue to focus on the threat that colonial expansion poses to the established systems of authority. Our expectations thus defeated, we might speculate, alternatively, that when the "popular body" seems more unruly, as it certainly did during the civil war, then the exalted figure of the English common body preferred by colonial promoters would have struck English readers as rather more than less threatening to the aristocratic body. Such critics of the colony as Thomas Lechford in *Plain Dealing: Or, Newes From New-England* (1642) accuse the colonists of challenging "an hereditary, successive, King, the son of Nobles."[93] "States and Kingdomes" will be destroyed, Lechford prophesies, if the "chiefe Magistrates" of a colony are chosen by "popular elections" rather than appointed by the king.[94] Popular rule would thus be seen as a threat to the purity of hereditary rule because it allows the body to overrule the head.

Those who write in support of the colony during the same period of crisis refute these arguments by drawing on the representation of the common body developed by the colonial promotion writers I will examine in subsequent chapters of this book. These later seventeenth-century writers endeavor to show that the body politic must rely on the common body if it is to survive its internal crisis. The common body has by then such status that it can provide the colonists with a symbolic resolution to the conflicting models of power troubling England. In *The Simple Cobbler of Aggawam* (1647), Nathaniel Ward acknowledges the monarch's body as the ultimate ground for political authority, claiming this body has been jeopardized by the conflict between the king and Parliament. Nevertheless, we have in Ward a figure that has come a long way from its appearance in pre–civil war literature, for he thinks of the head in an inverse relation to the body politic: "The body beares the head, the head the Crowne;/If both beare not alike, then one will downe."[95] Ward thus places the head and body in a dependent relationship. Nor will this body become unruly once it "leaves the head." The common body may lack aristocratic authority, but it can claim authority of another kind. The colonial experience tests the common body and, through that experience, the common body demonstrates the knowledge and self-discipline that makes it superior to the Native Americans. It has to be superior in these respects, after all, or it would not survive. Thus "experience" makes the difference between an unruly populace that inverts the natural order of body to head and a common body that exists in a relation of mutual dependence with that head. Ward cites the "[e]xperience" he has gained "here" in New England on "politicall, domesticall, and personall" matters. New England is, to his way of thinking, simply one part of the three bodies (England, Scotland, and North America) on which the king's "Crownes" are "set," and which have, in turn, "helpt [the king] beare them so honourably."[96] In such statements, the idealized version of the popular body emerges as a model in its own right in potential competition with a symbolic economy maintained by the Bakhtinian bodily duo. These statements represent the common body as integral rather than antithetical to the survival of the body politic. That is to say, the "experience" gained "here" in New England represents a specific kind of knowledge that the aristocratic body proper will never possess in and of itself.

By the time of the English civil war, then, colonial writers were thinking of the English common body as a prop for an aristocratic England. What I hope to demonstrate in the pages to follow is the degree to which this common body, characterized by knowledge based on experience and the discipline it takes to survive outside of England, is not only a distinctly modern development but a product of colonial culture as well. This figure grows out of the rhetoric developed by colonial promoters in their effort to show that the English body could withstand any climate and still remain English. This figure also entails a cultural logic that enables colonial writers to maintain their own political position vis-à-vis the monarchy. Thus I now turn to an examination of how this refiguration of the social body took place in particular texts. Only the texts that developed this new symbolic economy can show us how an image of the body that the monarchy used to justify aristocratic privilege came to represent state power itself. To those texts, then, we must look in order to see how the rhetoric of experience became an alternative basis for political, hereditary, and legal authority.

Chapter Two

THE MAN OF EXPERIENCE

IN WHAT is arguably the founding text of New Historicist criticism, *Renaissance Self-Fashioning*, Stephen Greenblatt explains that "[s]elf-fashioning is always, though not exclusively, in language."[1] Indeed, as if in anticipation of recent studies that equate the onset of modernity with the rise of writing, Greenblatt focuses on the role representation plays in how certain "middle-class" English writers established their "personal identity" and obtained social authority within the relatively rigid hierarchical structures of early modern England.[2] In theory, at least, these attempts at self-fashioning by "middle-class men" who lacked social power posed a challenge to English monarchy.[3] As Greenblatt explains, however, systems of power like the monarchy actually reinforce their own authority by containing potentially subversive cultural practices. These attempts at self-fashioning by English subjects outside the seat of power pose a threat to the reigning monarchical system, but, according to Greenblatt, such systems of power maintain their authority through the containment of such potentially subversive movements. In fact, Greenblatt's final condition for successful self-fashioning specifies that it "always involves some experience of threat."[4] All this has become commonplace. But I would like to call attention to a component of Greenblatt's theory that early modern scholarship has not satisfactorily mulled over, one that has specific resonance for scholars of seventeenth-century British America.

To describe the precise nature of the threat that self-fashioning poses to established structures of power, Greenblatt shifts his focus and terminology from "representation" to "experience." Experience, not representation, is what the courtly tradition of English culture had to contain. For Greenblatt, "experience" denotes a way of knowing that is distinguishable from the representational component of self-fashioning because it resists historicization and qualification. He writes that the "interpretive constructions the members of a society apply to their experiences" vary according to time and place. Apparently, though, for Greenblatt the experiences themselves and the value of experience remain the same.[5] But why would experience so threaten the powers that be; and what in Renaissance England made it an attractive way of knowing?

Greenblatt's failure to problematize "experience" becomes even more conspicuous when in *Marvelous Possessions* he shifts attention from the English court to the European colonies. This examination of colonial writing concerns itself precisely with the representation of what he calls "particular experiences."[6] He contends that the category of wonder is so important to early modern representations of the New World because wonder was "the decisive emotional and intellectual experience" of Europeans there.[7] Having established that what he means by experience ultimately authorizes existing structures of power, Greenblatt can proceed to argue that experience connects seemingly autonomous discursive systems; he claims that the "ambiguous experience of wonder . . . is the feature that most decisively links [colonial] discourse . . . to both philosophical and aesthetic discourse."[8] Once he has begun this discursive slide, moreover, there is nothing to prevent Greenblatt from considering colonial discourse an integral part of the attempt to regulate both native and European populations. Experience emerges from *Marvelous Possessions* as one among several ways of extending English cultural hegemony, and colonial literature can therefore be read as evidence of those hegemonic operations. This completes the tautology. As both a ground for representation and a key effect of representation, the "experience of wonder" serves as one more public exhibition of the monarchy's power to extend itself to the farthest reaches of the globe even as it extends its reign inward, as Foucault contends in *Discipline and Punish*, to regulate the European subject. I have no quarrel with what Greenblatt and Foucault have to say about early modern Europe.

By focusing on the rhetoric of experience in colonial writing, I will suggest not only that this term takes on a different political meaning in British America but also that such a focus yields a different account of where, why, and how the modern subject emerged. If we understand the authority of experience as something that is achieved primarily in and through representation, it is then entirely reasonable to ask, as Peter Stallybrass does of continental English literature in relation to the idea of the individual, "when and how was the specific signifier" experience "deployed" in colonial English writing?[9] To approach colonial writings from this vantage point is to understand experience as a way of knowing the world that did not support but competed with and ultimately undermined the tropes of political authority that dominated seventeenth-century Europe. Indeed, I will go so far as to argue that this competing epistemology was forged in the colonies to authorize colonial subjects over and against their European counterparts.

More important than any natural resources, I will suggest the colonies provide Europe with a potentially new way of authorizing the individual subject, one that required nothing less than a revolutionary reshaping of the early modern social order. Indeed, the emphasis on experiential forms of authority in colonial discourse suggests why the most important influences on New Historicists, Foucault prominent among them, have been able to describe in detail what new forms of authority emerged during the modern period but have been unable to say why such a process should occur, why it should occur in one way rather than another. Foucault, for example, uses the spectacle of the scaffold to demonstrate, as Greenblatt does, that early modern power inhered in the object of the gaze. That is what made both courtiers and criminals potentially subversive; they could, momentarily at least, attract the gaze. What made them ultimately harmless was their inability to hold the gaze and to display aristocratic power.[10]

Not so during the modern period, according to Foucault, when the situation is exactly reversed and power inheres in an invisible observer whose ability to represent the things and people that he sees gives him authority over such things and people. Foucault represents the advent of modernity as a genealogy or a before and after story that circumvents the question of why this particular shift at this moment in time.[11] His avoidance of causality is only to Foucault's credit, in my opinion, given his strictly European focus; the cause lies not only in Europe, but also in the colonies, as I will explain. If we think of the rhetoric of experience that was forged in the colonies as a competing but residual early modern base of authority, we can explain both where the modern individualist theory of knowing emerged and why scholars who look for its origin strictly in Europe fail. Modern authority was made in English writing, I am suggesting, but not on English soil because it was made in colonial literature.

Not surprisingly, a number of intellectual and cultural historians have disregarded Foucault and sought evidence of a continuous linear development of the observer's authority over object observed in seventeenth-century English culture. Nor is it surprising to find these scholars calling attention to experience—both its increasing authority as a concept and its redefinition as such. Charles B. Schmitt, for instance, argues that "[o]ne of the tendencies which clearly marked the intellectual development of the seventeenth century was an increasing emphasis on experience," while Peter Dear contends that "the seventeenth-century reconstructed the pre-existing concept of 'experience' to fit new ends" and, in the process, created "a new conception of experience."[12] According to Dear, early modern English writers tended to favor knowledge that came from reasoning, and they generally ignored or denigrated what they considered the relatively uninteresting information that could be obtained via common experience. Influenced by Aristotle, these writers explicitly excluded the observation of a "singular event" from the category of experiential knowledge. What Dear calls a "new conception of experience," though, emerged in the later half of the century and inverted the Aristotelian system. While the Aristotelians excluded singular events from the category of experiential knowledge because such knowledge relied too heavily on the testimony of individual observers, the new experimentalists made such observations the foundation for their claims. They championed singular experiments conducted by individual experimenters, and they downplayed the importance of rhetoric in assessing scientific claims. They wanted their results to emanate from nature itself, rather than from the process of abstract reasoning that Aristotelian scholastics favored, and they cast the individual experimenter in the role of reporter.[13]

While Dear and the others who describe this transformation provide a powerful narrative of how experience gained its rhetorical force in various early modern English discursive systems, they fail to see any relationship between this discursive event and the shift in personal and political authority that begins at about the same time. Nor do they consider what role colonial writings might play in the transformation they describe. Lest one conclude that the tendency to think about the cultural past in terms of present national boundaries is a European habit, I must add that American literary historians are equally prone to do this. When, for instance, Wayne Franklin and J. Leo Lemay describe the significance of "experience" in colonial travel writings, they ignore the impact that such new ways of knowing the world must have had on European systems of thought, so concerned are they to identify the "independent feature[s] of American . . . rhetoric" and the distinctive nature of the "American experience."[14] Like Schmitt and Dear, Franklin and Lemay fasten onto "experience," making it indicative of an emergent modernity in the one instance, and of emergent nationalism in the other.[15] These are not separate results but counterparts and even causes of one another.

This chapter will consider what the colonies might have contributed to modern British culture more generally by examining how John Smith revised the traditional aristocratic bases of authority in favor of "experience" for the very limited purpose of influencing colonial policy. I believe Smith's writings of his travels in British North America represent a point of intersection between new forms of authority and the reconceptualization of experience. They suggest that the modern subject, which appeared along with this new use of experience, develops as a way of advancing colonization in the very genre designed to promote the colonial project. To authorize his colonial observations and theories for

readers in a pre-Enlightenment England, however, Smith had to overcome several conceptual problems. If, as the Aristotelians held, experience was valid only when used to describe shared phenomena, how
could one claim that descriptions of an environment, people, and culture unknown to most English were "experiential"? Smith's lack of social standing exacerbates this problem. Were he a gentleman, he might
not be able to categorize his observations as experiential, but his place in
the social hierarchy would lend credence to his findings. Lacking such
distinction, Smith and his observations and theories faced ridicule, dis-
missal, or worse.[16] To give his observations the ring of authority, then,
Smith relies on the rhetorical strategy of early experimental philosophers: he represents his particular experiences as natural phenomena and
therefore as *potentially* common even if, so far, they had been observed
by and thus known only to Smith. As Dear says of early modern experimental science writers, Smith subtly shifts the terms of experiential observations and conclusions "from 'this is what I saw when I did this' to
'this is what happens when this is done.'"[17] To overcome the lack of
credibility that came with his lack of social status, Smith, in effect, disas-
sociates experiential knowledge from social standing and rhetorical presentation. In the process, Smith presents himself in terms that the experimental philosophers who emerged in the second half of the century
would use to describe the experiential subject. Smith describes himself
in proto-Lockean terms as a man whose ideas and identity are formed by
sensations arising out of his direct and particular experience of the external world.

Critics of Smith's work, as I have suggested, are quick to insist on the
importance of experience in his project. Lemay goes so far in this direction as to say that Smith's writings "focused on the effects of the American experience upon the individual."[18] Ultimately, however, Lemay uses
experience much as Greenblatt does: to indicate a transhistorical—and,
perhaps, universal—way of knowing. By ignoring the rhetorical basis of
experiential authority, Lemay is led by that very rhetoric to assume that
Smith learns through the hard work of colonization the value of experience that he tries to impart in his writings. This tendency to take the
rhetoric of experience on its own terms—as no rhetoric at all, as a trans-
parent record of the world outside of language—has led to a general
misunderstanding of Smith's importance. Interested in determining just
when experience becomes important in colonial travel narratives, Mary
Campbell places the turn to experience some years earlier than Smith,
beginning with Sir Walter Raleigh's *The Discoverie of . . . Guiana. . .* in
1596.[19] Michael McKeon, on the other hand, claims the process begins
in earnest only in the latter half of the seventeenth century.[20] In neglecting Smith, both Campbell and McKeon miss the moment when "experi-

ence" assumes the contours of a modern rhetorical strategy. In Smith, it seems to me, the notion of "experience" from which the modern observer draws authority makes its first appearance as the solution to specifically colonial problems.

In *A Map of Virginia* published in 1612, Smith criticizes the gentlemen colonists of Virginia on grounds they "never adventured to knowe any thing" while in Virginia, preferring instead to remain in Jamestown.[21] Yet these same gentlemen feel qualified, he complains, to "slander the Countrey" and, once returned to England, "spit at all things" relating to Virginia (1:176). Their rhetorical skills and social position are apparently all it takes to endow their gentlemanly opinions about the operation of the colony with authority. While the company's "true actors," who were those who, unlike the gentleman, performed the bulk of the labor, explored the surroundings, and fought with the natives, these unsung heroes are lower on the social ladder, and, as a consequence, their opinions go unremarked (1:176). As a result, the business of colonizing Virginia is being "miscaried" (1:176). The colony, consequently, faces financial ruin, and nothing is being done to improve the situation: people of elite social standing are "ever returning" to administrative positions in Virginia, while those who have the most "experience" in the colonies are passed over (1:176). Smith challenges the authority of these gentlemanly opinions in order to detach knowledge from rank. There is a kind of knowledge, he insinuates, that one can have and should be granted credit for independent of his rank. For Smith this is to suggest that his experience authorized his observations over and above those of his superiors in determining administrative authority. But how did Smith succeed in negotiating such treacherous political ground?[22]

Smith scholars have certainly noticed that "Smith repeatedly violated the standard social code that demanded deference . . . from those of a lower social order."[23] In doing so, however, these scholars tend to ignore the fact that Smith conscientiously develops ways also to seek approval from the very men he challenges. His second book, *A Description of New England* (1616), displays precisely this strategy. Rather than criticize his social superiors for respecting only rank in determining colonial policy, Smith invites his betters themselves to authorize experience. In the dedication to "worthy Lords, Knights, and Gentlemen, of his Majesties Councell, for all Plantations and discoveries," he writes:

> But, lest your Honours, that know mee not, should thinke I goe by hearsay or affection; I intreat your pardons to say thus much of my selfe: Neere twice nine yeares, I have beene taught by lamentable experience, as well in Europe and Asia, as Affrick, and America, such honest adventures as the chance of

warre doth cast upon poore Souldiers. So that, if I bee not able to judge of
what I have seene, contrived, and done; it is not the fault either of my eyes, or
foure quarters. (1:310)

Smith avoids the issue of rank entirely by focusing instead on the distinctions between different orders of knowledge. Experience here is one of
several ways of gaining knowledge—hearsay and affection, being the
others, each of which competes. He carefully phrases his endorsement of
experience over hearsay and affection so that it appeals to the "Lords,
Knights, and Gentlemen" who value experience over other forms of
knowledge. Smith accomplishes this by attributing to his social superiors
his own objections to hearsay and affection. He figures "his superiors"
as discerning readers who might regard his text as unreliable if he were
to depend on hearsay and affection, both of which are lower forms of
knowledge. It is to satisfy *their* demands that he draws strictly on experience. As a result, experience—and experience alone—without any attachment to rank is defined as the gentlemen's knowledge of choice.

It is worth noting that the dedication extends the issue of Smith's
authority. It moves beyond the question of whether Smith has had particular experiences of New England and ventures to discuss what
qualifies him to know experience when he sees it. The trustworthiness of
his observations and conclusions is made to rest on Smith's appeal to his
experience in Europe, Asia, and Africa, as well as America. Thus "his
Majesties Councell" should trust what Smith says not only because he
has experienced it, but also because his "lamentable experience"
throughout the world makes him the kind of person who can "judge"
what he has "seene, contrived, and done" in this particular situation.
The dedicatees are asked to value his colonial experience as a sign of his
character over and above any experience they might have of him person-
ally. Generic experience replaces individual familiarity: because Smith
himself is "experienced," his dedicatees need not experience him. In
thus laying claim to authority, it is crucial for Smith to demonstrate that
far from being unique, his knowledge is that of a generic subject. An
accumulation of experiential knowledge produces a subject who acts in
predictably responsible ways and sees the world much like other men
would under similar circumstances. Thus Smith distinguishes himself,
not on the basis of experience, but as the member of a new category—
the man of experience—that presumably any number of such individuals
could occupy.

Indeed, those who belong to this group can claim the experience of
others as their own without giving credit.[24] For virtually every text
Smith is said to have authored describes experiences that are not his
own. Smith often does acknowledge, as in *The Generall Historie* (1624),

that he uses someone else's experience, but when he incorporates other people's relation of their experiences into his own narratives, he plays fast and loose with their stories. Critics such as Everett Emerson have taken Smith's manner of incorporating this material as an indication he thought of himself as a "compiler, not a historian," who aspired to produce something like the collections of Hakluyt and Purchas.[25] This, despite what I regard as the crucial difference that Hakluyt and Purchas never claimed the experiences they collected were their own. What allows Smith to incorporate the experience of other men as if it were his own is the fact that he speaks for a category of men for which knowledge becomes common property. Such experience was not common to all, as the Aristotelians demanded. Quite the contrary, it was common only to colonial men and not necessarily to men of Classical learning.

Although experiences are so lacking in particularity that none can claim sole title to them, experience, nonetheless, becomes an object in demand. In the dedicatory letter to *An Accidence*, "To All the Right Honorable And most Generous Lords in England, and Others: Especially of his Majesties Privy Councell, and Councell of Warre," Smith calls the book "an intraduction for such as wants experience, and are desirous to learne what belongs to a Sea-man"(3:11). "Wants" operates here in both senses of the word: experience is both something that these readers lack and something they would like to have (they "want" experience). Thus Smith figures experience as an exchangeable good that can satisfy the desires of his audience. According to Smith, this audience consists of "many young Gentlemen and Valiant spirits of all sorts." Although the inclusion of gentlemen in the imagined audience provides the circulation of experience with a kind of social sanction, experience has replaced rank as the means of distinction; it is not where you are on the social ladder that determines whether you should read this book, but whether you want certain kinds of experience. Casting experience as a commodity that will satisfy the wants of "all sorts" makes men of experience into merchants, with experience as their wares. We can see this merchandising of experience at work on the title pages of Smith's later writings. Both *An Accidence, Or The Path-way to Experience* (1626) and *Advertisements For the unexperienced Planters of New England, or any where. Or, The Path-way to experience to erect a Plantation* (1631) use experience in an unprecedented way. Whereas earlier title pages had used experience to indicate how the information in the text was obtained, here it indicates what the text will provide. Experience is now understood as a consumer good.

Although Smith takes pains to disassociate knowledge from social hierarchy, authorize the man of experience, and commodify the category of experience, he also subtly reattaches experiential knowledge to the social status in the form of colonial administrative hierarchy. In effect, he proposes that colonial experience rather than traditional determinations based on rank should determine administrative positions in the colonies. What else if not experience, as Smith has defined it, can provide colonial administrators with knowledge of what is needed in a new colony: to make a profit and subjugate the natives? The same rhetoric asserts the value of experience in achieving both goals. In each case, he lets it be known how critics have attacked his administrative decisions, and then proceeds to document the successful outcome of those decisions. What better illustration that the right conclusions could only have been reached by a man of experience.

In making his case for the colony's profitability, Smith argues against those who claim Virginia can provide sufficient economic benefits to England only if such precious metals as gold and copper are discovered there. He contends, on the contrary, that even something so "mean" as fish will bring sufficient financial rewards to give England substantial international power. He points out that Holland, Spain, and Portugal are among the nations that use goods from their colonies to compete in the world market. Besides, he continues, New England soil can grow virtually any agricultural product. To prove his point, Smith compares the climate, culture, and commodities of New England with other regions well-known for wealth: the "best and richest parts of France," "the ancient Citie and Countrey of Rome," and the "most pleasant and plentifull Citie in Europe, Constantinople" all lie along the same parallel, as do the "temparatest parts" of Asia and the "richest of golde Mynes" of Chily and Baldivia (1:332). Such parallelism is a sure sign that similar wealth awaits discovery in New England. There is, however, only one way to open the treasure chest, according to Smith. New England's "natural" potential can be tapped, its waters fished and its lands cultivated, only if its "Land were cultured, planted and manured by men of industrie, judgement, and experience" (1:333). If this condition is met, he claims, then New England "might equalize any of those famous Kingdomes, in all commodities, pleasures, and conditions" (1:333). But experience is not only the element needed to transform the soil into English land; it also provides the magic that can reproduce English culture in the "uncultivated" New World environment.

Smith describes his attempt to form military and trading alliances with the natives as one that was initially considered "more bolde than wise" (1:351). Those who determined colonial policy back in England held that natives were deceitful, untrustworthy, treacherous, inconstant, and violent. Thus, Smith's critics reasoned that these same natives "desperately assaulted and betraied many others" soon after making similar agreements. In support of his policy, Smith counters, "I say but this (because with so many, I have many times done much more in Virginia, then I intended heere, when I wanted that experience Virginia taught me) that to mee it seemes no daunger more then ordinarie" (1:351). His announcement that his opinion is forthcoming on the matter under dispute ("I say but this") may be sharply distinguished from his statement of that opinion ("it seemes no daunger more than ordinarie") by their respective methods of authorization. Smith uses experience both to identify his way of making judgments and to provide evidence of the superiority of the judgments that result. For not only is this body of evidence simultaneously inaccessible to and ignored by his critics; it also is the basis on which he has taken action even more successful than the controversial policy he has just defended. In order to understand whether a given course of action is either dangerous or ordinary, Smith contends, one must have a basis for comparison, and such a basis comes only from having participated in or been witness to similar events—in this case, observing colonial events. Such knowledge allows those like Smith to develop alliances that will serve England's military and economic ends by displacing that other continental power, France, thus making Native Americans dependent on the English, all the while expanding potentially lucrative trading relationships in the area. It is the man of experience who can potentially turn adversarial peoples into dependent ones.

Smith makes experience more essential to the success of the colonial project when he demonstrates that military as well as economic success depends on experiential knowledge. After listing the various and abundant products of New England—from "Moos" to "diverse sorts of vermine" to "Mullets" to "Stugion" to cherries—and the place and season where each could be found, he notes still further that only careful planning can ensure a continuous supply of food. He then concludes: "hee that hath experience to manage well these affaires, with fortie or thirtie honest industrious men, might well undertake (if they dwell in these parts) to subject the Salvages, and feed daily two or three hundred men" (1:342). To be sure, his detailed catalogue of available food is designed to show that settlements would have abundant resources at their disposal, but the elaboration of that catalogue also allows Smith to show the necessity of experienced colonial management: only someone who has experienced colonial conditions and proved capable of managing the English under his charge has any chance of "subject[ing] the Salvages" (1:343). Under the guise of arguing for a commodity network in the colonies, Smith advocates subordinating English subjects to the leadership of experience. To bring the indigenous peoples of North America under English dominion, in other words, the English themselves must submit to the authority of experience.

Smith recognizes, however, the danger in this. Once experience provides a basis for political authority, what prevents anyone who should happen to have spent some time in the colonies or even to have read a book about life there from claiming authority over his social superiors when it comes to colonial matters? As if wary of the larger implications of his claim, Smith carefully restricts experiential authority to those who already possess a specific kind of information. First, Smith establishes a set of preconditions for "genuine" experience. The first section of *An Accidence*, for example, elaborates the shipboard hierarchy, including a detailed list of the various positions on a ship, the tasks performed at each of these positions, and the relation of each of these posts to others on the ship. After devoting a good deal of description to questions of who is in charge of whom, and what tasks each post requires of its holder, he goes on to explain "when the Captaine is to call up the company," who goes where during such calls to duty on the ship, "How to devide the Company," "Notes for a Covenant betweene the Carpenter and the Owner," and descriptions of various boat parts from "Masts, Caps and Yeards" down to the anchor (3:18–21). Despite this detailed display of naval knowledge, however, Smith devotes the bulk of the *Accidence* to terminology. He pummels the reader with terms for timber, ropes, harbors, winds, seas, anchors, searing, boats, and ordinances. Occasionally, the term in question comes with a definition, but more often he simply lists the words belonging to a given subcategory of navigation.

Such terminologies, listings, descriptions, and tables provide a framework for the reader who "wants experience." Here, Smith's habit of presenting information in distinct hierarchized units extends beyond the realm of human behavior into *all* aspects of the ship. As a result, the reader receives Smith's general principles of classification along with the highly detailed information it organizes. It is not just that experience depends on the enumeration and consumption of various kinds of information already bounded and categorized; it is also important to show that this knowledge holds together according to an internal logic that is predetermined and (paradoxically) immune from experiential alteration.

Although Smith delivers to the reader everything he knows, he also distinguishes those who have experience from those who have only read about it. Ultimately, writing cannot communicate what actual experience can teach; "every one that reads this booke can not put it in practice; though it may helpe any that have seene those parts" (1:353). In a manner that anticipates not only the experimental sciences, but also the practical information of *Robinson Crusoe* and the papers of the Royal

Society, Smith aspires to absolute transparency in his detailed account of life aboard ship. But this transparency turns out to be a rhetorical ploy as Smith proceeds to separate reading knowledge from experiential knowledge. Indeed, he explicitly widens the gap between what people want, namely, experience, and what a book can provide them, "relational knowledge." This gap opens whenever the administrative authority of the man of experience is at stake. The distinction between "Saying and Doing" structures his description of the qualifications for colonial management, and he attacks "relational knowledge" in defending his decision to live with a group of Algonkians.

Smith exploits this gap to greatest effect when he discusses military decisions. The section of *An Accidence* devoted to war terminology concludes with the claim, "there is as many stratagems, advantages, and inventions to be used, as you finde occasions, and therefore experiences must be the best Tutor" (3:23). Smith could, he implies, go on to describe additional strategic situations and enumerate the options available in each, but such an act of representation would be futile. Representation can only point to experience; it cannot provide it or substitute for it. One must be there—or have been there—to know what strategies a given situation requires. As a result, only those who have fought colonial battles are qualified to make military policy in the colonies.

Smith never quite explains how experience determines the appropriate action one should take in dire circumstances; he merely invokes the category. This in turn mystifies experience as something that cannot be adequately represented because—by an unabashedly circular process—experience is acquired experientially. The ease with which he deploys the tropes of inexpressibility suggests that the tautological character of experiential authority is so obvious as to require no further explanation. It is important to notice, however, how carefully this tautology limits the authority of experience in the very process of mystification. What Smith offers in *An Accidence* is merely a "path-way to experience" rather than experience per se. Even though one cannot acquire experience simply from reading a book, in order to be genuinely experienced, one must first read Smith. Knowledge based on experience thus becomes the source of Smith's authority as writer and limits what he can disseminate in writing. His book is paradoxically both inferior to experience as a source of information and required for all who want to be men of experience. Experience is quite literally both the precondition for representation and its by-product; only after reading the book can one convert experience into knowledge.

Finally, Smith limits the authority he has called into being by distinguishing the true man of experience from people who have merely been places and seen things. "Experienced observers" accumulate discrete bodies of information about the New World, but they lack the kind of experience necessary to serve in administrative positions. Many men can go to the New World and participate "in those actions," but few can return with more "wisdom" than they could have garnered from staying home in England (3:264). In this way, experience ultimately becomes a kind of cultural capital that offers a return upon return. Smith figures practical knowledge of the colonial project as a source of such enhanced status, the returns of which are visible. When one navigates correctly, for instance, the act of navigation signifies the invisible hand (the figure Adam Smith would use for the laws of the marketplace itself) guiding the ship toward a safe and prosperous future. Ironically, then, Smith begins *An Accidence* by linking experiential knowledge to reliance on visible evidence, only to perform an epistemological about-face near the end of his treatise and appeal to the ability of certain exemplary actions to represent much more than themselves.

Given the paradoxical terms in which he has proposed it, Smith's "theory" of experience ultimately authorizes England's colonial expansion even while it proposes that a new form of authority should rule there. In the end, this is how he avoids treason, by claiming that England can expand to embrace both aristocratic authority and the kind of authority that success in the colonies requires. Smith may mock those who claim that they "can by opinion proportion Kingdomes, Cities, and Lordships, that never durst adventure to see them," but he criticizes those who pretend to "tell . . . what all England is by seeing but Milford haven, as what Apelles was by the picture of his great toe" (3:264). In this way, Smith constitutes political entities, kingdoms, and nations as natural objects that can be "seen" by the naked eye. Experiential knowledge is, in turn, knowledge that depends on seeing such objects. Experience first illuminates particularity, and then unites those particularities into a single object of knowledge. Just as a complete view of Apelles, for instance, reveals all his parts and allows one to see the "whole man" they form, so one must experience all of England's territories in order to know the totality of England's political body. Smith claims that, unlike those he mocks, he knows the whole since he can record the position of the sun and the moon. His own experience is superior to the experience of those to whom his treatise is addressed. Visible evidence provides the best foundation on which to build that which cannot be seen, future colonization, and only a "man of experience" can write with authority on a nation that is by definition, then, not immediately before our eyes.

Smith transforms the threat that a specifically colonial authority might pose to the early modern monarchy by limiting that authority to the colonies, where it becomes necessary to the economic health, political future, and spiritual well-being of England as a whole, without changing the overall organization of that whole. To reap financial gains from its colonies, he claims, monarchy must rely on men of experience to direct the colonists toward producing exchangeable goods and forging trading relationships with Native Americans. Smith again conceals the fact that he shifts power from rank to experience by invoking historical analogies and suggesting that ancient peoples' trust in experience erected and maintained the "Monarkies of the Chaldeans, the Syrians, the Grecians, and Romanes." In offering this analogy, we should note, Smith raises the stakes significantly: the issue is no longer a matter of how experience can ensure the success of English colonial economic activities but rather one of how experience created "famous Kingdomes." Thus he suggests that the success of its colonies depends on England's ability to fashion itself in Rome's image (1:344). For, Smith argues, the "justice and judgement" that characterized Rome grew out of the "experience" it gained by extending its rule. He completes the analogy by attributing Rome's decline, in turn, to the "want of experience in [those] Magistrates" who were awarded posts on the basis of patronage. Besides being the chief requirement for a successful colonial administrator, experience offers a rationale for colonial expansion itself as essential to the success of the model state.

In his last work, *Advertisements*, Smith extends his definition of experience in another equally significant direction. Here he contends that English contempt for colonial experience and the policies to be drawn from such knowledge is leveled against both God and the man of experience. Respect for the lessons learned in North America in turn constitutes something like an act of piety. He explains that "the Devils most punctuall cheaters" (3:294), those people who obstruct the work of the godly, can be identified "by their absoluteness in opinions, holding experience but the mother of fooles, which indeed is the very ground of reason" (3:294). To stand in the way of experience is thus to oppose not only colonization but God as well. If in *An Accidence* Smith mystified experience as the force ensuring England's colonial expansion, then in *Advertisements* he demonizes those who advise the king against taking more territory, on grounds that God Himself authorizes the project of extending English rule outside England proper.[26] It is in the service of expansion in a more general sense that experience provides the most reliable basis for knowledge. Smith defines experience and reliance on this kind of knowledge as virtues requiring the relentless pursuit of totality within the twin domains of epistemology and politics. At the same time, paradoxically, he deliberately eliminates the possibility that any man— much less all men—can attain such comprehensive mastery. I would suggest, however, that this contradictory representation of experience operates in the service of a common goal: to promote English colonial expansion. There must be a new basis for colonial authority, Smith maintains consistently, in order for English monarchy to prevail.

Smith's emphasis on experiential authority marks a fundamental change in the genre of the colonial promotional tract.[27] Prior to Smith, writers in the genre invoked experience only rarely and certainly never to authorize an individual. Neither Richard Hakluyt nor Samuel Purchas indicates in their voluminous and oft-cited collections of travel narratives that we should trust the collected authors because their writing is based in experience, much less, as Smith would later claim, that experience should be the basis for colonial administrative authority. And none of the authors cited by Smith himself, including Thomas Hariot, Walter Raleigh, John Brereton, and James Rosier, express much interest in the power or authority of experience. In fact, only one of the many English travel narratives written about Virginia or New England from 1600 to 1616, Hariot's *Briefe and True Report*, uses experience in any way to establish the truth of its claims.[28] Following Smith, quite the contrary is true, and the tropes of experience I have identified in Smith assume priority over those of rank and Classical learning when it comes to authorizing the information presented in colonial narratives and promotional tracts. Subsequent writers such as William Wood apply the test of experience even more broadly, evaluating even the native inhabitants according to their experiential knowledge.[29]

These widely read tracts, I would venture to say, in turn helped create an intellectual climate that fostered the new experimental philosophy and, along with it, Enlightenment notions of the importance of experience in determining structures of authority. If the modern subject emerged out of the scientific revolution of the latter part of the seventeenth century, the authority required to grant this subject a place in the social hierarchy regardless of social standing grew out of the English colonies. More than simply providing material resources that helped fuel the English economy, the desire to subjugate English and native peoples produced one of the founding concepts of modernity.

Chapter Three

A BODY THAT WORKS

A S CLARENCE J. GLACKEN pointed out long ago, seventeenth-century English writers understood the relationship between "environment and national character" to be a causal one.[1] They thought that climate determined the character of a culture and, consequently, the character of those individuals who belonged to the culture. John Smith, for example, developed this theory of character into an argument that promoted the colonization of New England, claiming that New England would not only yield a bounty of natural resources but also flower as a culture because its climate resembled that of the "ancient Citie and Countrey of Rome" (1:333). This argument, as we have seen, solved the problem of when to authorize a hands-on colonial administration, namely, by granting experience authority over rank. In solving the problem of authorizing those of the king's emissaries who lived in the colonies, however, it managed to skirt the fear that English bodies would go native through long exposure to the North American climate. After all, since administrative positions offered no protection from the transformative effects of the local environment, what then was to ensure the Englishness of those Englishmen who carried out the king's will in the colonies?

This threat was thought to extend beyond colonial administrators. As I noted in my opening chapter, if the experience of place determined national character, then every English man and woman who took up residence in the colonies was putting his or her Englishness on the line. As the doctrine of experience gained weight as the basis for political authority, colonial promoters had to explain how the *American* experience could serve as the basis for *English* authority. They had to argue, paradoxically, that experience was instrumental in the production of individual identities but irrelevant to national identity. They had to explain, in other words, how the man of experience could remain a man of England. We have seen that the fear of going native was widespread enough to prompt the authors of colonial promotion tracts to defend against it. We have seen also that this fear overdetermined certain features of the body, making them, in Mary Douglas's words, "a symbol of society."[2] In allaying the fear that the "strange and alien" conditions in the colonies would adversely affect "English bodies," these promotion writers endowed the English common body with a rhetorical authority it had yet to enjoy, an authority that John Locke would establish elsewhere only later in the century. I have suggested in chapter 1 that colonial writers solved the problem of how to privilege the American experience without compromising the Englishness of the experiential subject by defining the common body as the ultimate ground for national community. Now that I have shown how Smith revised the rhetoric of experience so that it might serve as a form of supplemental authority, I can examine more fully the role experience plays in redefining the communal body. In order to focus this discussion, this chapter will examine how one New English colonial writing uses the rhetoric of experience to reimagine the ground for English national community.

Any number of early promotional tracts could be used to investigate my thesis, including *Mourt's Relation*, Eburne's *A Plain Pathway to Plantation*, White's *A Planters Plea*, or Higginson's *New Englands Plantation*. I will, however, focus on a work that is considered "one of the most influential guides" to colonization produced in the period, William Wood's *New Englands Prospect* (1634).[3] Among his contemporaries, references to Wood's work were frequent and frequently positive.[4] Jodocus Hondy in *Historia Mudni or Mercator's Atlas* urges any reader "that desyres to know more of the Estate of new England . . . lett him read a Book of the prospecte of new England & ther he shall have satisfaction"; *A Relation of Maryland* (1635) advises "Hee that hath a Curiosity to know all that hath been observed of the Customes and manners of the Indians" to consult "Captaine Smiths Booke of Virginia, and Mr. Woods of New England"; even the General Court of Massachusetts requested that "letters of thankefullnes [be] . . . sent to . . . Mr. Wood, and others, that have been benefactors to this plantation."[5]

Despite the attention it received in the seventeenth century, those literary scholars who work on colonial promotional tracts have entirely overlooked Wood's narrative, while those who study early American literature routinely mention it only dismissively.[6] When Wood's work is examined in detail, it is usually read solely in relation to developments within what can broadly be called the "American literary tradition." For them Wood provides evidence that supports the "continuity of experience" with "the American landscape" or the origins of an "independent American culture."[7] *New Englands Prospect* is seen as "representative" of other travel narratives in that it exposes issues that later American writers raise in more distinctively American terms.[8] If, however, one pays careful attention to Wood's use of the figure of the body, then *New Englands Prospect* can emerge for what it is: a compelling revision of English political authority. It is from this perspective that some of Wood's rather preposterous claims—the claim, for example, that New

England's climate enhances the Englishness of those who settle there—can be construed as a challenge to early modern conceptions of political power.

THE EXPERIENCED ENGLISH BODY IS A COLONIAL BODY

Wood first asks his reader to understand the body as a sign of national rather than individual identity that records the marks of experience. So, for instance, when he cites the case of "a certain man" and "a certain woman" to demonstrate "how some English bodies have borne out" the cold weather of New England, Wood does not bother to provide any individual names.[9] The names attached to individual bodies are irrelevant; what matters is the body's political affiliation. Indeed, as the "last argument" to demonstrate that the climate of New England does not adversely affect "the health of our English bodies," Wood cites his "own experience" (10).[10] Thus he suggests that even the experience that would seem to be most individuated, his own, is fundamentally and finally not his alone. There is no personal dimension to colonial experience. His is merely an "English body," and any English body that had spent time in New England could be used to prove the same point about the effects of New England on English health. Despite the difference in diet, housing, and climate, Wood suggests, the American experience sustains and even enhances the Englishness of an Englishman. All English bodies are thus understood to carry a political affiliation, and it is this affiliation—rather than the colonial climate—that determines their experience of a place.

Wood does not rest, though, with the claim that life in the colonies leaves English bodies unaffected. He proceeds, instead, to contradict himself by arguing that the New World experience actually makes English colonial subjects more English than their counterparts in England.[11] How does he support this apparently extravagant claim that New English experience enhances Englishness? More specifically, what is it about a distinctly "alien" environment that Anglicizes its population better than the home climate? Unlike those critics of colonization who say that the New England climate will destroy "our English bodies," Wood contends that life in New England actually provides a climate comparable to an earlier, purer England, the England of "quondom times" (8).[12] Colonial New English experience produces more truly English subjects than England, then, because its climate is closer to the historically original England. Over time, in the home country, the orderly division of days and seasons has broken down. In the colonies, however, "the days and nights be more equally divided" (8). The weather displays the lack of purity Wood is deflecting onto England in the hybrid seasons "Summer Winters" and "Winter Summers" (8). In a truly English climate the days and the seasons should be balanced and distinct. This balance not only helps produce Englishness, Wood suggests, but also shows the colonial England to be pure, coherent, and internally harmonious—all features that, paradoxically, once belonged to the aristocratic body alone. When Wood uses the notion of British America as a recovered English ideal, he silences those critics who think that the colonial environment poses a threat to the health of English subjects. Who, Wood asks, "will condemn that which is as England hath beene?" (8). He thereby suggests that anyone who opposes the colonial project in New England does "not wish" to "return" to the ways of old England. Wood thus associates colonial experience and, by extension, the entire project of colonization with the purification of English culture.

Wood argues further that in producing a more English body, New England also makes this English body more productive. In England, it is possible for people of a "dronish disposition" to "live of the sweate of another mans browes" but "all New England must," Wood insists, "be workers in some kinde" (47–48). In proposing that all colonial subjects not only can but in fact must work, Wood clearly means to quell concern among early modern English elites about what appeared to be a growing number of "idle" poor inhabitants.[13] By shipping such people to New England, England can put those "accounted poore" to work and improve her own financial stability (48).

These practical concerns notwithstanding, Wood's argument that colonialism increases productivity represents more than a simple appeal to the pocketbooks of English elites. The very productivity required by life in New England can transform the specifically English body into an ideal form. The abundance of goods meticulously documented by Wood in prose and verse provides something that England herself no longer can offer: the seemingly infinite chance to labor and transform the cornucopia of beasts, plants, and trees into salable goods. In other words, the natural environment of New England mirrors the English environment of "quondom times" in that its commercial possibilities remain unexploited. The Indians do not practice agriculture, or, at least, no agriculture that Wood and his other English chroniclers recognize as such. Indians hunt, fish, play games, and eat one another, according to Wood, but they do not "work" the land in his European sense of that term. His account of the possibilities that America offers the Englishman, possibilities derived in part from the native's failure to "work" the land, anticipates Locke's proclamation that "in the beginning, all the world was America." For Locke, the English body gains distinctive qualities because it performs the labor necessary to transform natural objects into commercial properties. For Wood, similarly, labor is a necessary precondition for the making of truly English bodies. But whereas Locke uses America metaphorically, *New Englands Prospect* argues quite literally that the climate and labor that made the original English body are available only in America. In order to save the crumbling English body politic located in England proper, Wood suggests, England must put its men to work in the colonies.

He goes so far as to suggest that increased productivity extends to the realm of reproduction as well, claiming that women's bodies reproduce the nation in greater numbers and with more efficiency in the colonies. In dispelling the "common aspersion that [English] women have no children" while living in New England, Wood argues that the colony has "more double births than in England, the women likewise having a more speedy recovery and gathering of strength after their delivery than in England" (9–10).[14] Wood exploits the grotesque qualities of the popular body and insists on its socioeconomic superiority over the body traditionally characterized as aristocratic. Because the popular body is, for Wood, more originary than the elite body, it is in a sense more aristocratic; and the present elite in England, then, represent a falling off from the ideal. While the common body is "unfinished, outgrows itself, transgresses its own limits," opening itself up and in the process absorbing and transforming territory into the common English body, the aristocratic body is static.[15] It is, as noted earlier, "finished, completed." The aristocratic body maintains its supremacy through replacement; in contrast, the common body gains its power through expansion and transformation.

Wood suggests, though, that not all of colonial America can restore the English body to its original form. He claims that unlike the purifying climate of the colonies in New England, the climate of some other colonies, Virginia, for example, can adversely affect the "natural" physical features of their colonists. Thus, when someone comes to New England from Virginia, the New England colonists "know . . . them by their faces," because the Virginia climate changes "their complexion not into swarthiness but into paleness" (8).[16] Here, Wood also addresses two of his readers' concerns. First, he reassures them that in the dangerous environment of colonial North America, with Native American, Spanish, French, and English forces at odds, one can still know one's fellow Englishmen. While the English bodies have been affected by their time in colonial Virginia, the transformation is not so great as to make them unrecognizable to other English colonists. Once an English body, always an English body, whether that body resides in England, Virginia, or New England.

Second, Wood translates his readers' fear of going native into an affirmation of "natural" skin color. "In New England," Wood claims, "both men and women keep their natural complexion" but also look noticeably healthier, "fresh and ruddy" (9). Life in colonial New England both enhances one's Englishness and makes it more noticeable to other Englishmen. One knows the English body from other bodies by its "whiteness," a distinction evident in the colonies, where one encounters people with other skin pigmentations. Wood thus represents as a fundamental characteristic of "our English bodies" what before had gone unnoticed. The colonies, Wood suggests, supply the English with more than mere material goods; they turn skin into a sign of English identity. This exterior condition has an interior counterpoint, for the colonists are "not very much troubled with inflammations or such diseases as are increased by too much heat" (9). English bodies are impervious to alteration in colonial New England, both "inwardly" and outwardly.

But Wood's claim that climate and labor combine in the New England colonies to enhance one's Englishness deals incompletely with an even more potent threat to English identity in the New World: cannibalism. As Myra Jehlen explains, cannibalism "became in Western culture the ideal type of alien behavior" and the very "sign of alterity."[17] For European writers of the early modern period, it drew a line between "civilized" and "uncivilized" cultures. Cannibalism represents the ultimate threat and the source of the fear of going native—because, through the act of cannibalism, one's body is literally incorporated by the native, annihilating both the individual and the self–other distinction Wood sought to establish by racializing the English body.

Wood tries to diminish this threat by establishing a safe distance between English colonial bodies and New World cannibalism.[18] The very presence of English bodies and the technologies their labor produces, he suggests, protects the English from cannibalism. Wood goes so far as to claim that the native practice of cannibalism ceased upon the arrival of the English.[19] Once the English align themselves with those Indian nations that do not practice cannibalism, he says, tribes that do engage in it, such as the Mohawks, apparently give up the practice because they "dare not meddle with a white-faced man, accompanied with his hot-mouthed weapon" (57). The English body itself, whose distinctiveness through color is produced in part through the very colonial encounters Wood is here describing, protects the English from cannibalism by frightening off those who would violate its cultural boundaries. Whiteness is frightening because it is linked with the body so marked and, in particular, with European weapons, weapons that invert the very terms of cannibalism. While cannibalism destroys by consuming an object, by literally ingesting it through the mouth, the "hot-mouthed" English musket projects a shot from the mouth that penetrates and destroys another body. Technological superiority not only shields the English from cannibalism but also humanizes the most "inhumane" of native peoples by putting an end to cannibalism (57).

Wood offers an account of Mohawk cannibalism that comes not from an English colonist but from "a near-neighboring Indian." In this story, the native's body corroborates his account, since he "still wear[s] the cognizance of their cruelty on his naked arm" (57). The marks displayed externally, this "lamentable experience" brands the author of this account as a native and a recipient of cannibalism, a practice the English never experience (57). Wood finds it necessary, we must assume, to represent cannibalism as something the English merely observe. Paradoxically, however, the very language that Wood uses to minimize the threat of cannibalism also connects English experience to native experience. Wood's choice of "lamentable" to describe the experience of the "near-neighboring Indian" echoes his description of English experience in *New Englands Prospect*, where the term supports his claim that servants who are well-provided for in the colonies are more productive laborers (57). John Smith uses the same term to describe his experiences in the colonies. The authority of experience rests on the belief that anyone who survives such "lamentable" hardships comes to much the same conclusion about their meaning and significance, regardless of their position within the English social system. Thus, Wood uses the phrase to describe how members of the English upper class have learned that it is not the number of servants but the quality of those servants that indicates whether one will make a profit in the colonies. To call on the notion of "lamentable experience," then, is to call on the role experience plays in breaking down categories that distinguish social groups.

Having situated cannibalism as a potential but absent danger, Wood can use it to reestablish English colonial identity on firmer grounds. That is to say, he can define all cultures, not just native ones, by their consumptive practices. On the basis of what they consume, for example, the Mohegans can be said to have an "inhumane" culture. At the same time, Wood suggests, the term "cannibalism" can be applied to English cultural practices as easily as native ones, once one understands that the consumption of English travel writing resembles cannibalism. Wood's opening address "To the Reader" explains that his "more light and facetious stile" in section 2 fits his discussion of what such practices have to offer English readers. The "mirth and laughter" inspired by his account of native culture should add some "spice" to his "serious discourse," making it more "pleasant" to digest. By adding "spice," he hopes to make his generous portions of "gravity and wisdom" taste better going down. Given that hope of opening new routes to the spice trade was one of the factors motivating English colonialism in the first place, his comparison of native experience with spice suggests the English reader can enjoy a dash of this culture, much as dinner plates and wallets are enhanced by imported condiments.[20]

The figure of England as a body consuming colonial texts fundamentally distinguishes English culture from those cultures indigenous to British America. Wood spends the bulk of the first eleven chapters detailing English consumption: what fish are available and where, what animals live in the area and how to trap them, what plants can be eaten and which avoided, and what commodities can reap a profit in the European market. At the end of this first section, Wood concludes, "if any man desire to fill himselfe at that fountaine, from whence this tasting cup was taken, his owne experience shall tell him as much as I have here related" (55). Thus, he converts his own experience into a form of eating (drinking from a fountain) that any Englishman would experience much as he does. As with eating, moreover, so with reading. Indeed, for Wood, the two are interchangeable. In lieu of drinking in the experience of the New World as Wood has done, other men can read what Wood has eaten. In addition to the agricultural goods and livestock, then, the English in America produce written accounts of experience that can be consumed to equal advantage by an English readership too. Indeed, we might say that Bakhtin's description of the grotesque body applies equally well to Wood's description of the common body, in this one respect: it "swallows the world."[21]

In order to elevate this nonelite, collective body so that it is no longer understood as the sprawling, inchoate, and inherently negative opposite of the early modern (elite) body politic, Wood must give it boundaries, internal order, and a foundation in the sensual, that is, the experiential body. The fact that the sensual body writes, reproducing its experience in words, makes all the difference between the popular body as represented in early modern England and the idealized version of that body that emerged in the colonies. In *New Englands Prospect*, Wood presents himself as merely a conduit, providing passages "from experience," as if parts of the book were written by a body known as experience. In the concluding chapter of Part One, for example, he writes:

> Many peradventure at the looking over of these relations, may have inclinations or resolution for the Voyage, to whom I wish all prosperity in their undertakings; although I will use no forcive arguments to persuade any, but

leave them to the relation; yet by way of advice, I would commend to them a few lines from the Pen of experience. (49)

Wood renounces almost all personal responsibility for the composition of portions of his book, handing that role over to experience. He announces that experience will pen the passages that follow; experience itself will write the forthcoming portions of *New Englands Prospect.* Moreover, the body that writes the text is a specific political body, initiated and reproduced by any Englishman who writes about his travels in the New World. Experiencing that world produces a common body of experience, one not tied to any particular person, and one that reproduces itself as such in writing. Thus it takes the "Pen of experience" to transform individual colonial bodies into a common English body that is originary and pure.

In proposing to substitute "the Pen of experience" for "forcive argument," Wood points the way to the unification of English subjects divided over the debates occasioned by colonization efforts of the 1630s. His mention of "forcive argument" alludes to the battles over the scope, method, and outcome of English efforts to colonize North America.[22] By abandoning the use of "forcive argument," his discourses no longer pit those Englishmen "estranged" from colonization against "such as are well willers to the plantations" (55). Instead, the "Pen of experience" addresses only those readers who "devote their states, and their persons, to the common good of their king and country" (55). The pen of experience, he implies, is a force for national unification. We can see, Wood suggests, that English subjects are unified when we observe them reduced to participation in the national body in accounts of their colonial experience. The English reader consumes a piece of this body when he reads colonial literature.

Placed immediately prior to the discussion of native cannibalism, this account of the consumption of the English body reads as a positive model of English consumption. Wood's paired examples of the eating of experience equate the English with the natives in that they are both what they eat. At the same time, these examples differentiate the two "cultures" by showing that only the English have a print culture to consume. The natives literally incorporate the other, while the English absorb its knowledge in the form of writing. Understood in this way, the English retain authority on experiential grounds alone because they are better consumers of experience.

But if all cultures are in some sense cannibalistic, as Wood indeed implies, what is to prevent the English from descending to the level of the natives once the colonists are connected to England only by print, and not by the more direct physical principle of eating the same food? Indeed, while in the opening chapters he claims that all of New England has more than enough food to sustain English communities, at a later point Wood claims that Mohawk land is not so fertile after all. He contends that the Mohawks consume human bodies in order to survive, not out of some inherent ferocity or because they cannot control this unspeakable appetite, but because Mohawk land is not good for agriculture and is "destitute of fish and flesh" (57). Human flesh serves as a substitute for more "natural" forms of consumption (57). If Mohawk cannibalism results from the harsh environment, then what is to keep all communities living in the area from this fate? Without rich land, might not the English themselves devolve into cannibals as well? This possibility threatens the foundational claim that experience purifies the English body.

What saves that body, according to Wood's account, is its ability to transform American land into English land through labor. The English body is a body that works. Wood contrasts English experiential methods with Indian methods. The natives have a passive relationship to the land: their experience enables them to take a living from the land, but they "fail" to "work" it. In a section devoted to native "games," he goes so far as to argue that the natives would "rather starve than work" (85). In order to work the land, one must rely on certain kinds of experience. His description of English "experiments" with potentially salable items obtained in New England suggests that the English can reap economic benefits from colonial products by testing them. Finding that a river which runs through the plantation of Saugus has a "great store of Alewives, of which they make good Red Herring," a number of colonists conduct an "experiment" to dry the herring, testing to see if the fish is as commercially viable as they suspect (41). If proven correct, their discoveries should prove a "great enrichment to the land" (42). Before the English, the land had been poor, and neither nature nor natives could enrich it. Only the English, using experimental methods, can do so. Their labor transforms nature itself into English culture—thus, into English land.

As Wood proceeds to contrast this "experiencial method" of achieving colonial productivity with other methods, he necessarily casts the means of acquiring colonial wealth in national terms. While he admits that "nobody dare confidently conclude, yet dare they not utterly deny" that gold deposits might exist in New England, he labels gold "the Spaniards bliss" (14). Wood thus deflects attention from the single-minded search for gold ("Spaniards bliss") among some proponents of colonization without totally discounting its presence. The English colonial method, though, as we saw above, relies directly on the body and its experience. This experiential method works to transform the land in a way that the Spanish method of simply extracting gold does not. Thus, unlike the Spanish who are enriched by the land through their acquisition of gold, the English make their own bodies more English through the process of enriching the land itself.

THE EXPERIENCED ENGLISH COLONIAL BODY
IS A GENDERED BODY

Even when the threats of climate and cannibalism have been neutralized, another threat to the English body remains: the transformation of that body through alien cultural practices. English bodies withstand the climate because they are English, and they avoid cannibals because they are inherently industrious and technologically innovative. But to survive in the colonies, even Wood concedes, the English must adopt certain native practices. They must learn to hunt as natives hunt, travel as natives travel, and eat what natives eat. Indeed, the English sometimes live among the natives, making one, in Wood's words, "home" to both native and English peoples (72). But if you live where the natives live, eat what they eat, hunt like they hunt, sleep where and how they sleep, what is it that makes you English? What makes the English "English" if they begin to emulate the natives in their habits and practices?

As a way to insist that the colonists retain their English identity even though they share certain native experiences, Wood creates separate categories of New World experience for the colonists and the Indians, respectively. Indeed, these experiential categories determine the structure of the book, the first part of which describes "the country as it stands to the English" and the second, "how it stands to the old Natives" (55). Wood differentiates between these two perspectives without demonstrating how people living in the same environment can see the same things so differently. If assertion is substituted for argument, however, rhetoric becomes fact, as if it made as much sense to separate Indian from English experience as to separate the birds from the fish of British America, or the "Beasts that live on the land" from those that "live in the water."[23] Thus Wood puts cultural differences on the same plane with differences in nature. English subjects will remain English, even though far away from England because they are English by nature.

Once experiences have been so categorized, furthermore, they can be compared and judged inferior or superior. Wood contends, not surprisingly, that while the English may lack experience of the local environment, the experience they bring from England to the New World allows them to overcome their lack of local knowledge.[24] So while the natives are experienced in matters of hunting, traveling, and planting in New

England, according to this logic, they lack experience in developing and employing "the inventions that are common to a civilized people" such as ships, windmills, and plows (77). Wood shifts attention away from the colonists' relative ignorance of New England geography onto their experience in a more civilized domain of trade. Indeed, whenever Wood concedes native superiority in some area of experience, he does precisely what he does here and takes away with the one hand what he just gave to native experience with the other. He demonstrates that any practical use of that experience depends on English know-how, and that any cultural exchange between the two groups results in a profit for the colonists. Noting that the natives are "expert" fishermen, "being experienced in the knowledge of all baites," he remarks that native "lazinesse" prevents them from producing as many hooks and lines as they need (89). Thus, native superiority in the fish trade is offset by native dependence on English products to maintain that trade. Indeed, Wood contends that the natives buy more hooks and lines than their profits from the fish trade require, creating a trade imbalance in the English favor.[25]

In Wood's telling, the natives themselves acknowledge the superiority of the Europeans' conception of experience, which derives from the term "experiment." Wood uses native behavior in response to the English colonists to legitimate his hierarchy. At "first view" of the medical, mechanical, and cultural "inventions" the English have brought with them from Europe, Wood reports, the natives are "ravisht with admiration" (77). He attributes these inventions to experimental procedures that natives lack. Smart enough to understand English superiority, the natives place themselves in the position of the student, hoping to learn how to make such "strange" things as the ship and the plow, as well as to overcome the infectious diseases to which the English seem curiously immune.[26] Wood congratulates the natives for displaying "no small ingenuitie, and dexterity of wit" in emulating English technology (78). He also assures his reader that natives will retain their inferior position because the "chains of idleness" will always prevent them from working as hard as the English. For Wood, while it may be true that the cultural differences between native and European knowledge are subject to the influence of cultural exchange between the two groups, the natives can catch up only by working like the devil to replicate English experience—in relation to which they will always display a lack. But Wood does not rest here. In the concluding chapter, he adds one last touch to his figure of the common body, a touch designed to allay fears that the English will become less English through their contact with any remaining native savagery.

To make his point, Wood tries to dispel one final "aspersion," spread by the plantation's opponents, about the effects of colonization on En-

glish culture, namely, that colonial Englishmen in the colonies have begun to treat English women with the same "churlishnesse and savage
inhumanitie" that native men treat native women (97). To refute the
charge made by critics of the colonial project that colonial men "learne
of the Indians to use their wives in the like manner," Wood appeals to
his "owne experience" (97). He has found that far from going native,
colonial Englishmen treat colonial women, in fact, in a way that repli-
cates the very social stratification that defines English society. He concedes that in New England, some "poore" women "carrie their owne
water" like native women do (98). But to say that such labor constitutes
the "mistreatment" of English women is to mistake the colonial reproduction of English class systems for nativization. He asks, "doe not the
poorer sort in England doe the same?" (98). In so doing, Wood transforms the gendered image that implies that colonists are going native
into an image of an orderly English class system.

It is ironic, I think, that to demonstrate how English men do not treat
women as the natives do, Wood uses female rather than male labor,
given that such a body image stands not only for the condition of colonial women but for the condition of the English body politic in general.
To make sense of this, we might begin by recalling what Wood has
stressed throughout *New Englands Prospect*: that English colonial life
does not replicate seventeenth-century English life; it reproduces the life
of England in "quondom times." What one sees in the colonies is pure
English life as it originally was, rather than what it has become under
Charles I. Wood establishes the treatment of women as a mark of civilization based on his observation that the greatest change occurs among
native women, not English men. Seeing "the kind usage of the English
to their wives," native women are likely to become "miserable" and
"condemne their husbands for unkindnesse and commend the English
for their love" (97). These women frequently seek out English women
for support against their husbands. Just as the English military presence
brings an end to "martial feats worth observation" between various
tribes, the English domestic presence creates dissent within the communities themselves that works to English advantage by making marginal-
ized persons in the native community publicly condemn their society's
behavior and argue for the transformation of native cultural life into an
English model (85). Wood again turns the head, rhetorically transforming the threat *of* native culture into a threat *to* native culture.

It is worth noting, at this point in my argument, how Wood strategi-
cally casts English women as England's defenders against native men.
The English colonial home is the site of gender differentiation. When
native women enter that home, they enter a space where "pares cum
paribus congregatae"—equals are gathered together with equals (97).

Within the home, however, women form an alliance across cultural lines in opposition to native male authority. Wood claims that if a native husband comes to an English home looking "for his Squaw," it is the English wife who repels him (97). Should the husband "beginne to bluster," the English woman will take up "the warlike Ladle, and the scalding liquors" against him (97). The English woman apparently displays her own version of English technological proficiency, as she transforms her pots and pans into weapons capable of staving off an invader. Domestic objects are thus transformed into objects of violence to be used against an invading enemy. The presence of native women in English households testifies to native male impotence: if they cannot defeat English women, how can they hope to defeat English men?[27]

In gendering the colonial body, Wood sets out to establish distinct categories of readers as well. Wood opens the final chapter of *New Englands Prospect* with the claim that it is designed to "satisfie the curious eye of women readers" (94). Wood has made it clear in the "Preface to the Reader" that he assumes all his readers to be English. In this final chapter, he divides the body politic into sexes. He takes care to define this chapter on women as supplementary material unnecessary to *New Englands Prospect* as a whole, and as added to prevent a relatively small group of potential readers from feeling "forgotten or not worthy a record" (94). Moreover, he contends that by reading his account, English women will not pick up any wild ideas but instead "see their owne happinesse, if weighed in the . . . ballance of these ruder Indians" (94). Something about its gendered nature gives the readership a different relation to the printed text than it would have if conceptualized as strictly male. Anatomical differences determine one's experience of reading colonial material, just as, by extension, they determine one's reading of all matters of life.

Thus, it can be argued, what Wood represents as a distinctively English way of imagining familial relations depends on the rhetoric of experience for its confirmation. In fact, this way of representing the family as distinctively English only becomes so when viewed in comparison with native practices. Indeed, experience of English familial structures results in the potential expansion of those structures, which surreptitiously work their way into native society when Indian women use their own experience to judge their husbands. But Wood must proceed carefully. By implying that the gendered body is the truly English body, he runs the risk of treason. English power is, after all, invested in the aristocratic body. To suggest another source of English power is to question the iconography that had for centuries authorized power. While the aristocratic English body is not gendered, the common English body survives at least in part through its very differentiation by sex.

In order to avoid antagonizing his reader, Wood devises a way to have the nobility itself authorize the very image that differentiates the colonial from the aristocratic body. Wood begins to do this in the opening pages of *New Englands Prospect* when he personifies the colonies as a living being with a physical body endowed with life by the king through his "Letters Patent" (1). The aristocratic body continues to support the growth of this body via his "Favors and Royall protection" (1). Thus Wood describes what could be seen as a direct outgrowth of the aristocratic body as oppositional; this outgrowth not only supports the growth of the colonial body by protecting it, but also supports that which produced that body in the first place. Indeed, figures of growth and expansion dominate the passage as Wood writes of "growing hopes," "the enlargement of . . . Dominions," and "further encouragement" (1). In return for protection, the colonial body in turn enlarges England's influence over a wider area of the globe. Far from opposing the aristocratic body, those who help the colonies grow "either by purse or person" are also acting in the service of the aristocracy.

England's support of the colonies extended, Wood would have us believe, to Wood himself. It was through the "grant of his Letters Patents," he claims, that the king gave "life to the plantations" (1). Without this support, Wood could not "see fit" to "set forth these few observations out of [his] personall and experimentall knowledge" (1). If these letters gave life to the plantations, then by implication they "gave life" to the very experiences Wood is relating and, by extension, to the body politic created by those experiences. The colonial body thus belongs to the monarch. Further, the same "letters" that authorize colonial experience also restrict it. When describing where the English have built New England, for example, Wood explains, it is "not my intent to wander far from our Patent" (2). In setting boundaries for the colonists' travel, the patent limits what they can and cannot experience. Thus, Wood suggests that, rather than experience producing writing, writing produces and restricts colonial experience. Born out of writing, the colonial body is held in check by writing.

Just as the aristocratic body gives life to the colonial body, Wood's patron serves as parent to the book itself.[28] In the dedicatory letter for *New Englands Prospect*, Wood describes his production of the book in terms of bodily "labors." Labor here means more than simply work, for Wood describes the book as his offspring, as both a "brat" and the "fruits" of his "far-fetched experience." This child "receive[s] life and courage" from Sir William Armyne. The patron's "foster[ship] of Wood's "brat" provides his writing with whatever authority it may have in the community. In return, Wood sees the child born of his own experience as an act of service to his superior. In his words, "I count it the least part of my service to present the first fruits of my far-fetched experience" to "the Right Worshipful, my much honored friend, Sir William Armyne, Knight and Baronet." In contrast with Wayne Franklin's claim that "Wood writes from the stance of an excited traveler for whom curiosity . . . is the primary impulse," then, this relationship between the book and the body implies that Wood writes in order to meet his social obligations to his patron.[29] Both evolve out of a series of exchanges where experience is one productive element in a larger framework, a framework whose series of interlinking chains must be present for both the experience and the writing to come into being. The experienced body does not exist outside or prior to the economy Wood describes, but, instead, is produced precisely within its boundaries.

Colonial expansion is necessary, according to this model, because the aristocratic body requires the colonial body in order to make itself whole. Wood concedes that "of late time there hath been great want" in the colonies (47). He blames the starvation of transplanted workers and men of estate on a "want" that "sprung up in England," rather than on any lack of food or shelter in New England (47). He contends that to understand the "roote of [Englishmen's] want" in the colonies one must look at the "originall"(47). England sends over people ill-prepared to survive because England does not have sufficient supplies to satisfy its people, not because New England fails to supply their needs. Those English who come to the New World without sufficient provisions will certainly perish, whether they are servants or noblemen. While "all new England must be workers [in] some kinde," even work is not sufficient at first to ensure survival (48). The working body requires the aristocratic body. Wood does not suggest, as Smith did, that aristocrats should labor in the same way as commoners do, but contends instead that the aristocratic body has something else to offer: capital. That is to say, Wood claims that New England offers a place where *capital* can be put to work and made productive. One does not have to perform physical labor in order to be a productive member of the nation, Wood suggests. Establishing an estate in New England requires the individual to "scatter" his cash: the "man of estate . . . must lay out monies for transporting of servants, and cattle and goods, for houses and fences and gardens" (48). Such a scattering of capital may seem like a "leaking" of the man of wealth's "purse," but in fact "these disbursements are for his future enrichments: for he being once well seated and quietly setled, his increase comes in double" (48). Thus Wood concedes that New English wealth and productivity depend on English importation of money, men, and technology; the increased productivity of labor and capital in England proper is, in turn, made to depend on New English experience.

Having established this reciprocal relationship between the aristocratic and colonial bodies in one body politic, Wood proceeds to use the figure of territorial expansion to define his ideal English reader as one who seeks to increase his body of knowledge. He describes that growth in physical terms: the ideal English reader of *New Englands Prospect* is one who seeks to increase his or her "mind" through reading. In his introductory address "To the Reader," Wood rather sarcastically suggests he will refrain from describing "anything which may puzzle thy beleefe" since some people are unwilling to concede the "possibility of those things he sees not." He goes on to "decline this sort of thicke witted readers," aiming his work at "more credulous, ingenious, and less censorious Country men."[30] What Wood does not say is that neither kind of reader actually "sees" anything in *New Englands Prospect*. No one does. Readers consume Wood's representation of things. The consumption of print is a form of mental labor equivalent to the labor of traveling in New England. Wood wants his account to have the same impact on those who merely intend to use his account for a "mind-traveling" adventure as on those who actually travel to New England. Thus, the reader expands her or his mind in reading Wood's account, much as the aristocratic body expands its sphere of control by colonizing America.

By aiming at a specifically English readership, Wood effectively nationalizes the consumption of colonial experience and simultaneously insinuates that those who are opposed to understanding life in the colonies do more than thwart colonization. In other words, print culture infiltrates the reader's mind in a way that aristocratic culture cannot, but always in the service of expanding the aristocratic body. A crucial component of Wood's genuinely English reader is his desire to expand his mind. Where a "decline[d]" reader may reject any bit of information that is outside the "straite hoopes of his apprehension," the ideal reader wants to know about the colonies. In this respect, the truly English reader does not limit his support for the monarchy to the dimension of geographic space but extends it over temporal space as well. Wood wants the "information" gleaned from his "observation" to prove "beneficiall to posteritie" (55). As a result, colonial experience will continue to expand England and keep it English as the years pass. What Wood is suggesting, then, is that colonial literature provides more than a temporary resolution to England's current crises; it provides a way of continually reproducing Englishness.

Moreover, his method of cultural reproduction is exceedingly economical, requiring little time or money. In fact, the prefatory poem to *New Englands Prospect*, "To the Author, his singular good friend, Mr.

William Wood" describes the book as a substitution of reading for travel that provides a "short cut to New England" (l. 10). Wood is thanked for having "comptly plac't" "much knowledge in so small roome" (l. 2). The "small roome" refers both to the site of the book's consumption and the relative brevity of the book itself. The poem figures Wood as literally entering rooms all over England to provide readers with his colonial experience.[31] By playfully suggesting that the object consumed is yet another small room in the English home, the poem domesticates the written record of colonial experience by demonstrating that such experience can be understood in terms of common and even mundane English social spaces. Any threat to Englishness posed by the consumption of the "stranger than ordinary" objects, places, and peoples described in colonial writing is rendered harmless. Read within the confines of the English home, colonial experience becomes—rather than a consumptive threat to English colonists—an object of English consumption. In order to claim that everyone can use the text to share in the experience of the colonies, the poem figuratively gives experience a body of its own. In then claiming that readers can "mount" Wood's experience, the poem suggests that experience is transformed into the body of a horse that will allow the reader to directly ride through or reproduce what has transpired to the writer (l. 6). As a result, all English subjects can "travel" great distances and participate in the colonization of distant lands. In the words of the title page, every English subject can become a "mind-travelling Reader." If this common experience permeates English bodies through the consumption of print, then, ultimately, it enters their homes as well. It is in the rooms of those homes—or, one might say, within the body of the house—that print works to return English subjects and England itself to their more English "quondom" bodies.

Wood's opponents had complained that colonial experience posed a threat to the Englishness of English subjects. *New Englands Prospect* proposes that, in fact, colonial experience produces subjects more English than those in England. What this address to the reader suggests is that the process does not end in the colonies but circles back to England as well. The poem's scene of reading provides the last link in an intricate chain of exchanges bonding the contrary embodiments of the English social order. By bringing colonial experience into homes back in England, *New Englands Prospect* will incorporate that home within the colonial project. "Home" indeed becomes the place where much of the work of English colonization is performed. All readers are in this sense colonists and by virtue of this fact become more truly English.

But housed within this body of experience imported from the colonies are what appear to be contradictory features, features that threaten to tear the body politic asunder. This imported body is associated with masculinity, as when Wood pictures it as a body at work transforming colonial ground into English land. At the same time, he also links this body with the feminine by having it defer to monarchical authority. Far from posing a contradiction, however, these diversely gendered features of the common body represent different aspects of a single body in which the feminine features are subservient to the masculine ones. Its masculine and feminine components represent different rhetorical uses of the common body, rather than incompatible elements within it. This compatibility of feminine and masculine, though, depends on the proper subordination of women to men. We will turn next to the Antinomian controversy of the 1630s in New England and observe how the church bureaucracy used the gendered body politic to put "men" in a position within the common body analogous to the position "aristocracy" occupied in relation to it. In this way, the Boston Church made the order and well-being of the English body politic depend on subordinating women.

Chapter Four

DISCIPLINE AND DISINFECT

AS PERRY MILLER noted long ago, New English civil and religious institutions were designed at least in part to be "a working model to guide" the political allies they had left behind in England.[1] New Englanders soon learned, however, that their institutions were often seen more as a threat to English government than a cure for its ills. In *Plain Dealing: Or, Newes From New England* (1641), Thomas Lechford claims that the years 1638 to 1641 during which he lived in Massachusetts Bay proved to him that the political system of New England undermined the political authority on which the stability of the English nation depends. The government of Massachusetts Bay endangered the monarchy, according to Lechford, because it assumed that patriarchal authority derives from the common body of the people rather than from "the great body, heart and hands, and feete" of the king, whose immortal body politic stands at the "head" of the ideal social body.[2] Lechford suggests that by locating the source of political authority in the will of the people, the colonists not only challenge the "hereditary, successive" monarchical system but also put the very Englishness of English government at risk, since national identity depends, he argues, on the purity of the aristocratic bloodline that popular sovereignty is not designed to protect.[3]

Colonial writers protested their innocence. They had no intention of undermining English government; they merely wanted to plant that government on firmer ground. They wanted England to adopt the Congregational church system, a system that called for the popular election of some political representatives by a carefully screened group of voters.[4] By publishing treatises in London during the monarchical crisis of the 1640s, Massachusetts Bay colonists hoped to make Congregationalists their allies in England.[5] They hoped that the English civil war would lead to a government on the order of their own Congregational churches.[6] But the colonists were in a precarious position. Since the king had issued the colony's charter, "political expediency" prevented the colonists from "publicly and officially endors[ing] the parliamentary cause," lest the king return to power and the magistrates be charged with treason.[7] So it was that the colonists refrained from publishing tracts that criticized the king and instead offered writings on Congregational "church order and discipline" to the English public.[8]

Colonial writers used the Antinomian controversy (1636–38) to demonstrate that Congregationalism safeguarded and even bolstered an English authority that would not challenge the old system of monarchical rule. The conduct of the magistrates and church elders during the controversy initially drew censure for what critics on both sides of the Atlantic saw as the colony's many violations of English common law.[9] Amy Schrager Lang points out that "the same English Puritans who had not hesitated to criticize New England's handling of the antinomians found themselves confronting a similar menace" during the crises of the 1640s.[10] Thus colonial New English writers hoped that the Congregational system that had drawn so much fire would now be viewed more favorably in England. It was at this point that colonial treatises could represent their own Congregational solution as one that might keep the English social order in place as well. Their argument to this effect began with the allegation that a group of "Antinomians" was engaged in "seditious" activities aimed directly at the authority of the colony's political and religious leaders.[11] Since the besieged leaders were the Crown's representatives in the colony, any threat to their power was also an attack on the king in particular and on English systems of authority in general. The Congregationalists' success in dealing with the seditious factions illustrated the superiority of the New England system. Thus, it was argued, the English government would be wise to follow the example of Massachusetts Bay if it hoped to maintain political order in already turbulent times.

All of this is well known to scholars of colonial American literature. Indeed, few texts in the period have generated as much commentary as the trial transcripts of Anne Hutchinson, the woman whom the magistrates considered the "root" of the subversive faction. I have no interest in participating in the ongoing debate over what precisely led the magistrates to banish Hutchinson and whether Hutchinson and the magistrates' theological differences represent competing orthodoxies or variations within a single religious ideology. I am interested, instead, in the rhetorical measures taken to represent and quell the threat posed to the colony.

As James Schramer and Timothy Sweet correctly point out, "[b]odily analogies are the controlling metaphors" in the Antinomian controversy's written records.[12] In telling the story of the controversy to an English audience, colonial writers cast the Antinomian threat as a "Plague" that had "infected" the colonial body. Magistrates and church elders subsequently "cured" that infection by subjecting Hutchinson and her allies to rigorous civil and religious examinations. Only after these hearings failed to convince the Antinomians of the danger their religious ideas posed to the health of the communal body did the magistrates decide to banish the Antinomians. Thus, the Congregational system drew on its authority to quell dissent by representing the colonial community as a body at risk.

To understand the significance of this use of the plague as a rhetorical figure, we must, I believe, look to Europe. The measures taken by the colonists against a spiritual infection are analogous to new procedures developed during the seventeenth and eighteenth centuries when the plague raged across the Continent. These new strategies developed for dealing with the plague in Europe are striking because they are also the very procedures that Foucault identifies with the onset of a modern bureaucratic system of inclusion and discipline that produces distinctively modern institutions for managing populations. Indeed, Foucault goes so far as to argue that "the plague gave rise to disciplinary projects."[13] When the plague struck a city in the sixteenth and seventeenth centuries, he reminds us, everyone, the populace as well as the aristocracy, were sealed into their homes. This change in policy represented a fundamental shift in the self-image of the nation: "Rather than the massive, binary division between one set of people and another," the nation comes to be imagined as many self-enclosed households "ceaselessly" under the surveillance of the local magistrates. Whereas previously the nation had been imagined as twin bodies whose separation was necessary to ensure the survival of the body politic, disciplinary society imagines the community as a single body whose health depends on the vigilant oversight of its constituent parts by an elaborate bureaucracy.

I do not mean to suggest that Foucault's analysis of continental responses to the plague can explain the Antinomian controversy. The spiritual plague infecting the Congregational community is not the same as the modern institutional culture that emerged as a new method of dealing with bubonic plague. But these differences between Europe and America should not prevent us from attending to certain similarities that offer new insight into this well-discussed controversy. The connection that Foucault makes between the treatment of the plague and the new ways of imagining and protecting the nation shows that the figure of the plague is used elsewhere to modify the basis, method, and goal of state government. To see the Antinomian plague as a threat to English systems of government, one must understand the nation in somatic terms. The colony, like the European nation, resembles a diseased body, because its membership/population has been infected—whether physically or spiritually figurative, the cultural logic is much the same. The remedy does not involve preserving the head, aristocracy, or elders, but weeding out the infection and making the whole body once again whole. This requires enclosure and examination, according to Foucault, rather than the kind of solution represented, for example, in Boccaccio's *Decameron*.[14]

Any number of seventeenth-century New England writings could serve as the site for an investigation of the figure of Antinomianism as an infection. Edward Johnson, Peter Bulkeley, John Cotton, and Cotton Mather—to name only a few—all cast the threat in terms of a plague-like infection of the colonial body.[15] In order to calculate the effects on the body politic of the figure of the plague, rhetorical and real, I have chosen to focus on the work not only considered the "first and most authoritative history of the Controversy," but also thought to have "set the conceptual terms for recounting the crisis" used by later chroniclers— John Winthrop's *A Short Story of the Rise, reign, and ruine of the Antinomians, Familists, & Libertines* (1644).[16] In this well-known "history," Winthrop, governor of the colony, shows how Massachusetts Bay's magistrates and church elders disinfected the colonial body of the Antinomian plague by transforming themselves into a bureaucracy capable of examining and weeding out the sources of contamination, and thus making the body whole.[17] In holding the magistrates and elders responsible for safeguarding the colonial body politic from disease, I will argue, Winthrop makes a subtle but significant shift in the national self-image. He suggests that for the colony's bureaucratic system to work, it must treat the national body as if it were made up of many different households rather than an aristocratic body in relation to which the common body represents, in Foucault's words, "a mass among which it was useless to differentiate."[18] This new figure of the body politic as an aggregate of individual members has at least one additional feature that the traditional body politic lacked. Winthrop's rhetoric suggests that the elevation of the common body to the status of a figure for the nation itself must be accompanied by a rather rigid internal division and hierarchy of that body along gender lines: for Winthrop, only the subordination of female to male members can ensure that this body politic does not revert to the older figure of the popular body as unruly or carnivalesque.

Scholars have long acknowledged the pivotal role played by images of women's bodies in Winthrop's version of the controversy. Their bodies, according to Ann Kibbey, are offered by Winthrop as "proof of the horror of antinomianism."[19] Thus, when Anne Hutchinson and Mary Dyer, both of the Antinomian party, bear stillborn children in the midst of the crisis, Winthrop orders the babies' bodies exhumed from their plots and examined as signs from God that the Antinomians have twisted His doctrine. The "monstrous and misshapen" body of the infant Hutchinson bears reflects the "misshappen" opinions she has "vented."[20] The author of the preface to *A Short Story*, Thomas Welde, wrote it while serving as the colonists' agent in England during the civil war. According to Welde, God has "caused the two fomenting women in the time of the height of the [controversy] to produce out of their wombs, as before they had out of their braines, such monstrous births as no Chronicle (I thinke) hardly ever recorded the like."[21] Indeed, Welde asserts that the children's dead bodies indicate God's "owne vote and suffrage" on the matter (12–13).[22]

Cultural historian Thomas Laqueur uses Winthrop's version of the trope of the monstrous birth to illustrate how women's bodies serve as figures for what Bakhtin calls the "grotesque body," the popular body in need of regulation. Winthrop's claim to have found "horns . . . claws, and holes in the back, and some scales" on one of the fetuses provides Laqueur with "an excruciating and dramatic" manifestation of the belief that "any perturbation of accepted order . . . could imprint itself disasterously on the flesh of [a woman's] child in utero."[23] Nor is Laqueur alone in equating women with the negation of the social order in seventeenth-century literature. Winthrop's macabre description of the dead babies has succeeded in attracting the attention of a number of scholars interested in demonstrating that representations of female bodies in early modern literature serve political ends.[24] For Welde, the traditional figure provides the "order and sense of [the] story" of Antinomianism (1). Winthrop argues that the Antinomians put this "order and sense" in jeopardy, as he translates the controversy's historical events and theological disputes into an account of how the colonial body politic body caught and fought off an infection. In England, the king's body stood at once for the secular government and for the Church of England, as if there were no difference between them. Winthrop invokes this figure of national leadership and puts the church in the place of the king in making the claim that "the whole Church of Boston" was "infected with [Anne Hutchinson's] opinions" (32). Hutchinson's opinions were so infectious that "where ever shee came [the infectious opinions] must and they should spread" (32). As a result, Antinomianism "spread so fast" that those of sound faith were powerless to stop its march through the colonial body; only "the most wise and mercifull providence of the Lord . . . prevented it by keeping so many of the Magistrates, and Elders, free from the infection" (33). As Welde notes in the preface, preaching provided the only "cure [for] those that were diseased already" and served as the necessary "Antidote" to "preserve [the rest] from infection" (10). Thus Winthrop sets the magistrates and elders in the place of the monarch as the protectors of the body politic, in much the same way that seventeenth-century bureaucracies did in European cities during times of plague.

It is only when Winthrop's remarks on babies' corpses are viewed as part of a larger discourse on the body politic that his detailed description of the grotesque features of the bodies of Antinomian babies can be seen as yet another contribution to the debate over the effects of the colonial body on the English social body. The figures he uses to describe the babies' dead bodies are identical to those used by English opponents of colonization to describe what would happen to the English body politic if colonization were allowed to proceed. In claiming that the child born of Antinomianism had "no head but a face, which stood so low upon the breast, as the eares (which were like an Apes) grew upon the shoulders," Winthrop appropriated a figure that opponents of colonization claimed would be the inevitable offspring of English bodies should they live outside England. In this single brilliant stroke, he equates the bodies of those who oppose his model of authority with those who have rebelled against colonial government and are thus no longer English. In his description, such people have not only reverted to a lower form in the natural chain of being; they have also gone to hell.

Thus does Winthrop devote such detail to these "Monsters" to show the dangers of colonial insurrection. Winthrop intends his method of dealing with unruly women to be a model for English rule in general. England requires such a model, he suggests, because the grotesque body, which anticolonial propaganda used to generate fear of extending the body politic to America, did not originate in the colonies. Nor did it "grow" within the colonial population. The "immediate revelations" that Hutchinson claimed to have received from God occurred before she arrived on New English shores (38). Indeed, there is nothing New English about the woman. Even the "skil[s]" necessary to "spread" the Antinomian "distemper" with preternatural speed through so much of the colonial population were "learned . . . in England" (31). By claiming that all of Hutchinson's opinions, practices, and abilities were in fact "brought into New-England" from England, Winthrop disarms critics who would suggest that she exemplifies the colonial woman. Pushing his argument for her essential Old Englishness still further, Winthrop validates Hutchinson's own argument that her rebellion was at least in part due to the authoritarian tactics of the New English court system. She arrived at what her judges contend are her most dangerous opinions only after they had locked her away from her most trusted religious counselors (58). According to Winthrop's version of the controversy, then, the order of the English colony was threatened by seditious thinking that came into the colony from England.

But Winthrop in no way suggests that England threatens the autonomy and internal order of colonial government, since that government is itself an extension and subordinate part of the English body politic. Indeed, Winthrop claims it is the Antinomians who challenge monarchical authority in defying the king's rightful emissaries in the colony: magistrates such as Winthrop himself. To the magistrates "the King" has "given . . . authority by his graunt under his great Seale of England to heare and determine all causes without any reservation" (27). Hutchinson, Winthrop concludes, was sent to New England by God to test the strength of an English body whose civil authority comes directly from the monarch and was established according to Biblical principles. The fact that Massachusetts Bay survived—which required nothing short of ridding itself of the infection attacking its body—defines the colonial government as an example of the well-regulated English social body that England herself should heed.

We receive an especially clear sense of how Winthrop rethinks the social body from his sermon written on the occasion of the Great Migration in 1630. In "A Modell of Christian Charity" (1630), he argues that what "knitts" the various parts of the social body together constitutes "its perfection."[25] The New England body politic comes as close to realizing the metaphysical body as can any body politic on earth, for nothing less than Christ's "spirit and love" "knitts" the "severall partes of this body . . . to each other."[26] Winthrop maintains that since Christ makes the various parts of this community cohere as one body, the political, theological, and social practices born out of the body will remain pure once the imported elements are disinfected (40). In calling attention to the English origins of the Antinomian threat, Winthrop means to point out England's own vulnerability to the very threat Winthrop himself is struggling to bring under control. That is, if a particularly strong part of the English body politic had to work so hard to shake off this infection, nothing would prevent an English body not modeled so closely on Christian principles from succumbing.

Imported opinions may put the pure New English body at risk, but the far greater threat comes from the sex of the body from which these trusted versions of the word of God issue forth. The importance of gender in understanding the controversy has long been a commonplace of colonial scholarship, and I have no intention of rehearsing the claim that Hutchinson was singled out as the "root of all [the colony's] troubles" simply because she was a woman.[27] Indeed, it is my hope that this argument has gained general acceptance and will require little further elaboration.[28] I simply want to suggest that gender becomes so important to representations of the body politic and eventually a source of tension within it because of the way that Winthrop used the Antinomian controversy to rethink the relation between England and her colonies. Hutchinson, he contends, is nothing less than "the head" of the infectious Antinomian monster that has been "breeder and nourisher of all these distempers" (31). Why, if not to represent the Antinomians as an upside-down version of the social body with its nether parts in place of its head, would Winthrop exaggerate her role in the controversy to the extent of naming her "the principal cause of [the colony's] trouble." Why would he do so, even though any number of influential male leaders, including the ministers John Cotton and John Wheelwright, lectured on Antinomian doctrine to larger groups on a more regular basis in an unambiguously acceptable context for religious teaching? Unless he had some larger rhetorical strategy in mind, it is hard to conceive of Winthrop contradicting his own (misogynist) assumption that Hutchinson's opinions were not her own. They were derived from radical English theologians whose ideas would have been familiar to any dissenter dissatisfied with the English church in the colonial environment of the 1630s.[29] Winthrop singled out the only female voice in the colony and proclaimed her opposition to points of theology, I believe, because it afforded the opportunity to suggest that the Antinomians were not only granting masculine authority to a woman, but thereby also neglecting the long-standing iconographic principle that the "head" of any legitimate political hierarchy was rightfully masculine.

Moreover, in casting the Antinomian communal body as threatening simply because it was female, Winthrop implied that the body politic should be understood as biologically rather than merely figuratively male. Particularly striking about this implication on Winthrop's part is his apparent willingness to fly in the face of a tradition that represented the body politic as a body without sex. Leonard Tennenhouse is among those who argue that at least through Elizabeth's reign "state power was not understood as male in any biological sense," even though it was certainly understood as masculine or patriarchal.[30] By insisting that the body politic should be thought of as biologically male, Winthrop has refigured that body and, by implication, the distribution of power itself.[31]

In making sex a precondition for political authority, Winthrop imperceptibly substitutes sex for rank as the chief division within the body politic. We can observe this shift more clearly if we return to the figure of the ideal body politic described in "A Modell of Christian Charity." In this earlier essay, Winthrop had figured the very same ideal body politic he describes in *A Short Story* divided by rank.[32] In fact, as he saw the political situation then, divisions by rank constituted the natural order of any social body, for "in all times some must be rich, some poore, some highe and eminent in power and dignitie; others meane and in subjection."[33] These differences within the social body were ordained by God, since "all men are ranked into two sortes, riche and poore" by "divine providence."[34] Winthrop believes that for the body politic to be just that, a body politic, distinctions between the various ranks "must" be maintained. Sexual divisions do not enter into this picture before the Antinomian controversy. To be sure, *A Short Story* still acknowledges the importance of rank in maintaining a healthy body politic, but sex has inserted itself into his paradigm of the orderly state as a more primary division on which all other forms of internal hierarchy—including rank—ultimately depend. The healthy body is the sexually differentiated body. In ignoring the consequences of having a biologically female head, a colonial government risks the health of the entire body of which the colony is a part. Indeed, this is precisely the insight *A Short Story* means to offer its English audience: that they, too, must reimagine the body politic along gender lines. The body politic can only be healthy when male bodies rule over female ones from head to toe, just as the members of one rank must rule those of a lower rank in the established model of the political order. What threatens the health of the body is not usurpation of aristocratic power by commoners so much as the usurpation of masculine prerogatives by women. At all costs, the political body must protect its masculinity.[35]

To make his point, Winthrop traces the Antinomian contagion back to the birth room. By locating the source of insurrection in this particular place, he loads his argument against female authority with the freight of ages to suggest at once blood, supernatural birth, women's gossip, and unsanitary conditions as the source of physical disease.[36] While Winthrop's call for a male presence in the birth room no doubt contributes to the well-chronicled "development of obstetrical science" dominated by males and the corresponding decline of midwifery, he wants more than simply to establish a male professional class to oversee and legitimate.[37] He draws on this repository of folklore about women's conspiratorial power in order to convince his readers to vest power in men. Embodied in women, power overturned precisely the order it was supposed to uphold.[38] When rank served as the basis of political power, the exclusion of males from the birth room posed little or no actual threat.[39] When, however, political authority depended on male regulation of the female body, any space where women might escape the watchful eye of male authority was a place where they were likely to stir up trouble. Such a space within the body politic was an inversion—or antibody, if you will—capable of undermining the health of the body politic from within.[40]

Winthrop goes well beyond merely placing a female head on the grotesque Antinomian body. So that there can be no doubt about the sexual character of the threat the female body poses to the authority that Winthrop would have us believe is naturally embodied in the male, he suggests that the infection spreads most rapidly when there are no men around; Antinomianism is born out of Hutchinson's "work" among women "during times of child-birth" (31). It was during such times that she "easily insinuated her selfe into the affections" of the female members of the congregation—so much so that she eventually usurps the rightful ministers in dispensing theological counsel. When he locates the origin of the Antinomian disease in childbirth, Winthrop means to show that men play absolutely no role in the "spread" of this infection. A perfectly healthy woman "contracts" the disease through contact with the Antinomian women attending at the birth of her child, and she "carries" the disease back to her own home when leaving the birthing room, "infecting" her own children in the process. I cannot overemphasize the graphically somatic character of Winthrop's metaphor for moral contagion. After Mary Dyer gave birth to the stillborn child, he tells us, for example, that "most of the women who were present at [Dyer's] travaile, were suddenly taken with such a violent vomiting, and purging . . . they were forced to go home" where "their children [were] taken with convulsions" (44).[41]

This account of an infection spreading outward from rooms that only women inhabit to the homes and families of those women helps Winthrop identify what he regards as the real target of Antinomianism. He contends that Hutchinson's diseased theology ultimately singles out the natural authority within families in order to destroy household by household the internal order of the body politic. Although weekly meetings were common among radical Protestants in England, in Hutchinson's hands these meetings become, according to Winthrop, a way of attacking the family; they do a "great damage," Winthrop claims, "to the Common-wealth" because the families of those attending are "neglected" (36).[42] The magistrates have no choice but to intervene in such a situation. To attack the family was to attack the very foundation of the church since, as Edmund Morgan argues, New England Puritans "thought of their church as an organization made up of families rather than individuals."[43] "As the Fathers of the Common-wealth," the magistrates were entrusted with protecting the family structure (36). Indeed, ministers in Massachusetts Bay "routinely referred to the family as a 'little church' or a 'little commonwealth.'"[44] It is this image of the household as "a little commonwealth" that Locke would use in his essay "On Paternal Power."[45] By invoking the image of the father, Winthrop suggests that the commonwealth not only be thought of as a single family but that its chain of command is as natural as the patriarchal chain from father, to mother, to child. To counter those who might argue that the meetings were of positive spiritual benefit to the families of all those in attendance, Winthrop argued that these meetings only misdirected spiritual energy away from the family and proper rearing of children. Hutchinson's meetings were designed, according to Winthrop, to lure people away from their rightful duties by appealing to their desire for "a very easie, and acceptable way to heaven" (31).

Let us pause at this point and consider what Winthrop has accomplished by means of the figure of the spiritually infectious woman. He has proposed that family units be closed off and contained within the individual household, each headed by a father who keeps his wife and children under supervision at all times and never allows women to congregate on their own. At the same time, and in apparent contradiction to this individualizing logic, he contends that such self-enclosure is the only way to ensure the integrity and inclusionary character of the English community as aggregate. Just such a set of procedures is proposed by Foucault as necessary for creating and maintaining a modern secular state. William Petty, too, proposed that such procedures were the best method for protecting the English nation from the next plague that might come to England from the Continent. By redefining the "head" of the body politic in gendered terms, Petty reconceptualized that body in terms of its people and the family as a self-enclosed social unit analogous to the state. I am not suggesting that Winthrop had anything like this European vision of modernity in mind when he rethinks the colonial social order in a way that will put Anne Hutchinson in her place. But he does seize upon a remarkably similar set of procedures and, in many respects, accomplishes the same goal even more powerfully than did his European counterparts, because his model is still shot through with divine purpose.

And what of Hutchinson in all this? What does Winthrop claim she used to attract so many colonists to meetings designed only to "seduce" them into separation from the very body that Christ had knit together? Winthrop does not, as we might first suspect, have Hutchinson advocate an earlier view of the social body, one that Winthrop would have us replace with his own. Quite the contrary. Winthrop's view resembles Hutchinson's in that they anticipate two contending components of a modern model of the nation.

According to Winthrop, Hutchinson's power is purely rhetorical and stems from her appeal to experience. He accuses the Antinomians of substituting experience for testimony sanctioned by God. One of Hutchinson's theological "Errors" is her belief that "No minister can bee an instrument to convey more of Christ unto another, than hee by his own experience hath come upon" (12). To suggest that a member of the church possesses knowledge equal to the minister's challenges the model of the church as a single body whose parts are held together by Christ's love and spirit. It substitutes the body of the individual who directly experiences God for the body of the church, which mediates between God and that individual. This, as Winthrop sets up the analogy, is tantamount to leaving Christ out of the picture.

Thus experience threatens to sever the ligaments connecting a community that Christ holds together. The "poyson" that Hutchinson injects into the pure New England body politic disguises itself as a cure for the anxiety felt by those members of the church who may not have achieved personal salvation (64). The body of the church may be immortal, but that does not eliminate the possibility that any individual member may perish. In this respect, Winthrop's model of the church resembles an early modern body politic in which perpetuity is guaranteed to the blood alone, not to any particular embodiment. According to Winthrop, Antinomianism fails to hook individual salvation up to the well-being of the whole social body. Since in Antinomianism the body of the saved remains healthy regardless of the welfare of the larger body of which it is but a part, why should such an individual bother, Winthrop asks, to worry about how his or her effects on the community? To demonstrate the falseness of Hutchinson's position in this respect, Winthrop calls attention to her claim that her "experience" of grace indicates that human judges "have no power over [her] body, neither can [they] do [her] any harme" (38).[46] From this, he concludes, the "practice of immediate revelations" could have "such dangerous consequences" for the community that the magistrates must "disarm" the Antinomians and all those "who had openly defended them" (41–42). What was finally wrong with Hutchinson, then, was her way of figuring the ordinary individual as outside and independent of the body politic.

In Winthrop's eyes, Hutchinson endangers the Congregational community because she believes that the saved have two bodies. Winthrop contends that the experience of immediate revelation allows her to disregard her place within the body politic, because this experience provides her with evidence of a second body housing the spirit. This spiritual body differs from the natural body in that it is immune from the diseases that will kill the common body of the church. According to Winthrop, Hutchinson has proposed that "[t]hose who are united to Christ have in this life new bodies, and 2 bodies," a conclusion she can reach only because she "knowes not how Jesus Christ should be united to this our fleshly bodies" (59). Her "admonition" from the church results from her "obstinately . . . maintain[ing]" her position on this issue in spite of "the many places of the Scripture . . . which were brought to convince her" that such views would lead her to deny the Resurrection (64 and 63). In fact, however, nowhere in the trial transcripts is Hutchinson actually quoted as saying that to be saved means that one possesses two bodies. She merely puzzles over how such a pure being as Christ could be united in any way to bodies that Puritan theologians consider the source and emblem of depravity.

It is important to remind ourselves at this point that neither Hutchinson's views nor Winthrop's attack on these views were unique to the colonies. Since the beginning of the Reformation, Protestants across Europe had been making much the same argument as Winthrop's whenever they refuted the various radical sects that arose on the fringes of Orthodoxy. Thus I am not claiming that Winthrop and Hutchinson have broken new theological ground in their debate over the problem of the resurrected body. I simply want to suggest that their rather conventional argument over how one evaluates individual experience does something new to the traditional iconography of the body politic, when that body is one and the same as the Church of Boston. However, inadvertently, Winthrop alters the theory of the king's two bodies on which English monarchical authority was founded when he tries to define Hutchinson's theology as not simply heretical but dangerous to the political order of the community as well. He, not Hutchinson, after all, proposes the idea of salvation as two bodies housed within a single human host. In doing so, he makes Hutchinson's position on the Resurrection look remarkably similar to the early modern figure of the monarch's two bodies.

Indeed, it might be argued that Hutchinson's central premise, that a human can have direct and continuing physical union with the Lord, is virtually the same theory used by political theorists to explain the king's two bodies.[47] Like the metaphysical body politic, the spiritual body created by Christ's direct intrusion into the individual's consciousness produces a corporate spiritual body that corresponds component by component to that older figure of the metaphysical body politic, in that it exists outside of time and knows no form of natural deterioration. In Hutchinson's representation, the "fleshly body" corresponds to the natural body of the monarch. In place of this figure incorporating Christ's spirit in individual flesh, each person saved being thus a little monarch in the kingdom of the elect, Winthrop substitutes the sexed body of the church community. This body, too, is immortal, but it is not housed within the body of any single individual. Nor, then, can it be represented by any such individual. It is a collective entity whose internal coherence demands the subordination of the female components to male. Winthrop claims that tolerating any other theory of the body will risk "the peace of any State." No body politic, neither New England nor England herself, should consider itself immune to the doctrine that issues from women. Hutchinson's individual encounter with God gives her a personal story to tell about a body she possesses as individual with Christ, a story that relies on the doctrine of experience for its authority. This is the basis on which Winthrop condemns her for having put herself outside and above the community.

In showing what is wrong with experience, however, Winthrop does not dismiss it. On the contrary, he demonstrates its flaws in order to appropriate its infectious powers for his own rhetorical use. In fact, I would argue that both Winthrop and the Antinomians more generally are the champions of experience. Though Winthrop would have us believe that his refutation of Hutchinson's doctrine merely provides the antidote to the disease of false theology, he appeals to experience to put forth the true theology. Nowhere in her two trials nor in other contemporaneous accounts of the Antinomian controversy does Hutchinson describe or defend her actions through recourse to the authority of experience. Yet Winthrop's condemnation of her views on experience has led scholarship to cast Hutchinson in precisely the role that Winthrop wanted. Hutchinson becomes the spokesperson for individual experience. In accepting Hutchinson's role in precisely these terms, I would contend, we fail to understand the role that her chief opponent played in authorizing his own position by empowering the doctrine of experience.[48]

Winthrop manages to shift the whole argument over church authority: whereas before colonists had argued whether institutional doctrine or personal experience should underwrite power, Winthrop asks them to consider different qualities and kinds of experience. His critique of experience proceeds on the premise that experience must be regulated because it is necessary for community health. He blames the Antinomians for overemphasizing what can be learned while one is involved in an experience and charges that in valorizing experience as is happening, they neglect the superior insights acquired during reflection on our past experience. It is only by reflecting on "bitter experience" that one sees the "true love" one has for Christ (33). "[F]ormer experiences" bring "comfort" to the true Christian by reminding him of his "Covenant" with God (13).

Immediately following the controversy and thus well before *A Short Story* was published, the conception of experience I am ascribing to Winthrop was actually institutionalized. After the controversy, according to Michael G. Ditmore, churches began to require prospective members to give a narrative of their conversion experience as a condition for membership.[49] Because the right to vote and hold civil office depended on belonging to the church, this required self-narration and allowed church leaders to set limits on what constituted an acceptable experience. Winthrop's account of a body politic imperiled by "monstrous"

views of experience served to legitimate precisely the disciplinary practices of Massachusetts Bay that had drawn so much fire from English
Puritans. By revealing the dangers of experience, Winthrop suggested
that while political authority in the colony derived from the *common*
body of the church, and was thus subject to the whims of that body, no
English institution oversaw the spiritual composition of the common
body with the care and consistency that Congregationalism did. In this
argument, we see the same kind of disciplinary logic that Foucault identifies with the management of the plague. Since all members of the community would want to belong to the church—their spiritual survival
depended on it—admission procedures made everyone feel their experience as subject to constant scrutiny. Far from being exclusionary, the
required narration includes all the community in the process of self-ex-
amination. In this way, the procedures Winthrop recommends to his
English audience anticipate modern institutional cultures that regulate
the body through the mind.

Rather than drive a wedge between English and New English Protestants, Winthrop aims the rhetoric of experience in *A Short Story* at all
true Christians, showing that those on both sides of the Atlantic must
align themselves against Hutchinson's attempt to define unregulated experience. Contrary to what some in England might think, Winthrop reasons, the English and New English Protestants constitute a single community of Christians in this respect, for "the servants of God, who are
come over into *New England*, do not thinke of themselves more spiritual then other of their brethren whom they have left behind, nor that
they can or doe hold forth the Lord Jesus Christ in their ministry, more
truly then he was held forth in *England*" (40). Such attempts on
Winthrop's part to defend New English Protestants against charges of
spiritual arrogance tend to be understood as self-interested. New England Puritans publicly disavow their criticism of their English counterparts, for fear of incurring the same forms of persecution that drove
them across the Atlantic in the first place. I cannot attest to the sincerity
of such disavowals except to mention how often, as in the case at hand,
they seem designed to create alliances between colonial factions and to
pit English Protestants against another colonial faction. It seems to me
that in insisting on the similarity of true Christians regardless of geographical location, Winthrop wants to portray Hutchinson's views as
not only spiritually deformed but also unEnglish. By insisting on his kin-
ship in this respect with English ministers, Winthrop reminds his readers
that after all is said and done, the colonists are fundamentally English.
Moreover, because they have met and conquered an enemy the English
have not, the colonists know how to solve certain problems. They have
the advantage of this experience. His account of the Antinomian contro-

versy thus invests Winthrop's faction of the church with the authority of an experience unique to colonial Protestants.

As if to demonstrate the power of this knowledge, Thomas Welde adds a "Postscript" to his "Preface" to Winthrop's account. In it, Welde explains how Winthrop's method of handling the crisis within the Congregational Church does more than it set out to do. These procedures both find a "cure" for the "poyson" within the church community and incorporate into that body representatives of the native, pagan population. This inclusionary strategy is the mark of discipline. A good modern institution can incorporate and deracinate almost anyone and make potential outsiders feel that they have gained rather than lost by acquiring the membership we equate with a modern identity. Welde claims, for example, that "two Sagamores (or Indian Princes) with all their men, women and children, have voluntarily submitted themselves to the will and law of our God . . and put themselves under our government . . . in the same manner, as any of the English are" (14). The implication is clear: the very body politic that saved the colony from a potentially lethal infection, in Winthrop's account, now subjugates the native population without violence or acrimony in Welde's postscript. Indeed, one might even see the postscript as a subtle criticism of those who would say that Winthrop's reformation of the body politic was hostile to English monarchy. In showing how the natives submit to the English monarch by submitting to Congregational doctrine, Welde suggests that such fears are completely unjustified. It would not be misreading his postscript to say that those in England who fail to see the benefits of the New English Way are less sensible than the Indians.

Chapter Five

THE INSIGNIFICANCE OF EXPERIENCE

SCHOLARS of American literature concluded long ago that the writings of the seventeenth-century Puritan poet Anne Bradstreet could well be the origin of American women's literature.[1] Bradstreet's work is said to provide "a model for future generations of women" because of her "insistence on the primacy of personal experience."[2] In the face of masculine "denial" "of the value of her experience and abilities" as a woman, Bradstreet remained "[t]rue . . . to her Puritanism and her female experience" and produced the "glorious gynocentrism" that marks her "as a forerunner of other women struggling to enter (and therefore subvert) the male-dominated tradition" of poetry writing.[3] Indeed, Patricia Caldwell goes so far as to argue that it is Bradstreet's "femaleness" that "force[s] [her] into a confrontation with language and meaning and identity that must come in time to any serious New World writer."[4] It is no coincidence for Caldwell, then, that Bradstreet inaugurates two traditions simultaneously, that of American women's poetry and of American poetry itself. In Caldwell's estimation, "only a woman could have written" poetry that would come to be seen as "a paradigm of the early American literary experience" in its attempt to find an "authentic" poetic identity, since women were the ones to experience the New World up close and personal.[5] I will not deny that such readings of gender in Bradstreet's poetry have called proper attention to a tradition that had been almost entirely ignored by literary scholars for the first two hundred years of the country's existence. Critical arguments arising from and legitimated by Bradstreet are responsible for opening the field of early American studies to considerations of those voices that were excluded in producing and maintaining a white, masculinist definition of our national literature. In their insistence that Bradstreet's poetry expresses what is "most truly female" about her "experience" of the New World, these studies make it clear that there are "experiences" that fall outside the purview of the Anglo-male confrontation with another continent and preexisting culture, experience that must nevertheless be considered American.[6]

There is only one point with which I want to take issue. As in the case of Anne Hutchinson, I believe Bradstreet's critics too often use unselfconsciously the very terms that require historical explanation.[7] The understanding of male and female experience as incommensurable grew in part out of the Antinomian controversy of the 1630s. Indeed, as I read it, Winthrop latched onto the figure of Hutchinson's body, not to say something about that body, but to represent her words and the spirituality that prompted them as less than truly Christian in that they were based on a brand of experience that challenged church authority. Her sex was, in other words, an icon or metaphor (as was the natural body itself) for the individual's ties to a corporate spiritual body. By metaphorically linking the natural order of the corporate body to the well-ordered household in which the father ruled over his wife and children, however, Winthrop anticipated a modern institutional culture divided first and foremost according to gender. Winthrop picked on Hutchinson, I have suggested, not so much because she was a particularly bad *woman*, but because she was a useful figure of speech—or to be completely accurate, a good figure for bad women. By representing her as a woman who had gotten out of place, in other words, Winthrop, not Hutchinson, gendered the body politic. By seizing authority from the church to declare the truth of experience, he argued, she had sexed a truth that was essentially above sexuality.

It was the idea that the individual's experience was predictive of regeneration that the Antinomians disputed. This was the idea from which Winthrop and the Antinomians' opponents sought to disassociate themselves, on the grounds that such doctrine was like an unruly woman, contrary to the natural—that is, "saved"—order of things. It is one of the grand ironies of our cultural history that the notion of experience as story waiting to be read came to be championed by Hutchinson's opponents as the century wore on. As Janice Knight points out, the Antinomian controversy pitted two "orthodoxies" within Puritanism against one another—each with an "equal claim to legitimacy." When properly understood, Knight argues, the controversy represents not so much "a weeding out of heretics" as a "violent redefinition of orthodoxy itself."[8] In the preceding chapter, I argued that Winthrop chose Hutchinson to embody the Antinomian position in order to associate this quotidian domain of experience with that of women. As I also demonstrated, in the same breath with which he debased any truth to issue from the female body, Winthrop insisted that such experience, when properly disciplined, was the basis for the church's institutional authority. What was merely suggested in Welde's postscript would become conventional wisdom in the aftermath of the Antinomian controversy.[9] It is in relation to this "redefinition of orthodoxy" that I would like to read Bradstreet's poetry.

Far from being "alienated" from Puritan theology, Bradstreet was, like Hutchinson, an advocate of accepted dogma.[10] If there is any truth in this assertion, it is not entirely accurate to call her poetry either "subversive" or "rebellious." Nor was she attempting to express the particular experiences of her gender. In fact, it was Winthrop's party—the Preparationists—who endorsed the idea that experience was indelibly gendered.[11] By looking at Bradstreet's writing from the 1630s until her death in 1672, I will not only argue that Bradstreet held out for an earlier, sexless model of the body of the spiritual community throughout her career—much as Hutchinson had—but also that the persistence of her position throughout her writing demonstrates the existence of an alternative model of the body politic that implied an alternative view of experience within New England discourse.[12] Bradstreet did not share the Preparationists' commitment to the "conversion experience" as represented through a progressive narrative in which experience on earth—in clearly identifiable stages—prepared the unregenerate body for translation into the form it assumes through salvation.[13] On the contrary, her poetry rejects the view being advanced by Hutchinson's opponents: that experience determines one's individual and communal identity. Instead of positing an opposition between male and female bodily experience from which individual and communal identities can be said to grow, Bradstreet renounces the experience of the body altogether. Earthly experience, she contends, does nothing to prepare the natural body for its translation into the spiritual one, for the experience to be had in heaven by those fortunate enough to be saved.

To argue for the insignificance of the sex of the natural body, Bradstreet drew on what Nancy E. Wright has called—after Ernst Kanctorwicz—"the legal fiction" of the king's two bodies.[14] In her elegy "In honour of that High and Mighty Princess, Queen ELIZABETH, of most happy memory" (1650), Bradstreet claims "That men account it no impiety,/ To say, thou wert a fleshly Diety."[15] Bradstreet uses divine sanctification of a woman's natural body, a sanctification authorized by men, to disassociate "worth" from sex (100). Elizabeth has forever "wip'd off the' aspersion of her Sex" that "women wisdome lack to play the Rex" and, in so doing, challenges "Masculines'" contention that "women have [no] worth" in national or religious affairs (29–30; 102; 100). As Wright remarks, Bradstreet uses the queen's figure to refute "the argument that gender justifiably differentiates the positions and agency allotted to men and women."[16] This refutation is not based, however, on the fact that Elizabeth has something unique to offer as monarch because she is a woman.[17] On the contrary, Bradstreet claims that her sex should not be an issue. What matters is that she remained connected to the divine through the everlasting body politic of which she is a member. In order to demonstrate that Elizabeth's skills as a ruler are based not on her natural sexed body, Bradstreet uses Elizabeth's saved body as evidence of her superiority. Elizabeth will "rise," Bradstreet contends, to "rule Albion" after "the heaven's great revolution" (112–14). Further, it is only by virtue of the fact that Elizabeth's "living vertues" "speak" from the "dead" that such virtues have become the "pride of Queens" and "the pattern of Kings" and can "vindicate" women's worth (125; 122; 103). Bradstreet, in other words, contends that women have the "wisdome" to be king, because they have equal access to a body that knows no sex (30).

Bradstreet does not simply insist that the insignificance of sex determines human worth. She raises the stakes by suggesting that all those who would insist that distinctions based on the natural body are important are at best traitors and at worst heretics. After all, as she insists, the monarchy itself requires, in compliance with Protestant theology, that the natural body is relatively insignificant. Bradstreet reminds her readers that when Elizabeth was queen it was "treason" to "say" that women were "void of reason" (104–5). Even after the queen's death, Bradstreet maintains, any challenge to the superiority of the spiritual body represents an act of heresy as well as an act of treason.

Using the monarch's metaphysical body to make a case for the insignificance of sex is problematic for the poet in that it renders the "glorious body" that rises from the dead unrepresentable except as a negation or metaphor ("As Weary Pilgrim," 30). We have already seen how Winthrop insisted that the resurrected body must be the very same body that lived on earth. Bradstreet agreed with Winthrop on at least this one issue—-that the materiality of the human body made it unfit to enter the world of spirit. How, then, to describe that body which was everything that the natural body was not? Bradstreet arrives at a purely Protestant solution to this problem by insisting that regeneration so fundamentally alters the human being that it no longer resembles its natural form. This being the case, however, the natural body can no longer serve as a living icon of the spiritual body. It serves instead as a negative embodiment— the sign of what the spiritual body is not. So, in order to indicate that Elizabeth's body is now in heaven, Bradstreet writes that the queen "moves not here" (109). She makes no attempt to describe the heavenly body, except to say that it no longer exists on earth. She thus twists the logic of Elizabethan iconography for theological purposes. Whereas Elizabethan iconography took the presence of the natural body of the monarch as a sign of the continuing presence of the metaphysical body of blood, Bradstreet argues that it is the very absence of the queen's natural body that should be taken as a sign that the spiritual body cannot be figuratively represented. Thus, Bradstreet uses Elizabeth's corpse to vindicate women's wisdom rather than describing the spiritual body

Elizabeth occupies once she is redeemed. So, after she writes of Elizabeth's "rise" following the "heaven's revolution," she moves on to describe Elizabeth's grave site without stopping to provide any details of the body that will "rule Albion" in this new age (103–5).[18]

When Bradstreet does try to represent the spiritual body in her poetry, she resorts to metaphors which, nonetheless, are inadequate to describe the glorious body of those who are saved. In "The Flesh and the Spirit" (1678), however, the character of Spirit is able to see the body that is "invisible" to the Flesh (79). But Spirit does not describe that body—or any part of the spiritual world, for that matter—so much as insist that human figures are inadequate to describe it.[19] Indeed, the inadequacy of the body is precisely the point. The "garments" worn in heaven "are not silk nor gold,/Nor such like trash which earth doth hold" (80–81). Heavenly crowns are made "not [of] diamonds, pearls, and gold" (84). Even the soul's heavenly surroundings are defined by the earthly qualities they lack: "Nor sun, nor moon, they have no need" (98). Visuality itself is both total and inaccessible in earthly terms. As the Spirit tells Flesh, "No candle there, nor yet torchlight,/For there shall be no darksome night" (100).

Indeed, it would not be stretching a point to say that for Bradstreet, resurrection brings an end to bodily experience. Far from preparing the earthly body for what will happen to it after it has risen from the grave, as the Preparationist theologians who came into power after the Antinomian controversy claimed, heaven provides Bradstreet with an escape from experience. Earthly experience demonstrates only what the resurrected body will not experience and, as such, all embodied experience represents what must be cast off in becoming spirit. In "As Weary Pilgrim" (1669), for example, the first fifteen lines describe the sufferings a representative pilgrim's body might endure over a lifetime.[20] The "burning sun" "heats" the body while "stormy rains" "beat" it (7). Briars and thorns scratch the pilgrim (7–8), thirst "parch[es]" the tongue, "rugged stones . . . gaule" his feet, and "stumps and rocks" cause him to "fall" (14–16). The speaker of "As Weary Pilgrim" understands her earthly body not as a figure for the "glorious body" she will inhabit after death but as the difference between one life and another:

> Mine eyes no more shall ever weep
> No faiting fits shall me assaile
> nor grinding paines my body fraile.
> Wth cares and fears ner' cumbred be
> Nor losses know, nor sorrowes see.   *(25–30)*

The "glorious body" that emerges out of the ground may be "sown" from the "corrupt carcass" that was laid in the grave, but it is completely other than that carcass (35). Produced "by Christ alone," the heavenly body can only be defined as the negation of the negative: it will experience "lasting joys" of a kind "ear ne'er heard nor tongue e'er told" (38–42). Once in heaven, experience is so unlike that which we know through sight and hearing that it can only be represented as the absence or failure of sensory description.

The language of experience thus serves as the rhetoric of absence and alienation, which are the condition of the natural body. So, for instance, in the manuscript "To My Dear Children," Bradstreet employs this language to describe how children know when they are *out* of God's favor. Bradstreet thus casts in the negative the "spirit[ual] Advantage" her children gain by reading the account of her own "experience."[21] Experience cannot *transform* the natural body into its spiritual other, but it can make one "look home" to God and "search what was amisse."[22] Although her experience can teach her children—and anyone else who might read this letter—how to recognize the "absence" of God, it can do nothing to help make Him present.[23] Since this absence is all one can attain on earth, it is the only legitimate form of authentic pleasure to be had from reading as well as from experience itself.

It is in this sense that exile becomes the paradigmatic experience. The burned-out house in "Upon the Burning of Her House" (1668) represents the individual's exile from home.[24] Counter to every impulse inspired by the New World experience, such exile represents a fulfillment of the narrator's desire. The speaker says as much in the fifth and sixth lines of the poem: "That fearful sound of fire and fire/Let no man know is my Desire." By claiming that the house has been reduced to "dust," then showing how this "dust" has been magically transformed into a "permanent" house in heaven, the narrator is obviously talking about the death and resurrection of the body (19; 43; 50). The house is more than a figure of home and community, then. It is also a figure of the person that must be destroyed before the individual can return to his spiritual home.[25] When she contends, "That fearful sound of fire and fire/Let no man know is my Desire," the narrator reveals her wish for deliverance from her earthly home. The poem, in other words, transforms human longing for material things into a longing for immateriality itself.

This longing for immateriality poses a problem of representation. After all, how can the poet represent the absence of materiality when representation is itself the representation of materiality? It is in order to solve this problem that Bradstreet turns to the image of homelessness. The poet cannot be at home on earth, once her house has burned. But neither can she make her home in heaven. From this home, too, she is an exile. Houses thus become figures of the natural body denied in favor of the spiritual body that can only be represented by virtue of one's separation from it. Paradoxically, then, the only kind of home that can be satisfying on earth is a home from which one is exiled. Thus the narrator walks "by the ruins oft" in order to "spye" the home she can no longer occupy: this home is at once the antithesis of heaven and, in its unavailability, a figure for the spiritual abode (27–28):

> My pleasant things in ashes lye,
> And them behold no more shall I.
> Under thy roof no guest shall sitt,
> Nor at thy Table eat a bitt.
> No pleasant tale shall 'ere be told,
> Nor things recounted done of old.
> No Candle 'ere shall shine in Thee,
> Nor bridegroom's voice ere heard shall bee.   *(31–38)*

Though the narrator proceeds to "chide" her "heart" for its attachment to the things in the house that are no longer there, neither her self-criticism nor her experience of loss alters her desire (40). They merely provide the terms of disembodiment and emptiness that are appropriate for desire—even the desire for one's spouse. Unlike for so devout an English poet such as John Donne, secular love cannot represent the individual's relationship to God any more than God's relationship to the mortal individual can represent the most devoted marital love. I realize that critics like to read Bradstreet's poems to her husband as emblematic of divine love.[26] In the context of her other poetry, as I am reading it, however, this metaphoric relationship would violate the relationship she consistently maintains between embodied—read "gendered"—existence and that of the spirit. Thus when the poet professes, "Let's still remain but one, till death divide," I would read this statement as a declaration of the differences rather than the resemblance of two kinds of devotion ("Another," 32). My reading has the virtue of accounting for the antiseptic quality of her secular love poems.

"Upon the Burning of My House" thus concludes not by denying desire for things of this world but by converting the object of earthly desire into a figure for divine love. The final section of the poem substitutes the image of a new house for the one lost, a "house on high" that cannot be "consume[d]" by flames for it "[s]tands permanent" (47; 16; 50), an attempt to redirect longing away from family and toward God. Scholars have often taken the speaker's final claim that she "need[s] no more" than the home heaven has to offer as a sign that she has arrived at new understanding of the superiority of the spiritual over the material world (55).[27] I would argue, to the contrary, that the poem concludes with a statement of a prayer for help:[28] "The world no longer let me

Love/My hope, and Treasure lyes Above" (57–58). The speaker asks for assistance here, rather than announcing some kind of achievement. In that the concluding lines represent no new revelation, only a restatement of dogma, they could as easily come at the poem's beginning as at its end. In this way, Bradstreet persists in distrusting experience, for it never becomes the teacher who prepares her for spiritual existence or a discourse that negates experience replaces experience. Even at that, this discourse is not one that yields intimations of immortality but one that is reformulated over and over again.[29]

While experience can only demonstrate the absolute difference between the spiritual and material bodies, writing at least offers a way to witness the spiritual body, if only in negative terms. In "Memory of My Dear Grandchild Anne Bradstreet," Bradstreet explicitly rejects the experience of holding her grandchild-surrogate in favor of writing that elaborates on her absence. The death of her grandchild has transformed "delight" into "sorrow" (2). While "Experience might 'fore this have made me wise,/To value things according to their price," the poet chose to regard the child as her own permanent possession, rather than as a source of joy "lent" to her by God (10–11; 13). Experience is valuable in this case, for canceling out the new very propositions that it fosters. Thus, it is the failure of experience to be of service that leads to the search for another means of comfort. Writing, rather than experience, provides the means: as the poet's "throbbing heart's cheared up" by the child that can now be materialized only by the "trembling hand" that writes the poem (23).[30]

In what may appear to be her proto-Romantic celebration of writing, Bradstreet never presumes to overcome the absolute difference between spiritual and material states of being. Writing merely provides a figure for the deferral of a permanent home and purely spiritual existence in contrast with the emptiness of experience per se. Writing provides a purely figurative solution for the problem posed by experience, namely, the problem of the lack of meaning. We can only read that absence as a figure for a presence, but we cannot experience what is fundamentally lacking. So, for instance, in "Contemplations" (1678), a poem traditionally read by critics as Bradstreet's celebration of the power of experience, I would argue that writing is what Bradstreet offers rather than experience, as compensation for a body that has yet to undergo "divine translation" (211).[31] A 239-line poem broken into 33 stanzas, "Contemplations" tells the story of a narrator's musings on salvation during a walk through the woods. The poem's concluding lines—"wit nor gold, nor buildings scape times rust;/But he whose name is graved in the white stone/Shall last and shine when all these are gone"—simply repeat the conventional wisdom that Bradstreet voiced in other poems:

that "neither honour, wealth, nor safety" can be found on earth (231–33; 224). Human identities, systems of exchange, and material productions ("names," "gold," and "buildings") will be forgotten and turn to dust (229–31). All that remains is writing to indicate the "name . . . graved in the white stone," the existence of an identity that is impervious to human experience (231).[32] What one learns from experience, then, is that heavenly intervention alone produces the spiritual body.

But what of the natural body that leads Bradstreet to resort to writing in order to compensate for its inadequacies? What kind of body does material experience produce if it cannot produce the desired spiritual body that only writing can manufacture? In contrast to the developmental narrative advanced by the Preparationists, Bradstreet represents experience as necessarily fragmentary, producing only partial and temporary identities that are, by definition, different and excluded from the supreme wholeness of the saved. So, for instance, experience provides the narrator of "Contemplations" with multiple and conflicting identities rather than producing cumulatively some larger coherent self.[33] I agree with Ann Stanford's claim that "the poem may . . . be read as a series of short emblematic poems."[34] Each stanza in the poem stands as a separate and discreet experience of the natural world and, as such, provides a separate and discreet emblem of self-negation in terms of which the spiritual meaning of that experience can be read. The initial quatrain sets the scene or asks a question, and the closing triplet interprets the scene or provides an answer. The question is posed in terms of experience and finds an answer in some figure of self-negation or disembodiment. There can be no "story" of the speaker's "transformation" if there is no beginning, middle, and end to her "Contemplations."[35]

Narrative is further defeated by the lack of an identifiable protagonist.[36] Indeed, any one scene can have multiple selves. A glance at the stanza that scholars identify with the moment of the poet's conversion, stanza 21, should make my point:

> Under the cooling shadow of a stately elm
> Close sat I by a goodly river's side,
> Where gliding streams the rocks did overwhelm,
> A lonely place, with pleasures dignified.
> I once that loved the shady woods so well,
> Now thought the rivers did the trees excel,
> And if the sun would ever shine, there would I dwell   (42–48)

There is no preparation for or transition between the speaker's first assertion of faith in stanza 20, an internal monologue, and the riverside scene in stanza 21 with its vision of nature as a new external environment.[37] The scene at the riverside puts the speaker in an entirely new location and is linked, if it is linked at all, to the moment when she was last in the woods, some eleven stanzas earlier, before she began a meditation on human history.[38] Even though this is the twenty-first stanza of the poem, it could easily stand by itself. It is, one might say, self-enclosed. Within this small enclosure, furthermore, the speaker offers three separate "I"s in the space of seven lines. The first is situated on the river's bank contemplating the scene before her. A second represents a previous incarnation recalled by the first. The act of thought that created this second "I" not only eradicates the "I" who began the stanza, but also implies its own replacement, a future conditional "I" who distinguishes itself from the previous versions of the self by its very conditionality. This is the position the speaker wants to occupy, but that "I" implies a body that she can occupy only in and through writing. It is a body that can be known only figuratively and through self-negation, that is, only by virtue of the fact that the body she does know and can occupy is *not* this body.

The poem argues, then, that during the course of one's life—indeed, during the brief course of a walk through the woods—experience may succeed in constructing a variety of unstable and fleeting "I"s, but the end product of such experience is a body and soul that dies and is no more. The ideal self in Bradstreet's work is thus one who learns from experience to be indifferent to experience, who learns that a stable sense of an "I," of a self housed "inside" the body, is *not* constructed through the discrete and transitory components of human experience. For Bradstreet, experience is *not* the story of a forward movement in which the character tries to shape the end in his or her favor. Meditating on experience cannot alter one's behavior because appropriate behavior is the result of a faith that is produced by an external agent who has no need for experiential means.

I have tried to show how Bradstreet's writing differs from Preparationist writers such as Winthrop—who took control of seventeenth-century New England culture—at least in their use of the rhetoric of experience. Of course, the argument that Bradstreet's poetry challenges the theological orthodoxy that took control through the Antinomian controversy is, in itself, nothing new. Debates over whether Bradstreet's poetry is complicit with or critical of the dominant theological and political ideologies of seventeenth-century New England have been a part of Bradstreet scholarship for as long as scholars have written on her work.[39] What tends to be overlooked, however, is how these two traditions describe a major departure of ways when it came to representing the body politic emerging in the wake of the Antinomian controversy, a refiguration authorized in both cases by the rhetoric of experience. Winthrop's model converts the monarch's body into the body of the church community, which, like Christ, provides a living icon of the metaphysical body of God. This model retains the pre-Elizabethan insistence on the masculinity of the monarch's body and the monstrosity of female rule. Whether in charge of the household or church, the female body represented an inversion of the metaphysical order—an unruly household, political order, and soul. How Bradstreet diverged from this model is best understood from a poem that explicitly addresses the question of the body politic during the monarchical crises of the 1640s. In "A Dialogue Between Old England and New; Concerning Their Present Troubles," Bradstreet casts England as a body "dissect[ing]" itself, that is to say, quite literally tearing itself apart through civil war (16).[40] She subtly modifies the traditional image of the body politic, but only in order to save the monarchy; the supposition is in and only by what she claims are even more traditional terms than those professed by Winthrop.[41] The poem casts the English body politic as a mother with New England as its daughter. To be sure, the figure of mother–daughter as an image for England and New England is an old one. John White, for instance, used it as the definition of a colony. While the image itself is hardly unique, Bradstreet is doing something new, I believe, when she uses this image to assert the independence and authority of New England over that of England.[42]

Bradstreet represents the body politic as a family composed entirely of women, a family in which England embodies the mother, New England the daughter, and Scotland the sister. Thus the traditional parts of the body politic—king, nobles, commons, populace—are included within a feminized body. Whereas Winthrop had associated female rule of the household or church with the monstrous distortion of the metaphysical order, Bradstreet contends that only such a female-centered household can restore order to this unruly home. Two parts of the body, "king and peers," are divided against one another over "a question of state" (165). According to "A Dialogue," these two body parts cannot agree over who should be their head, or "which is the chief, the law, or else the king" (166). "Old England" claims that the real "Disaster" is the "Contention" between "Subjects and their Master" that threatens to "overthrow" the order on which the strength of the entire body politic depends (191–92; 200). Thus, we might say, Bradstreet takes issue with Winthrop's claim that New England's power comes from its role as a model to be emulated. Whereas he asked that all eyes be cast on New England, she suggests that New England acquires its power by observing mother England. Old England finds a "cure" for its "woe" by "shew[ing its] grief" to its progeny (31; 59). New England can offer nothing for England's "releif"; she herself is in such "poverty" that she has neither "Armes . . . nor Purse" to give (61–62). Thus Bradstreet sets New England in the relation of "suppliant" observer to Old (62).

In this scenario, Old England exercises the traditional power of display that Foucault has analyzed in his study of early modern executions, where the sovereign unleashes punishment on the bodies of her enemies for all to see. It is through the spectacle of such punishments, Foucault tells us, that the sovereign gains his or her power over an observant multitude, who can see their bodies are his to nurture or destroy. Bradstreet predicts that England will transform kings from other nations into "nursing" babes who "shall come and lick thy dust," thus turning rival nations into dependent suppliants (261). This may sound like Royalist talk, but in having Old England display its sorrow to its daughter, Bradstreet has in fact inverted the patriarchal model of the family: parents are supposed to observe their children, are they not, and when observed, present those children with an example to emulate?

Moreover, this poem casts Mother England in terms of the unruly woman or monstrous body, the very terms in which Winthrop described Hutchinson's stillborn fetus. Bradstreet makes it clear that this female body politic is not a kindly nurse but a woman committed to exacting "vengeance" on the enemies of her Protestant Church (277). Indeed, Mother England will "send out" her "Armies brave" to "sack proud Rome," "tear the flesh, and set [its] feet on's neck" of the Catholic "beast that rul'd the world," and "lay . . . wast" to Turkey (270–84). Ultimately, then, Mother England more closely resembles the savage Indian than the English men and women who obey God's laws. The poem suggests that England herself is subject to the gaze of a most unlikely examiner, her own daughter, and examination "is the technique," according to Foucault, of modern disciplinary power "which, instead of emitting the signs of its potency . . . holds them in a mechanism of objectification."[43]

I am not suggesting that the position of observer is, in Bradstreet's scenario, the position of power. But neither is that of the observer a subordinate position, any more than Bradstreet's position is inferior to her husband's. Instead, it seems to me the poem's figuration of the body politic is situated between one model of power and another. Far from weakening the nation through its own self-destruction, the early modern version of the body politic brings into being the New Jerusalem. Since the secular and heavenly kingdoms exist in the same antithetical relation as the natural and spiritual bodies, the one cannot, as Winthrop argues, represent the other.

We should therefore be careful of the tendency in scholarship to classify Bradstreet as feminist or even protofeminist on the basis of her poetry's use of domestic imagery and privileging of familial relations. One need only look at the love poetry of Bradstreet's contemporary John Saffin, for instance, to see that such issues were not necessarily gendered female in Puritan New England. Like Bradstreet's later work, Saffin's poetry focuses on his love for his wife, the death of his children, and the struggles of domestic existence.[44] Indeed, these subjects constitute the entirety of Saffin's corpus, so that, if anything, his exclusive focus on matters of the heart and home make him even more "feminine" (as we currently understand the term's meaning) than Bradstreet herself, who wrote long historical and scientific poems in addition to her domestic verse.[45] In language, too, Saffin mirrors Bradstreet. In referring to his wife as "My love, my Joy, my Dear, my Better part" in a poem where he laments his absence from her, Saffin identifies his wife as a part of his own body in precisely the same way Bradstreet claims when her husband is away that they are one "flesh" and "bone"—even though she is at home and he is away on business.[46] Indeed, Saffin goes so far as to claim that he experiences the very same bodily sensations as his wife. He can "feel those paines that have opprest,/thy tender Body with whole Nights unrest."[47]

What we should conclude from this, it seems to me, is that understanding such sentimental attachment to the things of the home as distinctively feminine is in part the result of those narrative structures that Preparationist ministers began to circulate in seventeenth-century New England in order to promote a gendered hierarchy within both church and home. In using the very terms these morphologies of conversion helped naturalize, we tend to overlook how masculinity came to be associated with certain kinds of narratives and femininity with others in a rhetorical battle that used experience for ammunition. By the nineteenth century, that is, the private, lyrical notion of experience that Bradstreet articulates would come back with a vengeance, but this time it would be seen as a feminine protest against the progressivist narratives of adventure in the wilderness or the marketplace that identified the nation's destiny with men.[48]

Chapter Six

A NATIONAL EXPERIENCE

I T IS AN article of faith among scholars of colonial American culture that American national consciousness can be traced to the experiences of New English colonists in the latter half of the seventeenth century.[1] In the words of Richard Slotkin, these experiences mark the "beginning of the century of struggle over royal government that would end in the War of Independence."[2] Scholars typically cite two events as crucial to the story of America's experiential birth. First, the restoration of the Stuart monarchy in 1661 is said to have brought the Puritan colonies under greater scrutiny and exposed the rather lenient terms of their charter. By 1675, relations with the Stuart king had become so strained that his agents were claiming that the colonies had "committed . . . high crimes in contempt of the King and to the oppression of his subjects." James II also formed the Dominion of New England in order to wrest back much of the governing powers that the colonies had assumed for themselves.[3] Such dissatisfaction with New England's political structure extended well beyond agents of the royal government. As Stephen Saunders Webb has shown, English pamphlets in the 1670s routinely criticized "the magistrates of Boston" for their independence, arrogance, and greed.[4]

The year 1675 also witnessed what is said to be the second quintessential colonial experience—a series of battles that almost destroyed the colonies outright. As many as one out of ten adult males in the English population were said to have perished during King Philip's War, at least seventeen colonial towns were burned, and the New England economy suffered irreparable damage when trade was reduced to a virtual standstill.[5] All this at a time when the colonies were "already . . . at war with [themselves] over Indian policy and . . . economic, social, political, and religious issues, and divided along lines of class, race, interest, and generation."[6] By 1676, then, Massachusetts authorities were unsure that if they did manage to weather the political storm brewing in England, they would survive the war raging throughout the colonies and once again enjoy their precious political autonomy.

Perry Miller, Richard Slotkin, and Sacvan Bercovitch, among others, have each looked to the "experience" of King Philip's War and the simultaneous threat to the charter back in England as crucial turning points in the evolution of a nationalist rhetoric. For Miller, the war represented one of the "irresistible" forces of "American experience" and helped "launch" what he describes as the "process of Americanization" in the latter half of the seventeenth century.[7] For Slotkin, Puritan experience of the war played a "significant" role in the production of the "four basic narrative formats or mythological structures . . . at the core of the American experience."[8] And though Bercovitch has done a great deal to steer the study of American literature toward an analysis of ideological constructions and away from attempts to identify or uncover a homogeneous "American experience," he abandons his emphasis on ideology, when in *The American Jeremiad*, he comes to analyze the narratives of the war, and claims that he must "deal with some of the ways in which" the "hard facts" of "experience affected" the evolution of the jeremiad.[9]

I have no quarrel with identifying King Philip's War narratives as crucial to the development of an "American rhetoric." But I would like to suggest that by positing a domain of experience that happens outside of and prior to writing, these scholars have ignored the primary role that rhetoric played in making it possible to think of English subjects in the colonies as a separate national community. While all of these scholars point to this as a moment that defined the "meaning of America," they focus on how experience exposed the colonists to what are, ultimately, philosophical problems; they do not discuss how experience might have produced a political community in the first place. Miller, for instance, speaks of the results of the crises in existential terms, arguing that the colonist was suddenly thrust into a position where he was "left alone with America" in search of its "meaning"; Slotkin empties the events of their political significance by casting them as part of all human beings' struggle to fashion organizing myths out of an experience of place; and Bercovitch sees the narratives as part of a peculiarly American struggle to stifle the ideological dissent that began with Winthrop's speech on the Arabella and that continues fundamentally unaltered today in the work of, among others, American novelists and political speech writers.[10] All three positions depend on the assumption that a political community that came to be known as America grew out of an encounter with the land and peoples of North America. All three also assume that the narratives that follow these encounters demonstrate the inevitable evolution of this process. Political entities exist, they suggest, prior to writing.

But modern political communities owe not only their authority but their very existence to writing. Benedict Anderson maintains that during just the period these early Americanists describe, "print capitalism . . . made it possible for rapidly growing numbers of people to think about themselves, and to relate to others, in profoundly new ways."[11] This "new way" of "imagining communities" would help create nationalism, a concept that allowed, argues Anderson, people who did not live in close proximity to think of themselves as part of a "deep, horizontal comradeship" born through their participation in a community of readers.[12]

The shift from faith in religion to faith in the nation, which Anderson and others before him have identified as one of the key features of this period, appears in the very narratives of King Philip's War that Miller, Slotkin, and Bercovitch mark as the beginning of "America." As David Hall has made clear, the "consensus" over how to interpret God's Providence in New England "slowly dissolved" in the later decades of the seventeenth century.[13] He contends that the increasing popularity of interpretations "less keyed to special providences" demonstrates what he calls, using Peter Burke's phrase, "the reform of popular culture."[14] These new interpretative paradigms, which later came to define eighteenth-century, colonial New England popular culture, favor "scientific" over "supernatural" explanations of nature and history. If we couple this decline of traditional colonial religious authority with what Hall describes as the general population's growing dissatisfaction with the Puritan orthodoxy, we can see that New England's political system was threatened by more than the Indian violence and royal intervention. It would no longer be taken for granted that Puritanism would remain the source of New England's political authority.

Colonial New England writers in the latter half of the seventeenth century turned to experience to legitimate their claims to self-government because the corporate spiritual body used by Winthrop—among others—to represent and enforce the idea in England, Old and New, that the colony was an integral part of the English body politic no longer worked as an effective rhetorical strategy. We can best explain the development of the rhetoric of American experience by investigating how it helped colonial readers reimagine their relationship to one another on experiential rather than religious grounds.[15] Such a change in rhetorical strategies would also be more appealing, or so these anti-Providential writers argued, to those in England who were threatening to impose their political will on the colonies. Such an imagining of the Crown would suggest that New England's relative political autonomy would better serve Britain's interests than would a complete restructuring of colonial authority. This rhetorical project was, in short, an attempt to write into being a new kind of political community rather than an expression of a quintessential human struggle with existential, mythical, or even ideological problems.

To demonstrate the ways in which New England writers used the rhetoric of experience in an attempt to achieve their political goals, I will focus on two texts: William Hubbard's *Narratives of the Troubles with the Indians in New England* (1677) and Benjamin Tompson's *New Englands Crisis* (1676), neither of which has received a great deal of scholarly notice.[16] Most twentieth-century scholars of King Philip's War literature have focused almost exclusively on *A Brief History of the War with the Indians* (1676) by Increase Mather, Hubbard's "known opponent" in the ministry, or on Mary Rowlandson's captivity narrative. And Hubbard and Tompson were well known to their contemporaries. Hubbard served as minister in Ipswich, Massachusetts, for forty-five years, beginning in 1656.[17] While his theology was certainly "orthodox" enough, it has been characterized as "more rational" than that of other Puritan ministers of the time.[18] Indeed, this "rationalism" has been cited as the reason he was chosen to deliver an election day sermon during King Philip's War, "probably the highest honor which could be bestowed upon a clergyman," an honor rendered even more impressive by the fact that the sermon coincided with what was widely perceived to be "the greatest trial New England had undergone." Hubbard's historical account of the war was, moreover, officially sanctioned by the administrators of the United Colonies of New England.[19] Tompson, too, achieved considerable acclaim, including a reputation as the "renowned poet of New England." A native of New England and the son of a prominent minister, Tompson advocated for English colonial and commercial efforts.[20] Indeed, much of his poetry appears as introductory matter for histories and maps of the region (including a commendatory poem to Hubbard's *Narrative*) or as tributes to distinguished businessmen and leaders of British North American military campaigns. That is, he often provides framing devices for documents designed specifically to promote England's expanding empire.

Only by analyzing the work of Tompson and Hubbard can we begin to see how colonial writers used the rhetoric of experience to reimagine the grounds of English collectivity in the New England colonies. These writers argued that a unique brand of experience was available in the colonies and that only such experience could provide a reliable guide to political policies there: you had to be there, paradoxically, in order to know how to maintain the colonies for England. Whereas writers such as John Smith used experiential logic to forge a place for themselves within the English body politic, albeit on a place on the periphery of that body, Hubbard and Tompson use the rhetoric of experience to argue that their political authority—and the future of England's empire—depends on seeing the colonies as a wholly separate collective body. They suggest that the experience of native savagery—not the spiritual covenant that Mather cum Winthrop continues to invoke—binds the colonists together, creating a new political community. Hubbard and

Tompson thus transform what had previously been an outpost of bur-
geoning English expansion into a colonial community with its own autonomous space and sacred ground.

The differences between Mather's "spiritualized account" and Hubbard's "protohumanistic" narrative of the war have already been con-
vincingly described by a number of previous critics.[21] Dennis Perry, for
instance, concludes that "[w]hile Mather's history is a series of military,
as well as spiritual, disasters of a colony in decline, Hubbard's history
highlights a series of noble struggles of virtuous colonists supported by
occasional providential interventions."[22] Because it downplayed the role
of Providence in historical events, Hubbard's historical writing "must
be viewed," Perry thinks, "as a genuinely innovative . . . historical
strategy."[23]

But when they focus on the role that these narratives play in establishing a "scientific" historiographic tradition in America, critics like Perry
overlook the problem that both writers set out to solve.[24] For although
they disagree strongly on the Providential significance of the war,
Mather, Hubbard, and, I would add, Tompson all find common ground
on at least one issue: each believes he must legitimate colonial claims to
the land of New England over and against both native and English
claims. In England and in the colonies, as Webb has shown, colonial
claims to the land of New England had been under attack since the beginning of colonization. When New English writers sought to justify the
terms of their charter after 1661, their frequent implication that the land
belonged to them rather than to the natives or the king (a claim their
English readers found most offensive of all), drew the ridicule of their
English critics.[25] Disagreements over Providence thus begin as disagreements over the colonists' claim to "possess" what until very recently was
undisputed Indian land.

The different rhetorical figures that Mather, Hubbard, and Tompson
use to authorize colonial possession of New English lands suggest contradictory sources of political authority and at the same time establish
radically different notions of communal identity. Mather appeals to Biblical precedent, citing the Indians' perceived lack of agriculture as a sign
that "Land" belonging to the "Heathen . . . hath [been] given to [the
colonists] for a rightful Possession" by "the Lord God."[26] Hubbard invokes the Lord, too, but in his narrative, possession of the land derives
from the "industry and travels" of men like Sebastian Cabot, Captain
Gosnold, Captain Hudson, and Captain Smith, who "were [America's]
first discoverers."[27] Finally, Tompson begins his poem by citing Providence, but he shows such interpretations to be inadequate when he concludes that it is "hard to say" just what caused the war. It might have

been "Romish plots" or a hot sun inspiring a "feaverish heat" in the natives.[28] Or, more likely, he says, it might have been disputes over land. In the end, though, "Indian spirits need/No grounds but lust to make a Christian bleed" (ll. 100–101). Thus contrary to Mather, both Tompson and Hubbard suggest that natural enmity toward Christians in general, rather than God's decision to intervene and produce Scripture-confirming experience, caused colonial suffering.

Indeed, Hubbard and Tompson's focus on inherent Indian ferocity suggests that the war results from an accident of location and not from the guiding hand of Providence. Hubbard writes, for instance, that Native American prisoners of war had "confessed" that the Indians planned on "rising as one Man, against all those Plantations of English which were next them" (58). The attack is specifically directed at English land holdings rather than against the people themselves. By contrast, in Mather's narrative the exact cause of the sufferings is irrelevant because the French, the Spanish, or nature itself could serve just as easily as God's instrument. Their common fate in relation to this angry God holds the colonists together as a group and ties them to other members of the same religious movement outside the colonies. But for Hubbard and Tompson, English expansion into "Unheard of places" puts English subjects at the risk of attack by enemies who have particular ways of conducting war and inflicting suffering (25).

According to Hubbard and Tompson, the experience of these localized forms of violence helps build a national community rather than a religious one. All New Englanders, Tompson suggests, have "experience" of the "Mildew, Famine, Sword, . . . fired Townes, . . . Slaughter, Captivating, Deaths, and wounds" inflicted by the "naked swarm" of Indians (87). Hubbard similarly contends that Philip's escape from capture near the end of the conflict and after the Indian leader's wife and family are taken hostage by the colonists, will make him "acquainted with the sence and experimental feeling of the Captivity of his Children, loss of his Friends, slaughter of his Subjects, bereavement of all Family Relations, and being stript of all outward Comforts" (1:263). The different religious beliefs and experiences of colonists in Connecticut, Plymouth, Massachusetts, and Maine are irrelevant to community formation in Tompson and Hubbard. Both authors require the reader to imagine that all English colonists have experienced native violence regardless of their adherence to Puritan beliefs. Such collective experience can only be imagined, however, for it is simply not true, as their lines suggest, that every New Englander has had an acquaintance captured, a friend die, their property destroyed, or any of the other sufferings they list. Collective experience of native violence is no more a "hard fact" of

New England colonial existence than was the idea of a uniform religious system in Mather.[29]

One obvious consequence of grounding English identity in the experience of native violence is in the dehumanization of native peoples. Scholars have indeed acknowledged that such accounts of native violence helped reclassify the Indians as nonhuman.[30] Both Tompson and Hubbard certainly fit this paradigm. Tompson refers to the natives as, for instance, "Monsters shapt and fac'd like men" (l. 230). Alden T. Vaughan says that this sort of renaming was *the* turning point in English policy toward native peoples. After the war, he contends, "British colonists in New England joined those in the Chesapeake and elsewhere in a growing conviction that the Indians in general were their enemies."[31]

Scholars have not, though, considered the relationship between the removal of Providence from the world of human affairs and this dehumanization of the Indians. When a war is attributed to land disputes rather than to religious ideology, human suffering comes to be seen as the result not of spiritual awakening but racial antagonism.[32] Until the last decades of the century, English colonists argued over whether God had sent them to the colonies to convert the natives. Wars, diplomatic successes and failures, and religious conversions were attributed to God's intervention rather than native agency, but colonists rarely questioned whether the natives were human enough to receive God's grace. As Karen Kupperman has shown, the English "exploited" the Indians in the first half century of colonization "not because they were seen as [an] alien or inferior" racial category of people, but because they were seen as belonging "to the mass of people at the bottom of society whose role it was to serve others."[33] In Mather's history of King Philip's War, for example, the natives' humanity is never in doubt; they are merely God's instruments. But when Providence is no longer thought to be the unseen cause of natives and colonists' conflict, the blame for the murder, bloodshed, and terror falls entirely on native shoulders. In the service of legitimating the genocide of native peoples without invoking Biblical precedent, Tompson and Hubbard cast the Indians as fundamentally different than the English. The Indians are no longer like the members of England's lower classes, but are "monsters" and "beasts" who form a "naked swarm."[34] What Kupperman identifies as a nineteenth-century American attitude toward the Indians emerges here: the capacities of native peoples are now understood to be "not subject to change" and so "fundamentally" different than the colonists' as to be "forever set . . . apart from English people."[35]

The authority for this emergent racialist view of the native rests on the Indians' failure to heed the wisdom of experience. The natives may have greater experience of the local environment, and, as a result, would seem to have the superior claim to the land, given that Hubbard and Tompson cite experience to support colonial rather than English claims to it. According to Hubbard, though, the natives are fundamentally incapable of changing their ways based on information gleaned from experience. They are different from the English in that they reject what experience should teach them.

As a result, colonial Englishness becomes associated with adapting to experience, and inflexibility in the face of experience signals a fundamentally different and backward culture. So, for instance, when one of Philip's captains, Annawan, tries to absolve Philip of any guilt in causing the war, he is said to suggest that Philip willfully ignores the lessons of experience. Annawan claims that the "Praying-Indians . . . and others of the younger sort of his Followers" told Philip tales of English injustice (1:277). These tales act like "sticks" on a fire, according to Annawan, raising Philip's passions against the English to such an intensity that it could not be stopped (1:277). The natural imagery is meant to absolve Philip of guilt: his actions are to be understood as an uncontrollable reaction to what now appears to be untrustworthy information. But Hubbard does not accept such reasoning. He contrasts the native's stories with Philip's experience. He writes that "Philip had large and long experience of the gentleness & kindness of the English, both to himself and to his People" (1:277). Such experience would be so persuasive, in fact, that Philip would "never have harkenend to these stories" (1:277). The only explanation that Hubbard will accept for Philip's behavior is that he "had born an evil and malicious mind against the English" from the start (1:277). This, Hubbard suggests, is one of the ways in which the English and the Indians are distinguished from one another: the English value experience, the natives value stories.

I think we should briefly pause to note how far we have come from when Smith used experience to authorize his administrative decisions. In those tracts fifty years earlier, Smith placed the English royalty in the position now occupied by the Indians. In rejecting the teachings of experience, Smith tried to convince his readers that English royalty threatened the success of the colonies. By this point, Hubbard can count on his readers to afford experience a high enough value in administrative decisions that the mere suggestion that native leaders ignore such evidence is enough to cast them as foolish at best and subhuman at worst.

Hubbard uses native rejection of the evidence of experience to criticize those in the colonies who still want to use everyday events as a way of unlocking the mystery of God's Providence. He mocks attempts by the "barborous" Indians to do precisely what Mather does in his *History*, read Providential signs into simple human failure, by including a story that reads suspiciously like an allegory of overzealous New England Puritans who use Providence to excuse incompetence. When a group of natives killed after "accidently" igniting "some Barrels of [gun] powder" are discovered in a search of an abandoned English fort, Hubbard blames native lack of "experiential Knowledge of its force and power" for their deaths. The Indians, though, see things differently. Hubbard tells us that they "conceived their God was Angry with them for doing hurt to the English" (2:252). Hubbard is quick to point out their mistake. One might think that Hubbard, as a minister, would agree with the natives on this issue, but he does not. Nowhere does he suggest, as Mather might, that this incident demonstrates how God has intervened on the side of the Puritans. Natural human depravity, "Covetousness," rather than God's direct intervention, kills the Indians (2:252). Hubbard thus subtly suggests that Mather and his fellow ministers are not unlike the Indians when they read a moral lesson into what is merely the product of human ignorance.

While the impact on colonial perceptions of the natives has been recognized in the scholarship, the full impact of Hubbard and Tompson's dehumanizing discourse has gone unnoticed: Hubbard and Tompson's anti-Indian rhetoric also distinguishes the colonists from their counterparts across the Atlantic Ocean. That is to say, by creating a fundamental difference between Englishmen and Native Americans, Hubbard and Tompson's substitution of the rhetoric of experience for religious ideology established a fundamental difference between the colonists and English subjects in Europe as well as between the colonists and the natives. In *New Englands Crisis* and *The Present State of New England*, the experience of native violence produces a New Englander who is fundamentally different from not only his counterpart in Europe but also the English men and women in other colonies. By casting experience as the product of a combination of location and racial tendencies (in that the colonists, unlike the Indians, are predisposed to value experience) rather than Providence, these writers authorize the popular belief that different places produce different experiences which, in turn, produce very different people—so long as those people are attuned to the conceptual gold buried in experience. To do so, Hubbard and Tompson transform what had been thought of as an outpost of England into a colonial community with its own autonomous space and sacred ground.

The experience of native violence is also presented as causing English bodies to merge with the land itself and, by so doing, to transform the natural environment from native to English. In his attempt to illustrate the sufferings inflicted on all members of the colonial community, Tompson uses the female body as a stand-in for that collective body. So, for instance, English "Mothers bodies" are "ript" open by the natives and "laid" on the town "field" (89, l. 247). In the process of murdering the women, the natives also kill the "half formd Infant[s]" by exposing the "secret Cabinets which nature meant/To hide her master piece" (89–90, ll. 249–51). The body of the slaughtered mother merges with the soil of New England, soil that quite literally (in its place-names and legends) embodies the history of sacrifice.[36]

In order to transform these signs of sacrifice into signs of an emergent nation, Tompson must demonstrate that the wilderness is shifting its allegiance to the English, that a fallen nature is, in other words, becoming a redeemed culture. Tompson achieves this rhetorical feat by anthropomorphizing the natural environment and making nature itself sympathize with the colonists' plight. Attacks on the bodies of English women prompt the colonial army to counterattack; these counterattacks manage to transform "miery swamps" and "shady boughs" into "houses" (90, ll. 263–64). Moreover, the attack on English women must be understood, he insists, as an attack on nature itself, for in killing the infants in the womb, the natives rip "open" what nature had meant to hide. Nature has organized the human body like the interior of an English house, with different "cabinets" serving different functions, and has decreed that only members of the English community should enter there (89–90, ll. 249–51). That violation of the colonial body is a violation of nature herself is also demonstrated when the "clouds" burst with "sympathezing tears" and the land of New England begins its transformation from wilderness to English colony (90, l. 257).

Just as nature can be said to be on the side of the colonists, the soil itself protects colonial bodies from native violence. The colonial military leader and the colonists' sense of this affinity for the land substitute for God's Providence. When Captain Benjamin Church, for instance, decides to order his men to fight a much larger Indian party rather than continue their retreat, some members of his company believe they face certain death. In order to give them confidence, Church "assured them not a bullet of the Enemy should hurt any one of them" (1:81). One member "could hardly believe" Church's claim, though, until "a bullet of the Enemy was . . . warded from his Body" by a rock he had been transporting on Church's orders (1:81). Hubbard ascribes no superhuman agency to this event. Captain Church, not God, serves as the agent of this soldier's salvation. Hubbard suggests that colonial military commanders can be on such intimate terms with the land that the soil itself comes to their aid.

In this way, Tompson and Hubbard replace God with soil. Whereas Mather cast himself as a messenger of God, speaking God's words through the medium of human language, Hubbard and Tompson claim that their words arise directly out of the merging of colonial bodies with English soil. Tompson suggests, for instance, that the mutilated colonial body writes the story of its sacrifice to native savagery. Tompson cites "reports" from "Posts" as his source for the "Brutish Murthers" of New England women, whose blood is said to "stain" the "paper" from which he reads (89, ll. 243, 245). Material experience thus inscribes itself directly onto the printed page, where colonial blood substitutes for the ink, pen, and writer in the production of English words. This image of textual production is inclusive in that anyone who can read English can encounter colonial violence in a rather direct way. At the same time the image of the wounded female body bleeding forth its own history suggests that only those bodies that have felt the force of colonial violence can represent it to the reader. English colonial administrators may cite their military training as the basis for their authority over colonial affairs, religious leaders in New England may read in such horrific acts the signs of God's displeasure, but Tompson's image suggests that such people lack the knowledge required to rescue the woman subject from native violence. Such knowledge is the exclusive property of those who live in the colonies and who experience its specific forms of violence.

Since not everyone will have experienced native violence in the form they, Tompson and Hubbard, describe, they cast print as a way of creating community. Indeed, the community of the land that they require their readers to imagine can exist only in print, since the soil of Maine and the soil of Connecticut, and therefore the experiences arising from that soil, are so very different. Tompson's address "To the Reader" opens with a standard Renaissance disclaimer on the value of the work: Tompson "never thought this Babe/of my weak Phantasie/worthy of an Imprimature" (83, ll. 1–3). What concerns Tompson is not his poetry's general value, but that such products of his "Phantasie" enter the realm of print culture. The print circulation of his work concerns him because he sees the poem and its circulation as a "Service to [his] Countrey" (83, l. 14). But what "Countrey" is he referring to here? Since the title page is devoted entirely to New English subjects, it would seem that Tompson means New England rather than England. He fears, then, that putting this work into print will do a disservice to New England, where service means helping the ongoing efforts by New Englanders to maintain their community in the war with the natives. Tompson suggests in this passage a constitutive relationship between the work of print and a culture. This is, as Tompson suggests, a fight for the community itself, and he casts the distribution and reading of printed material as integral to the maintenance of that community, at least as integral as the physical sacrifices made by the various towns. In his opening address, Tompson suggests that printed works will help the country of New England both survive as a political entity, as we might expect it to do, and live on in the imagination even after it no longer exists.

Indeed, Tompson and Hubbard foreshadow what Michael Warner calls the "cultural meaning of printedness" that he identifies with the mid-eighteenth century.[37] The different titles given to the London and Boston editions of both Tompson's and Hubbard's works demonstrate how they saw the cultural work of their writing as a function of the communities of print in which it was circulated. Scholars of Tompson and Hubbard have most often viewed the different titles as cause for "confusion."[38] Since the various editions of their works are substantially the same, critics wonder why essentially the same words warrant a new title.[39] But being printed in different places makes a work, for Hubbard and Tompson at least, very different, and the titles are meant to indicate that difference.

Tompson's poem, for instance, changes from *New Englands Crisis* in Boston to *New Englands Tears* in London.[40] The change from "crisis" to "tears" shifts the emphasis from community to sentiment. The latter title assumes the existence of a unified community known as "New Englanders," who can weep as one, whereas the former stresses a precarious moment in that community's existence. English readers, as a result, are directed even before the narrative begins to think of New Englanders as a body made collective through experience. In contrast, New English readers will be taught that lesson about New English collectivity through the narrative itself. To do otherwise and to suggest to English readers that a new way of imagining community is under way in the colonies (rather than making it appear always already true) is to risk providing the English public with evidence that the colonies are in disarray and need English political assistance. Colonial readers, on the other hand, must be taught to think of themselves in a new way, as a community of experienced colonists: by stressing the potential for dissolution in the very title of the poem, Tompson leads the reader to look for ways to keep the community alive, even if that means finding new ways of imagining oneself as connected to other New Englanders.

Hubbard's different title pages work in a similar way. The first words of the title change from *A Narrative of the Troubles with the Indians in New England* in the Roxbury edition to *The Present State of New England, Being A Narrative of the Troubles with the Indians in New England*. The New England title calls attention to its difference from Mather. This is a narrative, not a history, and with this change a new way of imagining the coherence of colonial events must be found. The English edition follows the same pattern as the Tompson poem by announcing with the word "of" what Englanders have not yet come to accept: that the colonies of Plymouth, Massachusetts, and Connecticut constitute a single community that is to be distinguished from England.

What applies to the titles applies equally as well to the contents of the two works. That scholars fail to see Tompson's and Hubbard's works as attempts to fashion an imaginary political community has led to bewilderment at the works' structure and content, as well as to general condemnation of them as literary artifacts. Viewed primarily as attempts at historical narrative, Hubbard's and Tompson's works cannot help but come up short. Jane Eberwein, for instance, writes of Tompson's poem that "[n]arrative poetry . . . ought to tell a good story with detailed attention to characterization and plot" or at least be able to "reconstruct the war's events" from such poetry.[41] With these standards she judges *New Englands Crisis* to be "spotty, impressionistic, inconsistent."[42] Indeed, she claims that these issues were "matters to which Tompson showed himself indifferent."[43] The same petard has been used to hoist Hubbard. Cecelia Tichi, for instance, calls the book "fragmented" and its prose style "pedestrian."[44] She contends that such fragmentation is a sign of Hubbard's mind, arguing that the book's seemingly incoherent structure demonstrates how the war "quite evidently baffled him, and his work suffers from his bemusement."[45]

But the chronological and causal relationship is only one of Tompson's and Hubbard's criteria in selecting and organizing material, and not the primary one. Instead, the structure and content of these works make more sense if we understand that the criteria for selection and organization are determined at least in part by how those elements will contribute to establishing various imagined communities of people. For the London edition of Tompson's work, for instance, he drops the opening passages on New England's fall from religious piety, the very passages that make New England's identity a function of the imagined collective experience of native violence. Instead, Tompson begins the poem with an address to Harvard writers asking them to produce poems about the war, an address in the Boston edition that was only a supplement. He follows the address with what he calls "elegies" to the English towns that have been destroyed as a result of the war, adding a few elegies that were not included in the Boston edition. Eberwein has argued that these changes "switch" the poem's "subject from God's judgment on New England's sins to the problem of the artist attempting to treat sensational material."[46] But Tompson's choice of materials is actually based more on what he deemed necessary for New England's future political autonomy and community, rather than on, as Eberwein suggests, what the two groups of readers might find "entertaining."[47]

In placing the "Supplement" and "Marburys Fate" at the beginning of the poem, Tompson foregrounds for his English audience the colonials' claim to the land. For Tompson equates his town elegies to the lists of the dead printed in the "Gazetts" published in England during the plague. Colonial towns in *New Englands Crisis* thus fill the role played by individual English bodies in English journals. By equating towns with dead bodies, Tompson suggests that those towns should be granted the same sacred status that Christian theology gave the human individual body. Further, just like those journals that cast England as a community bound together by death, Tompson's elegies suggest that we should afford New England at least some of the status granted England. Putting these poems first immediately suggests to readers that New England should be accorded a similar status as England on the basis of collective experience of death rather than on the basis of some Providential plan. By the same token, when the Boston edition begins by transforming Providential means of collective identity to experiential ones, it highlights the work that the poem is designed to do in its colonial audience.

Hubbard's decision to include in his narrative a description of the Pequot War similarly reflects his sense of the work that print will do to form communities of readers. No other historian of King Philip's War bothered to include a history of this earlier war. Hubbard does not claim that the first war helps cause the later one. Indeed, he writes that relations with the Indians in the forty years between the conflicts were peaceful, with the Indians abiding faithfully by the terms of the treaty. But why then include such incidents at all if they do not demonstrate a significant component of the development over time of Indian-English relations?

Hubbard adds this description of the Pequot War to unify the community of New England through the experience of reading. He writes that the "experience" of reading about the earlier war "may administer much matter of comfort and encouragement to the surviving Generation, as well as of praise and thanksgiving to Almighty God from those who have thus long quietly enjoyed the benefit, and reaped the fruit of their labour, and courage, who engaged therein" (131). It is entirely formulaic for a New Englander in the later years of the seventeenth century to compare his generation to earlier ones.[48] But in this striking passage, Hubbard uses the generational distinction to establish a relationship between colonial subjects in all the New England colonies in terms of specifically colonial incidents, war with the natives, and in relation to a specific process, reading a printed narrative of the colony's history rather than the Bible.

The invocation of generations is thus designed to link New Englanders over time and across colonial boundaries without regard for religious belief, rather than to distinguish between those generations on the basis of religious piety and practice. Reading this history will produce the sense of a distinct colonial community that originates in and regenerates itself through acts of violence against native peoples rather than, as Mather and others argue, a community whose common feature is its religious experience. The experience of reading produces a sense of continuity between New Englanders as colonists rather than as Englishmen. The narrative is meant to establish a New England colonial self against which the Other can be judged, an Other that includes both European English and Native Americans.[49]

Approaching the texts from this vantage point can open our eyes to the ways that these narratives create rather than just describe new ways of imagining relationships between people. The commendatory poem by Tompson in Hubbard's *A Narrative*, for instance, begins by acknowledging that the war is "a Churches War," but instead of offering thanks to God for providing help in writing such an accurate history or claiming that the local churches are forever indebted for his sympathetic portrayal of their cause, Tompson offers "Thanks" to the "Countrey" of New England (1:23, ll. 1–5). Unlike Purchas, Hacluyt, Smith, Williams, and Columbus, to whom he is compared, Hubbard writes in service of a "Countrey" that is distinct from England, a "Countrey" whose very existence, Tompson suggests, Hubbard is in some sense responsible for helping sustain, if not create, through the circulation of this printed text (1:23, ll. 7–9).

Tompson goes on to suggest that in producing community, print gives birth to new places as well. He praises Hubbard for putting in print "Unheard of places" and strategies, and he suggests that the very act of printing transforms these places from the realm of the imaginary to the material world (1:25, l. 29); "Unheard of places," he writes, are "like some New-Atlantis,/Before in fancy only, now Newlandis." Hubbard's narrative and the accompanying map add something new that requires more than a revision of Moxon's "two Globes"; it requires that a third globe be added (1:25, ll. 29–35). Something new is created in the colonies, Tompson suggests, rather than something old being revised. The communities formed in these locations represent neither extensions of the Old World nor displacement of native peoples. They are figured as part of colonial addition rather than acquisition, in that in taking possession of formerly native lands, colonists remake those lands into something entirely new. This implies, of course, that the colonies have far more to contribute to Europe than mere supplies; they have new peoples and lands made from the combination of colonial soil, European peoples, and print technology.

In turn, these authors suggest, new ways of writing emerge out of the printed production of these new places and peoples. Paradoxically,

Hubbard first distinguishes his own writing by claiming that he, unlike Mather, relies on the norms of public print culture that were already accepted by the great historians of times past. Both New and Old World historians, Hubbard claims in "An Advertisement to the Reader," face the same challenge: method. All true "Compiler[s] of History," he contends, tell their stories by sifting through various source materials to find the true story lurking beneath the different versions told by the participants (1:15). Hubbard thus establishes his authority as a historian by pointing out the diverse variety of his source material, including "Letters" and "the mouths of such as were eye or ear-witnesses" (1:16). His history is to be believed, like other European histories, because he has come closest to compiling a complete history, one that synthesizes the individual experiences of those involved into one imagined collective experience that no single person had had but which the historian claims structures all that took place. In so doing, Hubbard implies that he removes himself entirely from the narrative; in other words, the extent of the author's absence from the narrative will determine its success as history. This, of course, is a direct challenge to Mather's historiography in *A Brief History*, which claims its author is the messenger of God and thus must be present in every word for the story to be believed. As Anne Kusener Nelsen has argued, "Hubbard's *Narrative* was fashioned by the essential non-intervention of the two primary movers in Mather's *Brief History*—God and the author himself."[50]

In claiming that the most successful histories are those that seem to have no author but experience itself, Hubbard suggests that print can work to substitute collective experience for religious belief as the way in which the colonists imagine themselves. Indeed, the collective experience that Hubbard represents as the standard for historical writing exists only in print. Collective experience is purely a rhetorical construct, as Hubbard himself concedes when he admits that no historian can, in fact, represent the experience of everyone who participated in the war. Some people will have died and thus will be unable to relate their experiences, some will not be able to speak the same language as the historian, and others will simply never be contacted. Hubbard wants his readers to see that print makes this imagined community possible. God does not need the continued distribution of printed materials to intervene in individual lives and keep the community intact. God simply intervenes. But once Providence has been removed, some other force of communal bond must take its place, and Hubbard suggests that the technology of print can reach people in ways only God once could.

Although Hubbard claims that his history should be believed because he adopts Old World methods, he still uses land to differentiate between colonial and Old World writing. Colonial histories, Hubbard contends,

are distinctive because of the errors that inevitably creep into any historical account. Colonial writing, he suggests, is noteworthy in this respect
for what it cannot do: accurately resolve property disputes. The colonial
historian is expected to give the exact distances between locations
"which no Geographers hand ever measured," but since he lacks the sur-
veyors' precise methods of measurement his history will inevitably contain factual errors (1:16). Hubbard asks the reader's indulgence "in describing the bounds and definitions of some of the Patents, and grants
of land belonging to the other Colonies" (1:17). It is not the historian's
place, he contends, to "prejudice any peoples Jurisdiction, or persons
property" (1:17). Both land measurement and the assignment of specific
particles of soil are deferred to a realm outside writing—that is, to the
surveyor and the courts.

Hubbard seems to be suggesting here that the colonists have a very
different relation to the land than do their counterparts in England, and
thus, whereas the Crown might not grant its subjects who live on the
Island itself full voting rights, the different conditions of the New World
demand different political structures. On the Continent, property relations and spatial relations were established over the years through English possession of the land. No matter how much the English may
Anglicize colonial land, it remains fundamentally Other in a way that
continental land does not. The colonists are still dependent on technology to know the land in its most precise detail. For Puritans like Mather,
Biblical writing authorized possession of the land, so there was no need
for "Geographers" to intervene when God had already written. But for
historians such as Hubbard, writing comes out of experience rather than
preceding it. Understood in this way, writing can only be said to reflect
property claims and "scientific" measurements; it serves as a readable
expression of those features of colonial life rather than as their
foundation.

When natural science such as geography replaces God in providing
authority for English land claims, some form of writing is needed to ren-
der what the Europeans claim to have seen in a readable form. Thus,
unlike the Providential historians of King Philip's War, Hubbard provides a map with his narrative. While the map claims simply to "shew the
Situation of the Countrey," I would argue that it makes the land visible
to the colonists in a way that words never could and, in the process,
helps call into being a new place.[51] In Michel de Certeau's words, the
"mastery of places through sight . . . can transform foreign forces into
objects that can be observed and measured, and thus control and 'include' them within its scope of vision."[52] Where Providential historians
saw the colonial possession of native lands as part of a historical development preordained by God, Hubbard uses the map to "transform the

uncertainties of history into readable spaces."[53] The mastery of space through sight demonstrates colonial possession, and in the process makes the seemingly foreign experience of the colonial world readable to Europeans.

Hubbard's map thus transforms alien territory into a new English homeland that occupies its own sacred ground separate and distinct from the community back in Europe. It does this first of all by calling attention to its place of production: the legend informs us that this is the "first [map] that ever was cut here." Unlike other maps of the English colonies, this is literally a self-representation. For the first time, the colonists are visually representing themselves and the land on which they live. In this way, Hubbard's map calls attention to its difference from the most famous of all maps of New England, the Smith map. Though the map was literally engraved by Simon Passe, it was called Smith's map because, according to the map's "State of Leagures," it was Smith who had "observed and described" its contents. The map gained its authority, in fact, through the invocation of Smith's name. Other colonial promoters might exaggerate about the colonies, but according to the map itself, Smith represented the conditions with scrupulous accuracy.

By contrast, the map of New England included in *A Narrative* derived its authority from its place of production and the absence of any individual author. The map's claims to be "the first that ever was here cut, and done by the best Pattern that could be had" are placed where Smith's map had noted Smith as the source of the map's information. By linking originality to location, the map suggests the emergence of a new form of subjectivity that results from place. It implies that colonial and noncolonial English subjects might represent the very same physical environment differently, and that such differences can only now, with the presentation of this map, be seen. But this new subjectivity is that which enables one to remove himself or herself entirely from the scene, to eradicate self in the representation of space. For unlike Smith's map, no mention is made here of either the engraver or Hubbard. This is simply "A Map of New England," as though the images had come directly off the ground to represent the land without any intervention from human hand. The colonial geographer thus replaces the word of God with a form of spatial representation that visualizes the land from the perspective of heaven and removes any trace of itself rhetorically from the presentation of its object.

The spatial boundaries of the community that this map imagines are determined by deaths suffered on colonial soil rather than by patents granted in England. By labeling this a map of New England rather than a map of the war, Hubbard extends the link between community identity and imagined collective experience of native violence to include the

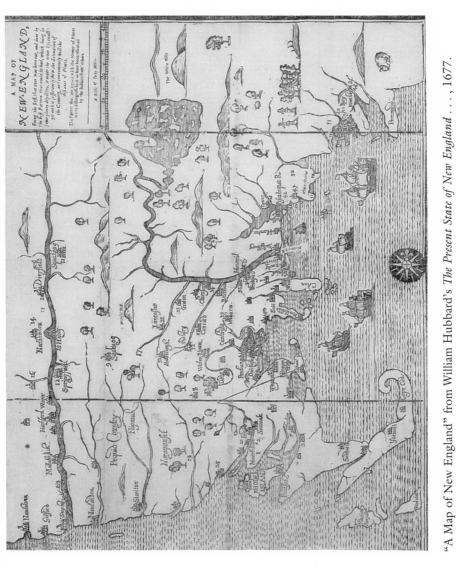

"A Map of New England" from William Hubbard's *The Present State of New England . . .*, 1677. (Courtesy of the John Carter Brown Library, Brown University.)

very possession of the land itself. That is, native violence not only produces an imaginary community; it is used to provide the imagined material boundaries of that community. And New England is afforded a communal status not so very different from England's. The dead men, women, and children are not seen as English emissaries sacrificed in the name of the expansion of the realm. They are colonial subjects who have lost their lives fighting to establish their "rightful" possession of "unheard of places."

What the map casts as neutral physical space it also transforms into sacred colonial ground. It accomplishes this by doing something no other map of New England had done: making the land itself a memorial to the colonial past. In order to achieve this effect, Hubbard incorporates elements of two early modern map styles, what Howard Marchitello calls the allegorical map and the scientific map, into this one map.[54] The allegorical map, according to Marchitello, presents a world where "divine meaning has already been written into the landscape," while in the scientific map "the landscape . . . is understood as essentially meaningless . . . as desacralized matter, natural phenomena."[55] Hubbard's map presents itself as a scientific map, providing no references to divine intervention or symbols of otherworldly mediation that might distract from its presentation of the world of seemingly natural phenomena. But the figures meant to represent natural objects, such as people, trees, hills, and so on, are relegated to the corners of the scene. The spaces normally occupied by these figures are instead filled with town names, Indian tribe names, drawings of forts, and, most numerous of all, the numbers that signify where English colonists have died in the hostilities.

It is these numbers, figures associated with the natural sciences rather than theology, that make the scene sacred. The numbers lead the reader to a table contained in the narrative, a catalogue of lost lives, possessions, even of entire communities lost. In this way, the map renders in visual form what Tompson had done in his poem in that it demonstrates how the colonists have become a part of the very soil of New England. New England becomes quite literally a colonial burial ground. Indeed, the map naturalizes the connection between New English soil and colonial bodies by placing the map's numbers alongside natural phenomena, making it appear that such figures are just another one of the natural features of New England.

By including the brief narratives of each battle in his table, Hubbard also suggests that colonial maps must combine verbal and visual representation to make good their claims on native lands. The table allows Hubbard to introduce historical materials into a genre, the scientific map, that, according to Marchitello, seeks to deny its historicity. In so doing, Hubbard once again combines two distinct early modern genres, cartography and choreography. Whereas cartography is "concerned primarily with . . . topographical characteristics" of an environment, choreography attempts to delineate "topography not exclusively as it exists in the present moment but as it has existed historically."[56] While the two genres were often not clearly differentiated in the late sixteenth and early seventeenth centuries in England, by the time Hubbard is writing the two are understood to be different, even competing modes of representing the environment. Hubbard's combination of the two suggests that he wants his reader to see that while the English map may no longer require detailed geographic histories and memorials to the land's past, colonial land claims require the visual and verbal representation of the mixing of English bodies with New English soil. Hubbard thus figuratively empties the land of any native. By combining the genres of cartography and choreography, Hubbard, in de Certeau's words, "delimit[s]" the "place" of New England as its own "from which relations with an exteriority composed of targets or threats . . . can be managed," an exteriority that includes not only the natives but also the English.[57]

Ironically, the table's historical detail makes New England land appear to be specifically colonial by obscuring the key element of historiography: chronology. While the numbers on the map begin with what Hubbard claims was the precipitating incident of the war at Mount Hope, they do not follow any chronological pattern. It is true that the narrative corresponding to each number includes the date or dates the Indians attacked, allowing the reader to construct a chronology of the war if he or she were to invest considerable effort. But the movement back and forth in time from one number to the next indicates that the table is not intended to be a chronology. Instead, the table and map lead one to see the events of the war as simultaneous. The table gives the impression that the natives are everywhere at once, attacking Hingham and Weymouth "in the same month," Deerfield and Squakbeag in September of 1675, Swanzy and Seconke in June of 1676, Sawco and Deerfield in September of 1675, and so on. It thus works in concert with the map to represent the colonists and the Indians as distinct groups, each united by the seemingly simultaneous timing of the attacks. The Indians come to represent one force acting in concert at the same time in different places, attacking a series of distinct entities that represent a counterforce. The map itself reinforces this sense of simultaneity by recording only the numbers without dates, giving the impression that the attacks occurred at the same time throughout New England.

As part of the process of establishing a collective identity for colonial English subjects, the table and map paradoxically also establish individual town identities. Each number tells a separate narrative of the war for a distinct location. While the numbers do not follow a chronology, the description of violence in each place adheres to one. A place in "New England" gains its status as a place in this text only if some act of violence involving the natives had happened there. Hubbard's detail, while it may seem overwrought, produces a dual effect: it attempts to locate the place and describe the events with such precision that each place can be absolutely distinguished from every other place in the war, but the similarity of the events described blurs the distinctions among places. Hubbard records the precise date of the attacks in most instances, sometimes even the time of day. He begins each narrative by naming the people killed, and, in several instances, he goes so far as to tell his readers the number of shots fired by the natives. He not only locates the exact location in the town where each person was shot but also describes it in relation to the local geographical features. Each community thus can be said to gain its identity through the very precise naming of what happened there, who was killed, how, where, and when. But this isolated identity depends on its comparison to and placement within a larger system of violence that the abundant detail works to illustrate and collectivize.

In *New Englands Crisis*, Tompson suggests what is at stake when these towns are destroyed by the Indians. While Tompson does lament the individual lives lost, he is more concerned to show how colonial experience Anglicized the very land of New England. Tompson concludes *New Englands Crisis* with the series of "elegies" to the English towns that were destroyed as a result of the war. For Tompson, New England towns represent the triumph of space over time. Native violence in *New Englands Crisis* is directed at specific colonial towns rather than at particular individuals. Tompson refuses to provide the names of exemplary individuals at certain points in the poem, but he goes on to claim that he will write elegies for the New England towns that have been destroyed during the war. While towns have a material component in that they take up physical space, have buildings, and house people defined as residents, they are fundamentally acts of imagination. Their identity grows out of their location rather than the material objects placed at those locations. Designating particular grains of soil as Marbury, Providence, Seequonk, and Rehobeth secures such places from the ravages of time: so long as the colonists bestow a name on that plot of land, its identity is fixed no matter what happens to the buildings, the people, or even the land itself. Though its residents might change over time, the colonial town gains its identity by occupying a certain space regardless of the moment in time. Providence is Providence whether the year is 1640 or 1675.

The geographer and the poet both make possession of the native land dependent upon the representation of colonial visual observation of what they cast as natural phenomena, colonial deaths and towns. Hubbard suggests that instead of receiving a new vision through the Word, as one does in Mather, wisdom comes from observing the natural environment. Thus, so-called natural law becomes the governing mechanism behind the seeming chaos of the world. Hubbard substitutes the rhetoric of empiricism for the magic of religion to bring order to what may otherwise seem an incomprehensible world. Hubbard calls on the Bible for the authority to make this substitution of one form of magic for another, using Biblical passages to very different effects than Mather.

Instead of Biblical passages as allegories that provide a blueprint for earthly events, Hubbard reads them as symbolic, suggesting that they offer structures for understanding the world rather than plotlines waiting to be lived again and again. For Providential writers, Biblical passages help predict the successive events of life. God has given humans the Bible so that they might understand his ways. They also believe that individual lives follow the same plotlines as Biblical stories.[58] For Hubbard, though, the Bible provides analogies for experience rather than typologies. That is, it provides common laws by which God operates, not stories that will be duplicated. Hubbard writes that the governors "have had so much experience" of the Biblical proposition, "Rejoyce not against me, O mine enemy; for when I fall, I shall arise; when I sit in darkness, the Lord shall be a Light unto me" (1:9). The governors know this to be true not because God has intervened to demonstrate it, but because God organized the universe in such a way that it cannot help but be true. Hubbard claims that the governors' experience of this proposition is confirmed by natural phenomena rather than by Biblical analogy. The governors know that their confrontation with the natives will end in the colonists' triumph, not because God has intervened, not because that triumph has been specifically predicted in Scripture, but because "there shall be a clear breaking forth of the Sun, after the Tempest is over" (1:9). Empiricism, then, merely substitutes one narrative, that of nature's cycles, for another, God's intervention.

While the rhetoric of experiential laws of nature suggests an intricately organized environmental system that anyone with eyes can understand, in fact, the knowledge derived from experience, Hubbard shows, is inconsistent, even contradictory. For instance, on the one hand, Hubbard cites experience when he wants to prove that the native population cannot be trusted. In a "Prologue" to the "particulars of the Tragedy" of "the first mischief . . . done by the Indians," Hubbard admits that English-Indian relations had been very good (2:96). The change in relations results not, he says, from any English action but rather from simply "News . . . of Philip's rebellion" (2:95). Hubbard recounts instances of "Indian duplicity," where Indians who "had joined with their Country-men in their rising against the English . . . returned back to the English" only to attack English settlements once they took what they needed from their friendly relations with them (2:95). He writes that "[i]t is hoped that we shall after some few more experiences of this nature, learn to beware of this subtle brood" (2:95–96).

But Hubbard also uses experience to demonstrate the *reliability* of the natives. He writes that the English "need never have suffered so much from their enemies" if "some of the English had not been too shye in making use of such of [the Indians] as were well affected to their interest." Hubbard suggests that when the English failed to convert the natives, they lost the talents of what might have been numerous Christianized natives. Hubbard cites several instances of ingenuity on the part of several Christianized natives in battle: one faithfully remains by his commander until it is clear that the Englishman cannot be helped, then disguises himself to look like the attacking Indians and returns to the English; two more Christian Indians trick enemy Indians into exposing themselves as Indians and shooting them. Each of these Indians could easily have switched sides, according to Hubbard. All demonstrate their faithfulness to the English cause and their abilities as strategists and marksmen. Hubbard's conclusion is that "it having been found upon late experience, that many of them proved not only faithful, but very serviceable and helpful to the English" (2:234).

It is no coincidence that the inconsistency of experiential knowledge is displayed in such discussions of the trustworthiness of Native Americans. The fact that experience can yield entirely different conclusions in regard to Native Americans actually serves to authorize the new system of thinking by confirming what will soon become the dominant view of native peoples. Just as Mather and other religious writers used claims of native inconsistency to demonstrate the direct intervention of God in world affairs, those who call on empiricism to authorize colonial politics use this same characteristic to show that natural laws do not apply to such fundamentally different categories of beings. Whereas Mather used the rhetoric of Providence to authorize the genocide of Native Americans, Hubbard suggests that Native Americans must be extinguished because political solutions are impossible. Since Indians act in contradictory ways and against what would come to be called human nature, they represent a never-ending threat that no diplomacy can overcome. The failure of experience that is used to explain Indian actions demonstrates the fundamental Otherness of the Indians rather than the inadequacies of the empirical system.

As I hope to have shown in the preceding pages, the new colonial rhetoric represented by Hubbard and Tompson both denied that it was rhetoric and substituted the power of "experience" for the power of the written word as well. It claimed that its authority grew, as all authority should, from the ground itself, not from the words of a poet, travel writer, or historian. Even the Word of God was insufficient. Moreover, this rhetoric of experience combined with the rapid expansion of colonial literacy during the seventeenth and eighteenth centuries to result in a new way of conceiving of people as a unified whole. People and the cultures that sustain them came to be thought of as more than casual products of their environment: colonial authors argued that a collective consciousness that followed from the sensory experience of a particular plot of land inextricably bound the members of a community together. These authors also refigured the political authority to govern these communities, claiming that only the dirt that was plowed up, the bodies that were plowed over, and the minute details of individual lives could legitimate a modern state and its rulers.

Only through these appeals to earthly experience could a people be said to exist even before documents like the Constitution had ratified their collectivity. Indeed, this very rhetoric of experience often leads us to mistake the growth of one nation on North American soil, the United States, for the inevitable outcome of experience. We forget that this nation grew not from experience but from the desperate writings of people who were far from what they considered to be their home. After the work of these texts was done, religion was still held to make New England a favored site in God's eyes. But experience was and is still understood to be the tie that binds the community. After these texts, experience could not sacralize colonial sacrifices to God or king. In this New World, experience made it sacred for colonials to sacrifice their bodies and lives to colony, to New England, and as now, to the nation.

NOTES

INTRODUCTION
INVERTING AMERICAN EXPERIENCE

1. Greene draws his quotations here from Madison's *Notes of Debates*. In "'An Instructive Monitor,'" Greene discusses what the framers meant when they used the term "experience" and what conclusions they drew from its lessons. See Jack P. Greene, *Imperatives, Behaviors, and Identities: Essays in Early American Cultural History* (Charlottesville: University Press of Virginia, 1992), 319–20. Douglass G. Adair claims that during the Constitutional Convention "no word was used more often; time after time 'experience' was appealed to as the clinching argument for a controverted opinion." See Adair, "'Experience Must Be Our Only Guide': History, Democratic Theory, and the United States Constitution," in *The Reinterpretation of the American Revolution*, edited by Jack P. Greene (New York: Harper & Row, 1968), 399. For further discussion of the importance of the term "experience" in American Revolutionary thought, see H. Trevor Colbourn, *The Lamp of Experience: Whig History and the Intellectual Origins of the American Revolution* (New York: Norton, 1965).

2. The phrase "new world" was first used by Amerigo Vespucci, while "Virgin Land" received its most notable application by Henry Nash Smith (*Virgin Land: The American West as Symbol and Myth* [Cambridge, Mass.: Harvard University Press, 1950]), "Unknown Coast" by Daniel Boorstein (*The Americans: The Colonial Experience* [New York: Vintage, 1958]), and "Frontier" by Frederick Jackson Turner (*The Frontier in American History* [New York: Holt, 1920]).

3. Perry Miller, *Errand Into the Wilderness* (Cambridge, Mass.: The Belknap Press of Harvard University Press, 1956), 9. For a discussion of Miller's "domination of the field" up to his death in 1963, see Philip F. Gura, "The Study of Colonial American Literature, 1966–1987: A Vade Mecum," *William and Mary Quarterly* 3rd ser., 45 (1988): 305–42, 306. See also Gordon Wood, "Struggle over the Puritans," *New York Review of Books*, 9 November 1989, 26–34. In "A Survivor's Tale," David Levin argues that Gura has overstated Miller's "domination" of colonial American literary scholars prior to his death. As Gura points out, this does nothing to refute the fact that Miller's work became the dominant paradigm after 1966. See Levin, "A Survivor's Tale," *William and Mary Quarterly* 3rd ser., 45 (1988): 345–47 and Gura, "Response" (350) in the same issue. It is important to point out that Miller's influence extends into the study of early American history as well. See Francis T. Butts, "The Myth of Perry Miller," *American Historical Review* 87 (1982): 665–94. Russell Reising provides an illuminating comparison of Miller's writings to other important twentieth-century critics' attempts to find a "beginning" for American literature. See Reising, *The Unusable Past: Theory and the Study of American Literature* (New York: Methuen, 1986).

4. Perry Miller, *The New England Mind: From Colony to Province* (Cambridge, Mass.: Harvard University Press, 1953), 51.

5. Ibid., 39.

6. To be sure, Americanists are hardly unique in emphasizing the problems with invoking experience as a relatively pure form of knowledge able to evade cultural influences. Alice Jardine (*Gynesis: Configurations of Woman and Modernity* [Ithaca, N.Y.: Cornell University Press, 1985]) has gone so far as to speak of the "demise of Experience," while Diana Fuss (*Essentially Speaking: Feminism, Nature, and Difference* [New York: Routledge, 1989]) has written that experience "can never be a reliable guide to the real" (118). Further, while critics of American literature have tended to see experience as subversive, Jane Gallop ("Quand no levres s'ecrivent: Irigaray's Body Politic," *Romantic Review* 74 [1983]: 77–83) has argued that "a politics of experience is inevitably a conservative politics" (83). For a provocative discussion of how experience can serve to unify a variety of different discursive positions, see Judith Butler, *Gender Trouble: Feminism and the Subversion of Identity* (New York: Routledge, 1990), 22–25. In light of these and other interrogations of experience as a way of knowing, Elizabeth J. Bellamy and Artemis Leontis ("A Genealogy of Experience: From Epistemology to Politics,' *Yale Journal of Criticism* 6 [1993]: 163–84) have called for a genealogy of experience to be done by literary scholars.

It should also be noted that colonial American scholars are hardly the only Americanists to interrogate the problems surrounding experience as a way of knowing, though as in early American studies, the category has not been historicized. The value of experience has been discussed, for instance, extensively by scholars of African American literature. See especially Deborah G. Chay, "Rereading Barbara Smith: Black Feminist Criticism and the Category of Experience," *New Literary History* 24 (1993): 635–52; Barbara Smith, "Reply to Deborah Chay," *New Literary History* 24 (1993): 653–56; bell hooks, "Essentialism and Experience," *American Literary History* 3 (1991): 172–83.

7. For a discussion of Bercovitch as the most influential critic of early American studies following Miller, see Reising, *Unusable Past*, esp. 74–91; Gura, "Study of Colonial American Literature," 310–13; and Donald Pease, "New Americanists: Revisionist Interventions into the Canon," *boundary* 2, no. 17 (1990): 1–37. While scholars of American literature have yet to interrogate the significance for literary analyses of the historicity of the term "experience," experience has come under scrutiny by historians of American culture. See, for instance, Joan W. Scott, "The Evidence of Experience" in *Questions of Evidence: Proof, Practice, and Persuasion across the Disciplines,* edited by James Chandler, Arnold I. Davidson, and Harry Harootunian (Chicago: University of Chicago Press, 1992).

8. Sacvan Bercovitch, *The American Jeremiad* (Madison: University of Wisconsin Press, 1978), xiv.

9. R. C. De Prospo also links Bercovitch with Miller using an argument similar to the one I use here. De Prospo claims that both Miller and Bercovitch, as well as virtually all other scholars of early American literature, employ what he labels an "environmentalist" (31) approach to colonial materials. De Prospo claims that such an approach reads the texts anachronistically, since, he argues,

no such environmentalism can be detected in the seventeenth-century writings under analysis. See De Prospo, *Theism in the Discourse of Jonathan Edwards* (Newark, N.J.: University of Delaware Press, 1985), 9–56.

10. Bercovitch, *American Jeremiad*, 16.

11. There are other examples in Bercovitch's work of how even he succumbs to the lure of experience to make his case. For instance, to identify the "turning points in the evolution" of the jeremiad, he decides to "deal with some of the ways in which experience affected the course of that unfolding" (*American Jeremiad*, 62). When explaining how "the eighteenth-century jeremiad established the typology of America's mission," Bercovitch argues that the Puritans "incorporated Bible history into the American experience" (*American Jeremiad*, 93). When it comes to explaining the origins of his own writings, moreover, Bercovitch claims that the "distinctive generational experience" he underwent "requires its distinctive form of expression" ("The Problem of Ideology in American Literary History," *Critical Inquiry* 12 [1986]: 631–53, 634).

12. It should be pointed out that Bercovitch has modified his position on the centrality of New England to the development of a distinctly American culture. But while he now speaks of a diverse colonial experience rather than a single American one, he has continued to cast experience as the thing that scholars have yet to uncover, even when he claims, as he does in the "Introduction" to the much anticipated *Cambridge History of American Literature*, that the book "marks a new beginning in the study of American literature" (Bercovitch, ed., *The Cambridge History of American Literature*, vol. 1, *1590–1820* [Cambridge: Cambridge University Press, 1994], 1). Bercovitch proceeds to praise Myra Jehlen's "sources" because they "are as diverse as the colonial experience" itself, while he notes with satisfaction how successfully Emory Elliott has described the way in which the Puritans "forged their vision of America out of the discordant (and finally uncontrollable) materials of colonial America" (ibid., 7).

13. Paul Lauter, *Canons and Contexts* (New York: Oxford University Press, 1991), 84. Lauter also argues that experience is the critical factor in producing scholarship as well. In his "Preface" to the *Heath Anthology of American Literature*, Lauter quotes Emerson to explain the need for a new anthology: "the experience of each new age requires a new confession." See Paul Lauter, ed., *The Heath Anthology of American Literature*, vol. 1, 2nd ed. (Lexington, Mass.: D. C. Heath, 1990), xxx.

14. William Spengemann has written the most influential critiques of early American literary studies. See William C. Spengemann, *A Mirror for Americanists: Reflections on the Idea of American Literature* (Hanover, N.H.: University Press of New England, 1989) and *A New World of Words: Redefining Early American Literature* (New Haven, Conn.: Yale University Press, 1994). For other critiques of the field of early American literary studies, see "Expanding the Early American Canon," Special Issue of *Resources for American Literary Study* 19 (1993); de Prospo, *Theism*; Philip F. Gura, "Turning Our World Upside Down: Reconceiving Early American Literature," *American Literature* 63 (1991): 104–12; and Annette Kolodny, "Letting Go Our Grand Obsessions: Notes toward a New Literary History of the American Frontiers," *American Literature* 64 (1992): 1–18.

15. Frank Shuffelton, "Introduction," in *A Mixed Race: Ethnicity in Early America*, edited by Frank Shuffelton (New York: Oxford University Press, 1993), 4.

16. Ibid., 6, 7.

17. Feminists have also argued that the traditional story of America's beginning defines America in terms of experience that is, in Nina Baym's words, "inherently male," effectively excluding women from primary roles in the myth of America since "their own experience" does not "fit" into the required plotline ("Melodramas of Beset Manhood: How Theories of American Fiction Exclude Women Authors," in *Feminism and American Literary History* [New Brunswick, N.J.: Rutgers University Press, 1992], 9, 15).

18. Amy Kaplan, " 'Left Alone with America': The Absence of Empire in the Study of American Culture," in *Cultures of United States Imperialism*, edited by Amy Kaplan and Donald E. Pease (Durham, N.C.: Duke University Press, 1993), 5, 4.

19. Ibid., 4. Indeed, scholars of postcolonial studies who do not work exclusively on American materials rely on experience to authorize their project. Postcolonial studies might even be said to be founded on a rhetoric of experience. Edward Said, the scholar credited with providing the impetus to studies of postcolonial literature, writes in *Orientalism* that his "starting point . . . has been the British, French, and American experience of the Orient taken as a unit, what made that experience possible by way of historical and intellectual background, what the quality and character of the experience has been" (16). See *Orientalism* (New York: Vintage, 1979). The authors of one of the first books attempting to synthesize postcolonial literary study claim that what "makes [a literature] distinctively post-colonial" is that it "emerged in [its] present form out of the experience of colonization and asserted [itself] by foregrounding the tension with the imperial power" (2). See Bill Ashcroft, Gareth Griffiths, and Helen Tiffin, *The Empire Writes Back: Theory and Practice in Post-Colonial Literatures* (London: Routledge, 1989).

20. Gura, "Turning Our World Upside Down," 110, 111. Gura also discusses the need for early American literature scholars to devote more attention to the southern colonies in "Study of Colonial American Literature, 1966–1987." See esp. pp. 309–10 and 315–23. Other advocates of an approach to early American literature that would stress the southern colonies include David S. Shields, *Oracles of Empire: Poetry, Politics, and Commerce in British America, 1690–1750* (Chicago: University of Chicago Press, 1990) and Spengemann, *New World* and *Mirror for Americanists.*

21. Jack P. Greene, *Pursuits of Happiness: The Social Development of Early Modern British Colonies and the Formation of American Culture* (Chapel Hill: University of North Carolina Press, 1988), xiii. See also idem, *The Intellectual Construction of America: Exceptionalism and Identity from 1492–1800* (Chapel Hill: University of North Carolina Press, 1993) and idem and J. R. Pole, eds., *Colonial British America: Essays in the New History of the Early Modern Era* (Baltimore: Johns Hopkins University Press, 1984).

22. *The Puritan Ordeal* (Cambridge, Mass.: Harvard University Press, 1989) drew largely positive reviews in *American Literary History* and *Early American*

Literature. Donald Weber called the book "the richest transcription we have of the hesitant, bewildered yet ultimately hopeful new-world inflections that register everywhere in early American culture" (113). See Weber, "Historicizing the Errand," *American Literary History* 2 (1990): 101–18. Frank Shuffleton concludes his review by saying that it should be seen as "a tribute to Delbanco's power of argument and scholarship," for, Shuffelton claims, the book "challenges our understanding of our history and our literature" (207). See Shuffelton, "Privation and Fulfillment: The Ordering of Early New England," *Early American Literature* 25 (1990): 200–207. I would argue just the opposite: the book relies on the same assumptions that have guided scholarship of American literature at least in the twentieth century and therefore represents a continuation of that scholarship rather than a challenge to it.

23. Delbanco, *Puritan Ordeal*, 1, 4. Delbanco goes on to criticize "contemporary American ideological criticism" (4) for its production of "a thin and colorless version of our history, as if all who lived before us were running on a treadmill" (5). Delbanco is not alone in finding fault with contemporary criticism of American literature. For a similar critique of the focus on ideology in literary studies, see Frederick Crews, "Whose American Renaissance?" *New York Review of Books*, 27 October 1988, 68–81.

24. Howard Mumford Jones, *O Strange New World: American Culture: The Formative Years* (New York: Viking, 1964), 107. See also his "The European Background," in *The Reinterpretation of American Literature: Some Contributions Toward the Understanding of Its Historical Development*, edited by Norman Foerster (New York: Harcourt, Brace, 1928), 62–82. Jones, of course, was not alone in his conviction that American culture owed much to European influences. Miller, too, made the case for the Englishness of the American Puritans. In the "Introduction" to *The Puritans*, Miller and Thomas Johnson assert that "about ninety per cent of the [American Puritans'] intellectual life, scientific knowledge, morality, manners and customs, notions and prejudices, was that of all Englishmen" (Miller and Johnson, "Introduction,"in *The Puritans: A Sourcebook of Their Writings*, vol. 1, rev. ed. [New York: Harper & Row, 1963], 7).

25. Jehlen, "The Papers of Empire," in *The Cambridge History of American Literature*, vol. 1, *1590–1820*, edited by Sacvan Bercovitch (Cambridge: Cambridge University Press, 1994), 36.

26. Ibid., 13.

27. See Peter Dear, *Discipline and Experience: The Mathematical Way in the Scientific Revolution* (Chicago: University of Chicago Press, 1995) and Steven Shapin, *A Social History of Truth: Civility and Science in Seventeenth-Century England* (Chicago: University of Chicago Press, 1994).

28. Very little is known of William Wood. For the most complete discussion, see Alden T. Vaughan, "Introduction," in *New Englands Prospect*, edited by Alden T. Vaughan (Amherst: University of Massachusetts Press, 1993).

29. Amy Schrager Lang, *Prophetic Woman: Anne Hutchinson and the Problem of Dissent in the Literature of New England* (Berkeley: University of California Press, 1987), 52. *A Short Story* appeared in four editions between 1644 and 1652. Thomas Weld's preface was not included in the first edition, but did appear in the three subsequent editions.

30. Wendy Martin argues the reverse. She claims that Preparationism "restrained" what she terms "Bradstreet's rebellious inclinations" (*An American Triptych: Anne Bradstreet, Emily Dickinson, Adrienne Rich* [Chapel Hill: University of North Carolina Press, 1984], 57). While I find Martin's readings of Bradstreet's poems and her discussion of the role of women in seventeenth-century Massachusetts Bay illuminating and insightful, I think my examination of experience will show that Bradstreet cannot be labeled a Preparationist.

31. For a discussion of the "narrative quality" of Preparationist doctrine, see Sargent Bush's analysis of Thomas Hooker, who has long been considered the preeminent spokesperson for the Preparationist cause in early America (Bush, *The Writings of Thomas Hooker: Spiritual Adventure in Two Worlds* [Madison: University of Wisconsin Press, 1980], 164).

32. Indeed, Nina Baym has shown how the focus on New England developed in the early nineteenth century in response to the felt need to provide some history to a young nation that seemed without one. Baym argues that the New England story of America's founding can be traced to Whig historians of the early nineteenth century, who "install[ed] New England as the originary site of the American nation" in order "to stimulate . . . those qualities they thought the nation needed to survive" (82). See Baym, "Melodramas of Beset Manhood." The critique of early Americanists' focus on New England at the expense of writings from other colonies has a long history. Its most recent formation can be traced to the 1980s, when William Spengemann in *Mirror for Americanists* and Gura in "Study of Colonial American Literature" each used the work of colonial American social historians to challenge the New England focus of early American literary studies. While much early American literary scholarship still focuses on New England writing—including my own—I think it is fair to say that scholars can no longer, in Gura's words, treat "the literature of colonial America as though it were that of New England writ large" (337).

33. Carla Mulford, "What *Is* the Early American Canon, and Who Said It Needed Expanding?" in "Special Issue: Expanding the Early American Canon," *Resources for American Literary Study* 19 (1993): 165–73, 170.

34. Shields, *Oracles of Empire*, 2.

35. See Larzer Ziff, "Text and Context," *William and Mary Quarterly* 3rd ser., 45 (1988): 348–49.

36. I want to be clear that I did not choose to focus on New England writing out of any sense that this material is somehow more American than the poems, tracts, histories, and so on produced in the other colonies. Larzer Ziff makes a similar point in discussing his exclusive focus on Puritanism in *Puritanism in America*. What he says about his study of Puritanism applies equally well to my study of New England discourse in general, so that while "[t]he influence Puritanism exerts on modern life is great . . . it is far from exclusive." He would not, he adds, "want to be misunderstood as offering a modern version of the silly theory that the real history of America is the history of the spread on the continent of Anglo-Saxon habits and Anglo-Saxon ideals." See Larzer Ziff, *Puritanism in America: New Culture in a New World* (New York: Viking, 1973), xi.

37. Shields, "Literature of the Colonial South," 176.

38. In claiming that New England texts might be connected to the development of distinctly modern ways of understanding the world, I am, of course, only following the tradition of other scholars of colonial American literature. For instance, Miller quite famously linked Jonathan Edwards to the modern world. Edwards, Perry Miller argues, "maneuvered a revolt by substituting for seventeenth-century legalisms the brute language of eighteenth-century physics. He cast off habits of mind formed in feudalism, and entered abruptly into modernity" (Miller, *Jonathan Edwards* [Amherst: University of Massachusetts Press, 1981], 77). And Bercovitch claims that New England "culture was committed from the start to what recent social scientists have termed the process of modernization" (*American Jeremiad*, xii).

CHAPTER ONE
HOW THE ENGLISH BODY BECOMES THAT OF THE ENGLISH NATION

1. Several scholars have discussed early modern English views of the North American climate. See John Canup, *Out of the Wilderness: The Emergence of an American Identity in Colonial New England* (Middletown, Conn.: Wesleyan University Press, 1990); idem, "Cotton Mather and 'Criolian Degeneracy,'" *Early American Literature* 24 (1989): 20–34; Joyce E. Chaplin, "Natural Philosophy and an Early Racial Idiom in North America: Comparing English and Indian Bodies," *William and Mary Quarterly* 3rd ser., 54 (1997): 229–52; David Cressy, *Coming Over: Migration and Communication Between England and New England in the Seventeenth Century* (Cambridge: Cambridge University Press, 1987), 1–20; Clarence J. Glacken, *Traces on the Rhodian Shore: Nature and Culture in Western Thought from Ancient Times to the End of the Eighteenth Century* (Berkeley: University of California Press, 1967); Margaret T. Hodgen, *Early Anthropology in the Sixteenth and Seventeenth Centuries* (Philadelphia: University of Pennsylvania Press, 1964); Karen Ordahl Kupperman, "Fear of Hot Climates in the Anglo-American Colonial Experience," *William and Mary Quarterly* 3rd ser., 41 (1984): 213–40; idem, "The Puzzle of the American Climate in the Early Colonial Period," *American Historical Review* 87 (1982): 1262–89.

2. Quoted in Chaplin, "Natural Philosophy," 235.

3. George Best, *Experiences and reasons of the Sphere, to proove all partes of the worlde habitable, and thereby to confute the position of the five Zones* (1578), in *The Principal Navigations, Voyages, Traffiques & Discoveries of the English Nation*, vol. 7 (Glasgow: James Machehorse, 1904), 252.

4. Ibid., 253.

5. Glacken, *Traces on the Rhodian Shore*, 358.

6. Ibid., 454. Glacken argues, in fact, that "there was a conspicuous interest" in the "subject" of cultural differences relating to climate "in seventeenth century . . . England" (451), precisely the period of my study.

7. Quoted in Canup, "Cotton Mather and 'Criolian Degeneracy,'" 22.

8. Kupperman, "Fear of Hot Climates," 215. John Canup has discussed the fear of the loss of English identity evident in colonial writings, a fear he describes

as a "concern that transplantation into an alien environment would transform English people into 'Americans'" (*Out of the Wilderness*, 4). In fact, while Canup provides an important discussion of the issue, which is the most extensive one I have seen, his project relies on precisely the assumptions I analyzed in the introduction. Canup writes that he hopes his book will "illuminate the anxiety these English colonists experienced as they became, despite themselves, American" (*Out of the Wilderness*, 7).

9. Richard Eburne, *A Plain Pathway to Plantations* (1624), edited by Louis B. Wright (Ithaca, N.Y.: Cornell University Press, 1962), 12.

10. Ibid., 12. Kupperman, Canup, Chaplin, and James Axtell also discuss the fear that colonists would lose their Englishness if they moved to the colonies. See Canup, Chaplin, and Kupperman above, and Axtell, *The Invasion Within: The Contest of Cultures in Colonial North America* (New York: Oxford University Press, 1985).

11. I do not discuss here a fear related to but distinct from the fear of alien climates: the fear that exposure to "alien" cultures like those of the Native Americans would nativize English colonists. As Canup has pointed out in *Out of the Wilderness*, the fear of "going native" caused a great deal of concern among early modern colonial writers. Jeffrey Knapp claims that "the most serious charge against Smith" was "the slander that he had proven himself so debased as to want to live not just like a savage but with one" (210). See Knapp, *An Empire Nowhere: England, America, and Literature from Utopia to The Tempest* (Berkeley: University of California Press, 1992). David D. Smits, in fact, claims that one of the most powerful reasons why the English were reluctant to marry natives, in comparison to other European colonizers, was the English fear of cultural transformation. See Smits, "'We Are Not to Grow Wild': Seventeenth-Century New England's Repudiation of Anglo-Indian Intermarriage," *American Indian Culture and Research Journal* 11 (1987): 1–32. Scholars concerned with the captivity narrative have explored the issue of the fear of nativization in some detail as well. See Nancy Armstrong and Leonard Tennenhouse, *The Imaginary Puritan: Literature, Intellectual Labor, and the Origins of Personal Life* (Berkeley: University of California Press, 1992), 196–216; Mitchell Robert Breitwieser, *American Puritanism and the Defense of Mourning: Religion, Grief, and Ethnology in Mary White Rowlandson's Captivity Narrative* (Madison: University of Wisconsin Press, 1990); Roy Harvey Pearce, *The Savages of America: A Study of the Indian and the Idea of Civilization*, rev. ed. (Baltimore: Johns Hopkins University Press, 1965), esp. 1–49; and Richard Slotkin, *Regeneration Through Violence: The Mythology of the American Frontier, 1600–1860* (Middletown, Conn.: Wesleyan University Press, 1973).

Also of particular relevance to my study is the work of Anne R. Jones and Peter Stallybrass on how the colonization of Ireland raised the same fears, what Jones and Stallybrass call "internal colonization," that English culture would go native as a result of colonization (169). See Jones and Stallybrass, "Dismantling Irena: The Sexualizing of Ireland in Early Modern England," in *Nationalisms and Sexualities*, edited by Andrew Parker, Mary Ruso, Doris Sommer, and Patricia Yaeger (New York: Routledge, 1992), 157–71. Indeed, James Muldoon argues that "[w]hen the colonists came to deal with the Indians, they did so in light of English experience in Ireland" (269). Muldoon, "The Indian as Irishman," *Essex Institute Historical Collections* 111 (1975): 267–89.

12. Kupperman, "Fear of Hot Climates," 213.

13. Canup, *Out of the Wilderness*, 3, 7.

14. Chaplin, "Natural Philosophy," 231.

15. Michel Foucault, *Discipline and Punish: The Birth of the Prison*, translated by Alan Sheridan (New York: Vintage, 1977), 25.

16. Michel Foucault, *The Order of Things: An Archaeology of Human Sciences* (New York: Vintage, 1970), 18.

17. Ibid., 18.

18. Ibid., 25.

19. R. H. Tawney, *Religion and the Rise of Capitalism: A Historical Study* (New York: Harcourt, Brace, 1926), 23.

20. Ibid., 22.

21. Ibid., 25.

22. Michel Foucault, "Nietzsche, Genealogy, History," in *Language, Counter-Memory, Practice: Selected Essays and Interviews by Michel Foucault*, edited by Donald F. Bouchard, translated by Donald F. Bouchard and Sherry Simon (Ithaca, N.Y.: Cornell University Press, 1977), 153. As Foucault himself acknowledges in *Discipline and Punish*, though, "[h]istorians long ago began to write the history of the body" (25). It is fair to say that the early modern colonial body has received little attention from scholars old or new. Chaplin has provided the most comprehensive analysis of the early modern colonial English body. See Chaplin, "Natural Philosophy," 229–52. For a discussion of how the body was integral to the reformation of manners in eighteenth-century British-American colonies, see Richard Bushman, *The Refinement of America: Persons, Houses, Cities* (New York: Vintage, 1992), 61–99.

23. Peter Stallybrass and Allon White, *The Politics and Poetics of Transgression* (Ithaca, N.Y.: Cornell University Press, 1986), 192.

24. Foucault, *Discipline and Punish*, 47, 50.

25. Ibid., 48.

26. Ibid.

27. Ibid., 49. Jonathan Goldberg makes a similar point in his analysis of theater during James I's reign. In using *Discipline and Punish* to illuminate his point that "[s]overeignty is a matter of sight," Goldberg writes that Foucault's analysis of torture argues that "what is done [to the criminal's] body is a manifestation of the power of the sovereign because his body belongs to the sovereign." See Goldberg, *James I and the Politics of Literature: Jonson, Shakespeare, Donne, and Their Contemporaries* (Baltimore: Johns Hopkins University Press, 1983), 149.

Such displays of the monarch's position as head of the social body were carried on at court as well as for the general public on execution days. Jonathan Sawday uses Foucault's insights on the body of the condemned to investigate Renaissance "anatomy theaters," where the bodies of executed criminals were dissected in front of the court. Sawday argues that these displays of the dissected body were designed so that "[w]ith each dissection, the onlookers were reminded of the great super-structure of religious authority which linked the bodies of the subjects to the incorporeal body of the king" (189). See Sawday, *The Body Emblazoned: Dissection and the Human Body in Renaissance Culture* (London: Routledge, 1995).

28. Leonard Tennenhouse, *Power on Display: The Politics of Shakespeare's Genres* (New York: Methuen, 1986), 105.

29. Ibid., 113.

30. Richard Helgerson, *Forms of Nationhood: The Elizabethan Writing of England* (Chicago: University of Chicago Press, 1992), 114.

31. Ibid., 117, 114.

32. Roger Chartier, *The Cultural Origins of the French Revolution*, translated by Lydia G. Cochrane (Durham, N.C.: Duke University Press, 1991), 134, 128.

33. Ibid., 134, 129.

34. Mikhail Bakhtin, *Rabelais and His World*, translated by Helene Iswolsky (Cambridge, Mass.: MIT, 1968), 29, 26. For discussions of how Bakhtin's analysis of the grotesque and classical bodies shed light on power in Renaissance England, see Armstrong and Tennenhouse, *Imaginary Puritan*; Stallybrass, "Patriarchal Territories: The Body Enclosed," in *Rewriting the Renaissance: The Discourses of Sexual Difference in Early Modern Europe*, edited by Margaret Ferguson, Maureen Quilligan, and Nancy J. Vickers (Chicago: University of Chicago Press, 1986); Stallybrass and White, *Politics and Poetics*; and Tennenhouse, *Power on Display*.

35. Bakhtin, *Rabelais*, 320, 29.

36. Ibid., 154.

37. Helgerson, *Forms of Nationhood*, 294.

38. Bakhtin, *Rabelais*, 27.

39. Stallybrass and White, *Politics and Poetics*, 26.

40. Ibid., 20.

41. Ibid., 193.

42. Englishness, of course, was hardly a static concept in the seventeenth century. For a discussion of how the English themselves might be imagined as "English" in the first place in light of English men and women living outside England proper, see Nicholas Canny, "Identity Formation in Ireland: The Emergence of the Anglo-Irish," in *Colonial Identity in the Atlantic World, 1500–1800*, edited by Nicholas Canny and Anthony Pagden (Princeton, N.J.: Princeton University Press, 1987), 159–212.

43. Leonard Barkan, *Nature's Work of Art: The Human Body as Image of the World* (New Haven, Conn.: Yale University Press, 1975), 75. Barkan is not alone in his assessment that the image of the body politic was especially prevalent in Renaissance England. David George Hale claims that it "flourish[ed]" in "Elizabethan literature" (7). See Hale, *The Body Politic: A Political Metaphor in Renaissance English Literature* (The Hague: Mouton, 1971).

44. For a discussion of the body in early modern England, especially but not only as it relates to the legitimation of structures of power, see Armstrong and Tennenhouse, *Imaginary Puritan*; Marie Axton, *The Queen's Two Bodies: Drama and the Elizabethan Succession* (London: Royal Historical Society, 1977); Francis Barker, *The Tremulous Private Body: Essays on Subjection*, 2nd ed. (Ann Arbor: University of Michigan Press, 1995); Lucy Gent and Nigel Llewel-

lyn, eds., *Renaissance Bodies: The Human Figure in English Culture c. 1540–1660* (London: Reaktion, 1990); Goldberg, *James I*; Helgerson, *Forms of Nationhood*, esp. 105–47 and 292–95; David Hillman and Carla Mazzio, eds., *The Body in Parts: Fantasies of Corporeality in Early Modern Europe* (New York: Routledge, 1997); Ernst Kantorowicz, *The King's Two Bodies* (Princeton, N.J.: Princeton University Press, 1957); David Lee Miller, *The Poem's Two Bodies: The Poetics of the 1590 Faerie Queen* (Princeton, N.J.: Princeton University Press, 1988); Roy Porter, "History of the Body," in *New Perspectives on Historical Writing*, edited by Peter Burke (University Park: Pennsylvania State University Press, 1991), 206–32; Sawday, *Body Emblazoned*; Roy C. Strong, *The Cult of Elizabeth: Elizabethan Portraiture and Pageantry* (London: Thames & Hudson, 1977); Stallybrass, "Patriarchal Territories"; Stallybrass and White, *Politics and Poetics*; Tennenhouse, *Power on Display*; and Linda Woodbridge, "Palisading the Elizabethan Body Politic," *Texas Studies in Literature and Language* 33 (1991): 327–54.

45. Miller, *Poem's Two Bodies*, 18.

46. Kantorowicz, *King's Two Bodies*, esp. 19–20. As Marie Axton points out, the body politic referred to with regard to the king's two bodies "should not be confused with the old metaphor of the realm composed of many men with the king as head. The ideas are related but distinct" (Axton, *Queen's Two Bodies*, 12). For a thorough discussion of the development of the idea of the realm as a body politic, see Hale, *Body Politic*. For a revealing reading of the metaphor of the body politic as it appears in Renaissance drama, see Claire McEachern, *The Poetics of English Nationhood, 1590–1612* (Cambridge: Cambridge University Press, 1996), 103–5.

47. Axton, *Queen's Two Bodies*, 12.

48. Kantorowicz, *King's Two Bodies*, 20.

49. My discussion of the shift in the grounds of political authority during the latter part of the seventeenth century is heavily indebted to Armstrong and Tennenhouse, *Imaginary Puritan*, 171–74.

50. John Locke, *Two Treatises of Government*, edited by Peter Laslett (Cambridge: Cambridge University Press, 1988), 2.55.7–8.

51. Ibid., 2.58.5–15.

52. Ibid., 2.27.6–12.

53. Locke was using the experiential body to argue against Robert Filmer's defense of royal absolutism. The body language I analyze here was specifically directed at Filmer's arguments regarding how order is maintained within the family. Filmer uses the image of the family in an attempt to show how the monarch's patriarchal authority is, in fact, a natural form of power that operates even in the smallest political unit. Thus we can see that the experiential body Locke proposes is fundamentally hostile to monarchy. As Armstrong and Tennenhouse argue, "[i]n opposing Filmer's representation of the English social body as the monarch's body, Locke imagines the social body as a genetic, or self-replicating, cellular structure" (Armstrong and Tennenhouse, *Imaginary Puritan*, 254). See also Armstrong and Tennenhouse, *Imaginary Puritan*, 168–69 and Bryan S. Turner, *The Body and Society: Explorations in Social Theory*, 2nd ed. (London: Sage, 1996), 144–47.

54. Christopher Hill, *Intellectual Origins of the English Revolution* (Oxford: Clarendon, 1965), 5.

55. Christopher Hill, *The Century of Revolution, 1603–1714* (London: Nelson, 1961), 3.

56. Locke, *Two Treatises*, 2.49.1. Locke's frequent references to things American in the *Two Treatises* has led at least one critic to advance the argument that the whole work should be regarded as a defense of the colonial project. Barbara Arneil argues that "the *Two Treatises* were written as a defence of England's colonial policy in the new world against the sceptics in England and the counter-claims of both the aboriginal nations and other European powers in America" (2). Arneil's argument places too much stress, it seems to me, on the colonial applications of Locke's work at the expense of the interventions it makes in political questions having little to do with the colonies. Nonetheless, the fact that a plausible argument could be made that *Two Treatises* is principally concerned with colonial issues only serves to illustrate my point, namely, that in order to understand how Locke intervenes in early modern political theory we need to understand the way in which he depends on figures developed in earlier colonial writings. See Barbara Arneil, *John Locke and America: The Defence of English Colonialism* (Oxford: Clarendon, 1996).

57. Best, 'Experiences,' 252.

58. John Brereton, *A Briefe and True Relation of the Discoverie of the North Part of Virginia* (1602), in *The English New England Voyages, 1602–1608*, edited by David B. Quinn and Alison M. Quinn (London: The Hakluyt Society, 1983), 300.

59. Sir Ferdinando Gorges, *A Briefe Relation of the Discovery and Plantations of New England* (1622), in *Publications of the Prince Society*, vol. 18, *Sir Ferdinando Gorges and His Province of Maine*, edited by James Phinney Baxter (Boston: The Prince Society, 1890), 229.

60. Edward Winslow, *Good Newes from New England* (1624), in *Chronicles of the Pilgrim Fathers of the Colony of Plymouth from 1602–1625*, edited by Alexander Young (Boston: Charles C. Little & James Brown, 1841), 355.

61. Francis Higginson, *New Englands Plantation* (London, 1630), 1.

62. For a discussion of how colonial writers interpreted Classical theories of the composition of the body and the concept of the five zones, see Chaplin, "Natural Philosophy," 234 .

63. Higginson, *New Englands Plantation*, 1.

64. Ibid.

65. Ibid., 9.

66. Mary Campbell, "The Illustrated Travel Book and the Birth of Ethnography: Part I of De Bry's *America*," in *The Work of Dissimilitude: Essays from the Sixth Citadel Conference on Medieval and Renaissance Literature*, edited by David G. Allen and Robert A. White (Newark, N.J.: University of Delaware Press, 1992), 182–84.

67. Anita Pacheco, "Royalism and Honor in Aphra Behn's *Oroonoko*," *Studies in English Literature, 1500–1900* 34 (1994): 491–506.

68. Vincent, "A True Relation," 34.

69. Ibid., 35. As Canup (*Out of the Wilderness*) points out, the theory of the humours allowed the English to diagnose the Pequot War "as the natural consequence of a humoral imbalance" (61).

70. Because scholars have found it difficult to be precise in determining the population of Native Americans prior to the beginning of colonization in the sixteenth century, estimates of just how many Native Americans died as a result of the many diseases brought over by Europeans vary widely. Among the Pequots alone, it has been estimated that approximately 90 percent of the Pequot population, about 18,000 people, died as a result of a single smallpox epidemic from 1616 to 1619. See Alfred A. Cave, *The Pequot War* (Amherst: University of Massachusetts Press, 1996), 43. For discussions of epidemics among New England Indians, see Dean R. Snow and Kim M. Lamphear, "European Contact and Indian Depopulation in the Northeast: The Timing of the First Epidemics," *Ethnohistory* 35 (1988): 16–38. For more general discussions of Native American depopulation, see Alfred W. Crosby Jr., "Virgin Soil Epidemics as a Factor in Aboriginal Depopulation in America," *William and Mary Quarterly* 3rd ser., 33 (1976): 289–99; idem, *The Columbian Exchange: Biological and Cultural Consequences of 1492* (Westport, Conn.: Greenwood, 1972); and idem, *Ecological Imperialism: The Biological Expansion of Europe 900–1900* (Cambridge: Cambridge University Press, 1986); Russell Thornton, *American Indian Holocaust and Survival: A Population History since 1492* (Norman: University of Oklahoma Press, 1987); Ann F. Ramenofsky, *Vectors of Death: The Archaeology of European Contact* (Albuquerque: University of New Mexico Press, 1987).

71. Chaplin, "Natural Philosophy," 244, 230.

72. John White, *A Planters Plea Or the Grounds of Plantations Examined, And usual Objections answered* (London: William Jones, 1630), 25.

73. Thomas Morton, *New English Canaan* (Amsterdam, 1637), 134.

74. Edward Johnson, *A History of New-England From the English planting in the Yeere 1628 untill the Yeere 1652* (London, 1653), 41.

75. Mary Douglas, *Purity and Danger: An Analysis of the Concepts of Pollution and Taboo* (London: Routledge & Kegan Paul, 1966), 122.

76. *A Relation or Journal of the beginning and proceedings of the English Plantation settled in Plimouth in New England* (London, 1622), 8. For other instances of the metaphor of the enlargement of the body politic in New England colonial tracts, see, for example, Robert Cushman, "Reasons and Considerations," included in *A Relation or Journal of the beginnings and proceedings*, 88–96, Edmund Winslow, and William Wood. Such metaphors were also used by writers who were promoting colonization in general rather than New England in particular. See, for instance, John Smith, *The General Historie of Virginia, New-England, and the Summer Isles* (London, 1624).

77. Sir William Alexander, *An Encouragement to Colonies* (London, 1624), 152.

78. White, *A Planters Plea*, 34.

79. Morton, *New English Canaan*, 122, 117.

80. Ibid., 313, 316. George Mariscal has shown that the same concern that colonial social practices might threaten established categories of rank can also be

seen in Spanish colonial writing. In the case of Spanish colonies, Mariscal argues, it was the insertion of "subjects . . . born of the union between nonaristocratic conquistadores and female members of the Indian nobility" that "called into question the entire structure of traditional Castilian life" (97). Mariscal contends that the "traditional categories" had to be "expanded if they were to hold together" (97). See Mariscal, *Contradictory Subjects: Quevedo, Cervantes, and Seventeenth-Century Spanish Culture* (Ithaca, N.Y.: Cornell University Press, 1991).

81. David Lee Miller argues that Spenser criticizes monarchical authority through a "structural adaptation of the metaphor" of the king's two bodies rather than via "specific tactical exhortation[s] or admonition[s]," while Marie Axton argues that Elizabethan dramatists used "the theory of the two bodies . . . to criticize and coerce the Queen" (Miller, *Poem's Two Bodies*, 110; Axton, *Queen's Two Bodies*, 146).

82. There is considerable controversy over the causes of the Pequot War, especially over whether the Puritans lied about their knowledge of the Pequots' involvement in the death of one of the colonists and if they demanded excessively high reparations in order to provoke a conflict. For a discussion of the various positions taken in this controversy, see Alfred A. Cave, "Who Killed John Stone? A Note on the Origins of the Pequot War," *William and Mary Quarterly* 3rd ser., 49 (1992): 509–21. Cave also provides a comprehensive narrative of the war in his *The Pequot War*. For a very different account of the causes, see Francis Jennings, *The Invasion of America: Indians, Colonialism, and the Cant of Conquest* (New York: Norton, 1976).

83. Captain John Underhill, *Newes from America; or, A New and Experimental Discoverie of New England* (London, 1638), 9.

84. Ibid.

85. Canup also discusses the question of English cultural identity in *Newes from America*, pointing out how the text represents an Indian's "alienation from his own people" when he is referred to by other Indians as an "English man" (*Out of the Wilderness*, 167).

86. Underhill, *Newes from America*, 25.

87. Ibid., 15.

88. Ibid.

89. John Winthrop, "A Modell of Christian Charity" (*Old South Leaflets* No. 207, edited by Samuel Eliot Morrison [Boston: Old South Association, n.d.]), 13, 20. For a discussion of Winthrop's use of the metaphor of the body politic, see Andrew Delbanco, *The Puritan Ordeal* (Cambridge, Mass.: Harvard University Press, 1989), 73–79 and Scott Michaelsen, "John Winthrop's 'Modell' Covenant and the Company Way," *Early American Literature* 27 (1992): 92.

90. Winthrop, "Modell of Christian Charity," 20.

91. Underhill, *Newes from America*, 19.

92. Ibid., 20.

93. Thomas Lechford, *Plain Dealing: or, Newes From New-England* (London, 1642).

94. Ibid., 139.

95. Theodore de la Guard, *The Simple Cobbler of Aggawam in America* (London, 1647), 46. *The Simple Cobbler* was originally published pseudonymously. For a discussion of Ward's choice to use a pseudonym, see Lawrence C. Wroth, "Introduction" to *The Simple Cobbler of Aggawam in America* (1647) (New York: Scholars' Facsimiles & Reprints, 1937), i–vii.

96. de la Guard, *Simple Cobbler*, 53.

CHAPTER TWO
THE MAN OF EXPERIENCE

1. Stephen Greenblatt, *Renaissance Self-Fashioning: From More to Shakespeare* (Chicago: University of Chicago Press, 1980), 9. It is important to note that Greenblatt first used the term "new historicism" not in *Renaissance Self-Fashioning*, but in his "Introduction" to the Winter 1981 issue of *Genre*, which appeared after the publication of *Self-Fashioning*.

2. Ibid., 9. For three views on the link between modernity and the rise of writing, see Benedict Anderson, *Imagined Communities: Reflections on the Origin and Spread of Nationalism*, rev. ed. (London: Verso, 1991); Nancy Armstrong and Leonard Tennenhouse, *The Imaginary Puritan: Literature, Intellectual Labor, and the Origins of Personal Life* (Berkeley: University of California Press, 1992); and Michael Warner, *The Letters of the Republic: Publication and the Public Sphere in Eighteenth-Century America* (Cambridge, Mass.: Harvard University Press, 1990).

3. Greenblatt, *Renaissance Self-Fashioning*, 7.

4. Ibid., 9.

5. Ibid., 4.

6. Stephen Greenblatt, *Marvelous Possessions: The Wonder of the New World* (Chicago: University of Chicago Press, 1991), 6.

7. Ibid., 14.

8. Ibid., 19.

9. Peter Stallybrass, "Shakespeare, the Individual, and the Text," in *Cultural Studies*, edited by Lawrence Grossberg, Cary Nelson, and Paula Treichler (New York: Routledge, 1992), 593.

10. See Leonard Tennenhouse, *Power on Display: The Politics of Shakespeare's Genres* (New York: Methuen, 1986).

11. For Foucault's most extensive articulation of this position, see Michel Foucault, *Discipline and Punish: The Birth of the Prison*, translated by Alan Sheridan (New York: Pantheon, 1977).

12. Charles B. Schmitt, "Experience and Experiment: A Comparison of Zabarella's View with Galileo's in *De motu*," *Studies in the Renaissance* 16 (1969): 80–138, 80; Peter Dear, "Jesuit Mathematical Science and the Reconstitution of Experience in the Early Seventeenth Century," *Studies in History and Philosophy of Science* 18 (1987): 133–75, 134, 175. For other discussions of the transformation of experience, see Peter Dear, *Discipline and Experience: The Mathematical Way in the Scientific Revolution* (Chicago: University of Chicago Press, 1995); idem, "Miracles, Experiments, and the Ordinary Course of Nature," *Isis*

81 (1990): 663–83; idem, "Narratives, Anecdotes, and Experiments: Turning Experience into Science in the Seventeenth Century," in *The Literary Structure of Scientific Argument: Historical Studies*, edited by Peter Dear (Philadelphia: University of Pennsylvania Press, 1991); Rose-Mary Sargent, "Scientific Experiment and Legal Expertise: The Way of Experience in Seventeenth-Century England," *Studies in History of Philosophy of Science* 20 (1989): 19–45; Steven Shapin, *A Social History of Truth: Civility and Science in Seventeenth-Century England* (Chicago: University of Chicago Press, 1994); Barbara J. Shapiro, *Probability and Certainty in Seventeenth-Century England: A Study of the Relationships between Natural Science, Religion, History, Law, and Literature* (Princeton, N.J.: Princeton University Press, 1983).

13. See Shapin, *Social History of Truth*, 191.

14. Wayne Franklin, *Discoverers, Explorers, Settlers: The Diligent Writers of Early America* (Chicago: University of Chicago Press, 1979), 5; J. A. Leo Lemay, *The American Dream of Captain John Smith* (Charlottesville: University Press of Virginia, 1991), 5.

15. Mary Fuller discusses the use of Smith as "the point of origin for a specifically American history" in *Voyages in Print: English Travel to America, 1576–1624* (Cambridge: Cambridge University Press, 1995), 103–6.

16. For a discussion of Smith's family background and his place within the English social hierarchy, see Philip L. Barbour, *The Three Worlds of Captain John Smith* (London: Macmillan, 1964), 1–73; Everett H. Emerson, *Captain John Smith* (Boston: Twayne, 1971), 35–36; and Alden T. Vaughan, *American Genesis: Captain John Smith and the Founding of Virginia* (Boston: Little, Brown, 1975).

17. Dear, "Miracles," 667. For a discussion of the "literary techniques and strategies" employed by early modern experimental scientists, see Dear, "Narratives, Anecdotes, and Experiments."

18. Lemay, *American Dream*, 5.

19. See Mary Campbell, *The Witness and the Other World: Exotic European Travel Writing, 400–1600* (Ithaca, N.Y.: Cornell University Press, 1988), 228.

20. Michael McKeon, *The Origins of the English Novel, 1600–1740* (Baltimore: Johns Hopkins University Press, 1987), esp. 100–105.

21. John Smith, *The Complete Works of Captain John Smith*, 3 vols., edited by Philip Barbour (Chapel Hill: University Press of North Carolina, 1986), 1:176. All subsequent references to Smith's writings will be to this text and will be made parenthetically.

22. Indeed, Smith is jailed by his fellow colonists in Virginia for the so-called treasonous nature of what his opponents claim are scandalous remarks (1:206–7).

23. Lemay, *American Dream*, 172.

24. Emerson provides the most detailed account of Smith's "borrowings" and the changes that are made in Smith's works in numerous different editions in which they appeared. In fact, Emerson provides a stylistic and thematic close-reading of a number of these alterations.

25. Emerson, *Captain John Smith*, 87, 65.

26. As Emerson has noted, Smith begins to shift his position on the impor-

tance of religion and colonization in his final works. See ibid., 114–16. In these later writings, Smith represents religion, as Emerson notes, as an "indispensable instrument of order, a preventor of factionalism" (115).

27. For a discussion of the genre of the promotion tract, see Howard Mumford Jones, "The Colonial Impulse: An Analysis of the 'Promotion' Literature of Colonization," *Proceedings of the American Philosophical Society* 90, no. 2 (1946): 131–61; and Paul J. Lindholdt, "The Significance of the Colonial Promotion Tract," in *Early American Literature and Culture: Essays Honoring Harrison T. Messerole*, edited by Kathryn Zabelle Derounian-Stodola (Newark, N.J.: University of Delaware Press, 1992). For a discussion of the colonial travel narrative in more general terms, see McKeon, *Origins of the English Novel*, 100–118; and Richard Helgerson, *Forms of Nationhood: The Elizabethan Writing of England* (Chicago: University of Chicago Press, 1992), esp. 149–91.

28. In the prefatory letter to the reader in *A Briefe and True Report*, Hariot writes that he "will set downe all the comoodites which wee know the countrey by our experience doth yeld of it selfe for victuall, and sustenance of mans life." See Thomas Hariot, *A Briefe and True Report of the New Found Land of Virginia* (London, 1588). At no other point in his narrative does Hariot invoke experience.

29. See William Wood, *New Englands Prospect* (1634), edited by Alden T. Vaughan (Amherst: University of Massachusetts Press, 1993).

CHAPTER THREE
A BODY THAT WORKS

1. Clarence J. Glacken, *Traces on the Rhodian Shore: Nature and Culture in Western Thought from Ancient Times to the End of the Eighteenth Century* (Berkeley: University of California Press, 1967).

2. Mary Douglas, *Purity and Danger: An Analysis of Concepts of Pollution and Taboo* (London: Penguin, 1970), 138.

3. David Cressy, *Coming Over: Migration and Communication Between England and New England in the Seventeenth Century* (Cambridge: Cambridge University Press, 1987), 203.

4. Cressy is not alone in his assessment. For a discussion of the book's publication history and its seventeenth-century reputation, see Alden T. Vaughan, "Introduction," in *New Englands Prospect*, edited by Alden T. Vaughan (Amherst: University of Massachusetts Press, 1993).

5. Quoted in the Prince Society edition of *New Englands Prospect*, viii; *A Relation of Maryland Narratives of Early Maryland* (New York: Charles Scribner's Sons, 1910), *Original Narratives of Early American History* 10, edited by Clayton Colman Hall, 83; Nathaniel B. Shurtleff, ed., *Records of the Governor and Company of the Massachusetts Bay in New England (1628–86)*, 5 vols. (Boston, 1853–54), 1:128.

The list of contemporaneous references to Wood's work could continue. Some of the most interesting are contained in Thomas Morton's *New English Canaan* (Amsterdam, 1637). Indeed, the frequency of Morton's invoking Wood in his satire of New England Puritan culture attests to the influence Wood was thought to have enjoyed. Whether Morton's comments are to be understood as entirely negative or at least somewhat praiseworthy is the matter of some disagreement. Vaughan labels the references to Wood's work by Morton "usually favorable" ("Introduction," 3), while Wayne Franklin claims that Wood served as an "available target for shots aimed actually at the Puritan elite" (*Discoverers, Explorers, Settlers: The Diligent Writers of Early America* [Chicago: University of Chicago Press, 1979], 38).

6. For instance, Stephen Greenblatt makes no mention of *New Englands Prospect* in any his numerous writings on European travel narratives, including his book devoted solely to the genre, *Marvelous Possessions*. In addition, Wood goes unmentioned by all the scholars in the collection of essays specifically on European representations of native peoples, *New World Encounters*, edited by Stephen Greenblatt (Berkeley: University of California Press, 1993). By contrast, historians of colonial America make frequent reference to *New Englands Prospect*. William Cronon, for instance, uses Henry David Thoreau's mention of Wood in his journal to open his colonial environmental history, *Changes in the Land: Indians, Colonists, and the Ecology of New England* (New York: Hill & Wang, 1983). Cronon is representative of colonial historians in general, who value the book primarily as a source of reliable information about the colonies. They rarely examine the rhetorical construction of the book. And, like the critics of American literature, they entirely ignore its relationship to European discourses of the body. See, for instance, John Canup, *Out of the Wilderness: The Emergence of an American Identity in Colonial New England* (Middletown, Conn.: Wesleyan University Press, 1990); Cressy, *Coming Over*; Neil Salisbury, *Manitou and Providence: Indians, Europeans, and the Making of New England, 1500–1643* (New York: Oxford University Press, 1982); and Alden T. Vaughan, *New England Frontier: Puritans and Indians, 1620–1675*, 3rd ed. (Norman: University of Oklahoma Press, 1995).

7. Franklin, *Discoverers, Explorers, Settlers*, xi; and John Seelye, *Prophetic Waters: The River in Early American Life and Literature* (New York: Oxford University Press, 1977), 4.

8. Seelye, *Prophetic Waters*, 152.

9. Wood, *New Englands Prospect* (London, 1634) 6. All subsequent references to *New Englands Prospect* will be to this text and will be made parenthetically.

10. Wood's language here follows almost exactly what other colonial promotion writers have written. See, for instance, Francis Higginson, *New Englands Plantation* (London, 1630).

11. Some critics have cited this as an instance of Wood's exaggeration and unusually positive presentation of life in the colonies. See note 12 below. In fact, Wood only reproduces what is said so often by other promotion writers that it might even be labeled a convention. *Mourt's Relation, New Englands Plantation*, *A Planters Plea*, and even *New English Canaan* all make the same claims.

12. Other critics have also examined Wood's claim that the New England climate resembled Old England's. These other critics have seen this claim as merely another attempt to make the colonies seem appealing to an English audience—a position I share—rather than as part of a larger rhetoric of experience

that Wood uses to achieve this goal. Even Canup, whose *Out of the Wilderness* examines how early modern English readers feared the effects of New World experience, concludes that Wood's representation was "perhaps too obviously seductive in a genre that constantly risked arousing suspicion through excessive enthusiasm or cleverness" (*Out of the Wilderness*, 17).

13. Wood was one of many promotion writers to argue that colonization would help solve the problem of English "idleness." Hackluyt, Raleigh, and Smith, to name only a few, made similar claims. Twentieth-century historians and literary critics of early modern England have examined these claims in some detail. See, for instance, Jeffrey Knapp, *An Empire Nowhere: England, America, and Literature from Utopia to The Tempest* (Berkeley: University of California Press, 1992).

14. According to Kupperman, Wood's claims about increased births were not at all unusual among colonial writers. See Karen Ordahl Kupperman, "Fear of Hot Climates in the Anglo-American Colonial Experience," *William and Mary Quarterly* 3rd ser., 41 (1984): 219.

15. Mikhail Bakhtin, *Rabelais and His World*, translated by Helen Iswolsky (Cambridge, Mass.: MIT, 1968), 26.

16. Kupperman uses Wood's claim that the Virginia colonists turned pale to support her argument that English colonial writers felt that the English body had to be properly "seasoned" like wood for about two years. See Kupperman, "Fear of Hot Climates," 215.

17. Myra Jehlen, "History before Fact; or, Captain John Smith's Unfinished Symphony," *Critical Inquiry* 19 (1993): 684.

18. Franklin and Seeyle also note the threat cannibalism poses in *New Englands Prospect*. Franklin writes, for instance, that cannibalism represents one of the "deeper hesitations" that Wood "will hint at," but that "even there his dominant stress [was] on the fruitfulness of America" (*Discoverers, Explorers, Settlers*, 41). Seeyle claims they constitute an essential part of the book's "dramatic irony," an irony that "encourage[s] an outward-moving, unstable rim of settlement" but which is "beyond Wood's intention and control" (*Prophetic Waters*, 154). I would argue that Wood's use of the threat of cannibalism plays a crucial role in the rhetoric of experience, a role that can be seen to operate on the surface and that is very much intended.

19. See Wood, *New Englands Prospect*, 76.

20. For a discussion on how the spice trade served as an impetus to colonization, see Kenneth Andrews, *Trade, Plunder, and Settlement: Maritime Enterprise and the Genesis of the British Empire, 1480–1630* (Cambridge: Cambridge University Press, 1984).

21. Bakhtin, *Rabelais*, 317.

22. For a discussion of the military conflicts that occurred among the various forces in North America, see Ian Steele, *Warpaths: Invasions of North America* (New York: Oxford University Press, 1994); Vaughan, *New England Frontier*; and David J. Weber, *The Spanish Frontier in North America* (New Haven, Conn.: Yale University Press, 1992).

23. Wayne Franklin also calls attention to the similarity of the divisions Wood makes between the natives and the English and between various catego-

ries of natural phenomena. While I find Franklin's reading of *New Englands Prospect* quite interesting, he uses this division to precisely the opposite end I am using it here, namely, to show that Wood was trying and failed to replace "the field of experience with a series of descriptive set pieces" (*Discoverers, Explorers, Settlers*, 42).

24. The representation of native populations as inferior in the field of economics is certainly not unique to Wood. Columbus claimed European superiority in economic issues, for instance, and the charge seemed to stick over the years. To name only a few in what would be a very long list, *Mourt's Relation*, *New English Canaan*, and *A Planters Plea* all use economics to distinguish between native and English cultures.

25. See Kenneth Andrews on the lucrative nature of the fish trade.

26. Paul J. Lindholdt offers a different reading of Wood's representation of the natives' response to English technology. Lindholdt claims that Wood sometimes "cunningly exaggerates the Indians' subjection to European settlement" and instruments of technology, such as the windmill ("The Significance of the Colonial Promotion Tract," in *Early American Literature and Culture: Essays Honoring Harrison T. Messerole*, edited by Kathryn Zabelle Derounian-Stodola [Newark, N.J.: University of Delaware Press, 1992], 63).

27. James Axtell reads this scene in relation to the argument common among colonial promotion writers that Indian women were far superior to Indian men in work habits. Axtell argues that Wood goes "one better" (*The Invasion Within: The Contest of Cultures in Colonial North America* [New York: Oxford University Press, 1985], 152) in this scene to demonstrate that native women have better work habits than native men, who blame English men for allowing English women to work shorter hours than they should.

28. For a discussion of how the New England colonies were financed, see Karen Ordahl Kupperman, *Providence Island, 1630–1641: The Other Puritan Colony* (New York: Cambridge University Press, 1993); and Theodore Rabb, *Enterprise and Empire: Merchant and Gentry Investment in the Expansion of England, 1575–1630* (Cambridge, Mass.: Harvard University Press, 1967).

29. Franklin, *Discoverers, Explorers, Settlers*, 41.

30. For a discussion of the importance of the figure of sight in Renaissance literature, see Patricia Parker, "Fantasies of 'Race' and 'Gender': Africa, *Othello* and Bringing to Light," in *Women, 'Race,' and Writing in the Early Modern Period*, edited by Margo Hendricks and Patricia Parker (London: Routledge, 1994).

31. I am indebted for this insight to Garrett Sullivan's discussion of the scene of reading maps in early modern England. See Sullivan, *Staging Space: The Theatre and Social Relations in Early Modern England* (Ph.D. diss., Brown University, 1995), 4.

CHAPTER FOUR
DISCIPLINE AND DISINFECT

1. Perry Miller, *Errand Into the Wilderness* (Cambridge, Mass.: The Belknap Press of Harvard University Press, 1956), 11. T. Dwight Bozeman has argued that Miller overemphasized the so-called New England errand, and thus drasti-

cally overstated the extent to which Massachusetts Bay's leaders thought of their system as a guide for their counterparts in England. See *To Live Ancient Lives: The Primitivist Dimension in Puritanism* (Chapel Hill: University of North Carolina Press, 1988).

2. Thomas Lechford, *Plain Dealing Or News from New England* (Rpt. New York: Johnson Reprint Corporation, 1969, rpt. 1642), 140.

3. Ibid. Even among residents of Massachusetts Bay, Lechford was not alone in calling attention to the potential consequences for monarchical rule of the actions of the colony's magistrates and church elders. Following his ouster as governor of the colony for his support of the Antinomian party, Henry Vane argued in *A Brief Answer to a Certain Declaration* (1637) that the colony would "fall to the ground . . . and fail" because its judicial system had "shut out" both "Christ and the king."

4. Though there were certainly differences in the areas of policy and practice between English and American Puritans, it does seem fair to say at this point that both groups were part of what Patrick Collinson has described as a large "movement" to reform the Church of England (11). See Collinson, *The Elizabethan Puritan Movement* (Berkeley: University of California Press, 1967). How one goes about defining Puritanism, however, remains a source of contention. For an illuminating discussion of this problem, see Peter Lake, "Defining Puritanism—Again?" in *Transatlantic Perspectives on a Seventeenth-Century Anglo-American Faith*, edited by Francis J. Bremer (Boston: Massachusetts Historical Society, 1993), 3–29.

5. For a more thorough discussion of these treatises, see Francis J. Bremer, *Puritan Crisis: New England and the English Civil War, 1630–1670* (Westport, Conn.: Greenwood, 1989); Harry S. Stout, *The New England Soul: Preaching and Religious Culture in Colonial New England* (New York: Oxford University Press, 1987), 50–56; and Stephen Foster, *The Long Argument: English Puritanism and the Shaping of New England Culture, 1570–1700* (Chapel Hill: University of North Carolina Press, 1991), 166–74.

6. I am, of course, rehearsing here in brief the argument that the Massachusetts Bay Puritans saw themselves as on an "errand into the wilderness." The classic statement of this position can be found in Miller, *Errand Into the Wilderness*. For a critique of this reading, see Bozeman, *To Live Ancient Lives*.

7. Stout, *New England Soul*, 52. As Francis J. Bremer points out, though, the colonists did make a rather bold move that might very well have been interpreted as antiroyalist "when the General Court struck the king's name from the oath of allegiance tendered to the freemen" (Bremer, *The Puritan Experiment: New England Society from Bradford to Edwards*, rev. ed. [Hanover, N.H.: University Press of New England, 1995], 126).

8. Stout, *New England Soul*, 52.

9. So, for instance, Nathaniel Ward notes that Massachusetts Bay has "been reputed a Colony of wild Opinionists, swarmed into a remote wilderness to find elbow-roome for [their] phanatick Doctrines and practices" (*The Simple Cobbler of Aggawam in America* [London, 1647], 3).

10. Amy Schrager Lang, *Prophetic Woman: Anne Hutchinson and the Problem of Dissent in the Literature of New England* (Berkeley: University of California Press, 1987), 54.

11. The controversy is one of the more well-documented events in New England colonial history, for, as David D. Hall has written in *The Antinomian Controversy, 1636–1638: A Documentary History*, edited by David D. Hall (Middletown, Conn.: Wesleyan University Press, 1990), "scarcely a book about seventeenth-century New England . . . fails to touch on the Antinomian Controversy" (443). For more recent scholarly accounts, see Edmund Morgan, *The Puritan Dilemma: The Story of John Winthrop* (Boston: Little, Brown, 1958), 134–54, who argues that Hutchinson's position on immediate revelation "threatened the fundamental conviction on which the Puritans built their state, their churches, and their daily lives" (139); Emery Battis, in *Saints and Sectaries: Anne Hutchinson and the Antinomian Controversy in the Massachusetts Bay Colony* (Chapel Hill: University of North Carolina Press, 1962), contends that Hutchinson's followers were motivated by economic as much as religious reasons; Larzer Ziff reads the controversy in *Puritanism in America: New Culture in a New World* (New York: Viking, 1973) in terms of a developing conflict within the colony between the demands of social responsibility and individual conscience; Philip F. Gura, *A Glimpse of Sion's Glory: Puritan Radicalism in New England, 1620–1660* (Middletown, Conn.: Wesleyan University Press, 1984), 237–76, places the Antinomian controversy in context with other radical religious movements in seventeenth-century New England; Stephen Foster's *The Long Argument*, 138–74, sets the events in the context of English influences; Andrew Delbanco contends the controversy divided the colony over what he calls "religious style," which manifested itself in the different understandings of evil (*The Puritan Ideal* [Cambridge, Mass.: Harvard University Press, 1989], 138); Janice Knight claims the controversy is a "moment of visible rupture" demonstrating that New England had at least two competing strains of religious thought rather than being, as Perry Miller argued, a monolithic view of the world (Knight, *Orthodoxies in Massachusetts: Rereading American Puritanism* [Cambridge, Mass.: Harvard University Press, 1994], 11).

12. James Schramer and Timothy Sweet, "Violence and the Body Politic in Seventeenth-Century New England," *Arizona Quarterly* 48, no. 2 (1992): 1–32, 6.

13. Michel Foucault, *Discipline and Punish: The Birth of the Prison*, translated by Alan Sheridan (New York: Pantheon, 1977), 198.

14. Armstrong and Tennenhouse have shown how English innovations for containing the plague "testify to nothing less than the presence of a new way of imagining the body politic" (Nancy Armstrong and Leonard Tennenhouse, *The Imaginary Puritan: Literature, Intellectual Labor, and the Origins of Personal Life* [Berkeley: University of California Press, 1992], 94). They associate this new body with a new body politic defined by work rather than perpetuated through blood. See pp. 92–96.

15. In *Wonder-Working Providence of Sions Savior in New England* (1654), for instance, Johnson writes of "infectious persons" who have "secretly broached" what he calls "grosse errours . . . in the dark like the Plague" (Edward Johnson, *Johnson's Wonder-working Providence, 1628–1651*, edited by J. Franklin Jameson [New York: C. Scribner's Sons, 1910], 131–32). Thomas

Shepard writes of the Antinomians as a "contagion" (*God's Plot: The Paradoxes of Puritan Piety, Being the Autobiography and Journal of Thomas Shepard*, edited by Michael McGiffert [Amherst: University of Massachusetts Press, 1972], 65).

16. Lang, *Prophetic Woman*, 52. *A Short Story* appeared in four editions between 1644 and 1652. Thomas Welde's preface was not included in the first edition, but did appear in the three subsequent editions.

17. It is ironic that while *A Short Story* was meant to demonstrate the benefits of the Congregational system to a skeptical English audience, it became one source for Congregationalism's opponents in the debates of the 1640s over just what religious system England should adopt. As Philip Gura points out, "within a few years" of the publication of *A Short Story* "such prominent presbyterians as Ephraim Pagitt, Robert Baillie, and Samuel Rutherford fleshed out their attacks on congregationalism with facts about New England gleaned from its pages, and predicted from events in the Boston church [England's] inevitable decline into heresy and immortality" (*A Glimpse of Sion's Glory*, 275).

18. Foucault, *Discipline and Punish*, 198.

19. Ann Kibbey, *The Interpretation of Material Shapes in Puritanism: A Study of Rhetoric, Prejudice, and Violence* (Cambridge: Cambridge University Press, 1986), 112.

20. Winthrop's interpretation of the significance of Hutchinson's stillborn child has drawn much attention. Anne Jacobson Schutte reads Winthrop's and other Puritans' remarks in relation to the growing European literature on "monsters," and she attempts to refute the claim that Winthrop read this birth as an act of God's "special providence." See " 'Such Monstrous Births': A Neglected Aspect of the Antinomian Controversy," *Renaissance Quarterly* 38 (1985): 85–106. Lang shows how Puritan readings of the body of Hutchinson's stillborn child deny women power by making them passive agents of God and Satan's active inscriptions. See Lang, *Prophetic Woman*, 57.

21. John Winthrop, *A Short Story of the Rise, reign, and ruine of the Antinomians, Familists & Libertines* (London, 1644), 12. All subsequent references to *A Short Story* will be to this text and will be noted parenthetically. Bremer discusses Welde's role in advocating the cause of New English Puritans in *Puritan Experiment*, 126.

22. It should be pointed out that John Wheelwright, one of Hutchinson's Antinomian allies who was also banished, objected to Winthrop and Welde's interpretation of the stillborn children. In *Mercurius Americanus*, he claims Winthrop "brings in defects of Nature, amongst defects of Manners" (John Wheelwright, *The Writings of John Wheelwright* [1876] [Rpt. New York: Burt Franklin, 1968], 197). Wheelwright argues that Winthrop's reading would thus allow him "under the same title [to] discover all the weaknesses and natural imperfections either of man or woman, and fix a kind of mortality upon them" (197). Whether Wheelwright was the author of this tract, though, has been cast in doubt. Sargent Bush argues that "internal differences between" *Mercurius* and *A Brief and Plain Apology by John Wheelwright* (1658), a work Bush recently discovered and whose author he argues must be Wheelwright, "sharpens the possibility that the authorship of Mercurius Americanus, now almost universally accepted as Wheelwright's, is much less certain than we have thought"

(42). See Bush, "John Wheelwright's Forgotten Apology: The Last Word in the Antinomian Controversy," *New England Quarterly* 64 (1991): 22–45.

23. Thomas Laqueur, *Making Sex: Body and Gender from the Greeks to Freud* (Cambridge, Mass.: Harvard University Press, 1990), 121.

24. This episode in colonial history and this passage in particular has, indeed, taken on the character of a scholarly touchstone for a postfeminist age, to the extent that anyone who wants to rethink early American culture must interpret this trope one way or another. I am no different. In revisiting the moment that established this misogynist foundation for religious and other rights in the English colonies, however, I am not so interested in the impact of men on women as I am in the impact of Winthrop's use of monstrosity on the reigning figure of the English body politic.

25. "A Modell of Christian Charity," *Old South Leaflets* No. 207, edited by Samuel Eliot Morrison (Boston: Old South Association, n.d.), 13.

26. Ibid., 14.

27. Indeed, these arguments have proved so convincing that virtually all commentators now concede that one cannot understand the controversy without understanding how gender contributes to it. Discussion of the controversy in relation to issues of gender is quite plentiful. Ross Pudaloff, for instance, argues in "Sign and Subject: Antinomianism in Massachusetts Bay," *Semiotica* 54 (1985): 147–63, that the controversy "constituted the individual, the subjective, and the female as separate entities, but did so by constructing these as culturally coded representations of powerlessness" (149). In *The Interpretation of Material Shapes*, Anne Kibbey links race with gender, arguing that the "events of 1637 established the legitimacy of genocidal war against nonwhite peoples and the sanctity of prejudicial attitudes toward women" (120). Amy Schrager Lang examines the significance of the controversy beyond the seventeenth century, to later representations of Hutchinson, and shows how Hutchinson, as representative "Public Woman," is used to figure "the larger dilemma of maintaining the law in a culture that simultaneously celebrates and fears the authority of the individual." See Lang, *Prophetic Woman*, 3. In "A Radically Different Voice: Gender and Language in the Trials of Anne Hutchinson" *Early American Literature* 25 (1990): 253–70, Lad Tobin sees "gender . . . as the root cause" (254) of the Antinomian controversy, and argues that Hutchinson's opinions represent those of a distinctly "feminine" voice and perspective. In *Female Piety in Puritan New England: The Emergence of Religious Humanism* (New York: Oxford University Press, 1992), Amanda Porterfield analyzes how the Puritan conception of "female piety," which she identifies as "humility and [the] control of anger, pride, lust and greed," functions in the controversy (13). Thomas Laquer also makes mention of Anne Hutchinson and the case of the Antinomians in *Making Sex*, 121, 230. Ivy Schweitzer discusses the role of gender in New England theology in general while making particular mention of Hutchinson and the Antinomian controversy. See *The Work of Self-Representation: Lyric Poetry in Colonial New England* (Chapel Hill: University of North Carolina Press, 1991), esp. 1–41.

28. As evidence of how this reading of Hutchinson has gained general acceptance, I would cite the analysis of the controversy in the *Cambridge History of*

American Literature. In it, Emory Elliot writes that the "fact that Hutchinson was a woman is very important in any interpretation of the texts of the case and in later writings about her. The Puritan authorities resented all defiance, but they were doubly disturbed by her assertions of spiritual independence because of her gender" ("New England Puritan Literature," in *The Cambridge History of American Literature,* vol. 1, *1590–1820,* edited by Sacvan Bercovitch [Cambridge: Cambridge University Press, 1994], 197).

29. J. F. MacLear, "Anne Hutchinson and the Mortalist Heresy," *New England Quarterly* 54 (1981): 77–91.

30. Leonard Tennenhouse, *Power on Display: The Politics of Shakespeare's Genres* (New York: Methuen, 1986), 103.

31. For a discussion of the connections between gender and the body politic in seventeenth-century England, see Phyllis Mack, *Visionary Women: Ecstatic Prophecy in Seventeenth-Century England* (Berkeley: University of California Press, 1992).

32. Knight contrasts Winthrop's vision of the social body with Cotton's. She argues that Winthrop's insistence in "A Modell" on the permanence of class divisions demonstrates that though his "vision" is no less "utopian" than Cotton's, "it is certainly less committed to a fluid reordering of this world in anticipation of a kingdom of saints in the next" (*Orthodoxies in Massachusetts,* 143). For a reading of Winthrop's vision of the social body in "A Modell" as a rejection of what Andrew Delbanco sees as an emergent "utilitarian ethic" aligned with capitalist modes of economic relations, see Delbanco, *The Puritan Ordeal* (Cambridge, Mass.: Harvard University Press, 1989), 72–74.

33. Winthrop, "Modell of Christian Charity," 7.

34. Ibid.

35. My argument here has benefited from Coppélia Kahn's analysis in *Roman Shakespeare* of how Shakespeare's Roman plays promote a masculinist political ideology "constituted by its opposition to the feminine" (77). Kahn goes on to argue that it was "through Machiavelli as well as Aristotle that a gendered discourse of the republic came to England" (85). See Kahn, *Roman Shakespeare: Warriors, Wounds, and Women* (London: Routledge, 1997).

36. Indeed, Winthrop's choice of the scene of childbirth seems overdetermined by the shared assumption among early modern European cultures that women were especially accessible during the final stages of labor. In fact, women were often asked late in labor to name the "real" father on the assumption that they would be unable to resist the questioner while in the "state" of labor. See John D'Emilio and Estelle B. Freedman, *Intimate Matters: A History of Sexuality in America* (New York: Harper & Row, 1988), 32.

37. Laurel Thatcher Ulrich, *Good Wives: Image and Reality in the Lives of Women in Northern New England, 1650–1750* (New York: Oxford University Press, 1982), 135.

38. As Ulrich points out, social rank played a greater role in a woman's status in seventeenth-century New England than did what moderns such as ourselves would consider the " experiences" unique to women's bodies. This is not to say that childbirth played little or no role in a woman's status. Ulrich argues that in order to be a "good woman," a female needed to bear children. An individual's

identity as a "woman" was thus dependent on a particular kind of experience, and, according to Ulrich, a hierarchy among women existed based on the number of children one had borne and under what circumstances. Those who had borne numerous children under the sanction of marriage were afforded greater respect and privilege than those women who had not yet given birth, and women who had given birth to illegitimate offspring were at the lowest rung of the social ladder.

39. Ulrich sees the absence of men in the delivery room as a threat to dominant structures of power—"momentarily at least" (*Good Wives*, 131). Indeed, she argues that "the decline of midwives in the nineteenth century" can best be accounted for by "the undermining of traditional social relations and the increasing privatization of the family," trends that I would contend are brought about in part by the change in how political authority is figured that I am describing here.

40. Of course, proper regulation of childbirth practices were maintained with vigilance at least in part because they were so crucial to colonization efforts. Indeed, Ulrich argues that the threat to New England patriarchal structures of power posed by childbirth stemmed in part from its importance to Massachusetts Bay. The colony's political and religious strength required a well-populated colony, and so, as the final stage in the reproductive process, childbirth was vital to the colony's influence and power.

41. For a discussion of women's role in childbirth practices in seventeenth-century New England, see Ulrich, *Good Wives*, 126–29.

42. For more detailed discussions of the controversy surrounding Hutchinson's public speaking, see Lang, *Prophetic Woman*, 43, and Gura, *Glimpse of Sion's Glory*, 243.

43. Edmund S. Morgan, *The Puritan Family: Religion and Domestic Relations in Seventeenth-Century New England*, rev. ed. (New York: Harper & Row, 1966), 135. For more detailed discussions of the family in seventeenth-century New England, see Bremer, *Puritan Experiment*; John Demos, *A Little Commonwealth: Family Life in Plymouth Colony* (London: Oxford University Press, 1970); Morgan, *Puritan Family*; and Stout, *New England Soul*.

44. Stout, *New England Soul*, 22.

45. John Locke, *Two Treatises of Government*, edited by Peter Laslett (Cambridge: Cambridge University Press, 1988), 2.52–76.

46. There has been much debate over why the magistrates reacted so strongly to Hutchinson's claim that she had an immediate revelation from God since it seems to have been a staple of Puritan rhetoric in England. Indeed, Winthrop's own description of his conversion experience contains numerous instances of God "speaking" to him (See John Winthrop, "John Winthrop's Relation of His Religious Experience," in *Winthrop Papers*, vol. 3 [Boston: Massachusetts Historical Society, 1929–47].) It seems to me that—as others before me have already pointed out—immediate revelation makes for very difficult government. Recognizing this, the New English magistrates set limits on what was and was not acceptable revelation so that the commonwealth they set out to establish in Massachusetts did not deteriorate into anarchy. For a discussion of

the shift in Puritan doctrine on this matter when it became institutionalized in New England, see Delbanco, *Puritan Ordeal*, 118–49.

47. For a discussion of the theory of the king's two bodies, see Marie Axton, *The Queen's Two Bodies: Drama and the Elizabethan Succession* (London: Royal Historical Society, 1977), and Ernst Kantorowicz, *The King's Two Bodies* (Princeton, N.J.: Princeton University Press, 1957).

48. According to Philip Gura, Hutchinson spoke for "the supremacy of personal experience with the divine over [ecclesiastical] creeds or platforms" (*Glimpse of Sion's Glory*, 255). Sacvan Bercovitch places Hutchinson in a tradition of thinkers such as Emerson and Wordsworth, who preach "self-reliance" and locate "the divine center in the individual" (*The Puritan Origins of the American Self* [New Haven, Conn.: Yale University Press, 1975], 176). And Larzer Ziff contends that Hutchinson values "inner experience"(*Puritanism in America*, 66).

49. For the most thorough history of the idea behind the test and its subsequent institution in New England's churches, see Edmund Morgan's *Visible Saints: The History of a Puritan Idea* (New York: New York University Press, 1963). More recently, Stephen Foster and Charles Cohen have elaborated further on the history surrounding the test's justification and enforcement. Cohen attempts to refute the claim that some churches, particularly Thomas Hooker's church in Connecticut, did not use conversion narratives as a qualification for membership. See Foster, *Long Argument*, and Charles Lloyd Cohen, *God's Caress: The Psychology of Puritan Religious Experience* (New York: Oxford University Press, 1986), 140–44. In "Preparation and Confession: Reconsidering Edmund S. Morgan's Visible Saints," *New England Quarterly* 67 (1994): 298–319, however, Michael G. Ditmore argues that conversion narratives were a direct result of the Antinomian controversy and were supported by Thomas Shepard and Hooker rather than by Cotton, as Morgan claims. For a literary analysis of conversion narratives, see Patricia Caldwell, *The Puritan Conversion Narrative: The Beginnings of American Expression* (New York: Cambridge University Press, 1983).

CHAPTER FIVE
THE INSIGNIFICANCE OF EXPERIENCE

1. See, for instance, Emily Stripe Watts, *The Poetry of American Women from 1632–1945* (Austin: University of Texas Press, 1977); Cheryl Walker, *The Nightingale's Burden: Women Poets and American Culture before 1900* (Bloomington: Indiana University Press, 1982); Adrienne Rich, "Anne Bradstreet and Her Poetry" and "Postscript," in *The Works of Anne Bradstreet*, edited by Jeannine Hensley (Cambridge, Mass.: The Belknap Press of Harvard University Press, 1967); and Wendy Martin, *An American Triptych: Anne Bradstreet, Emily Dickinson, Adrienne Rich* (Chapel Hill: University of North Carolina Press, 1984).

2. Pattie Cowell, "Anne Bradstreet," in *Heath Anthology of American Literature*, vol. 1, 2nd ed., edited by Paul Lauter (Lexington, Mass.: D. C. Heath, 1990), 290; Emory Elliott, "New England Puritan Literature," in *The Cam-*

bridge History of American Literature, vol. 1, *1590–1820*, edited by Sacvan Bercovitch (Cambridge: Cambridge University Press, 1994), 290.

3. The first two quotes are from Martin, *American Triptych*, 3; the second two are from p. 307 of Ivy Schweitzer, "Anne Bradstreet Wrestles with the Renaissance," *Early American Literature* 23 (1988): 291–312.

4. Patricia Caldwell, "Why Our First Poet Was a Woman: Bradstreet and the Birth of an American Poetic Voice," *Prospects* 13 (1988):1–35, 2.

5. Ibid., 2, 27.

6. Ibid., 2.

7. Timothy Sweet makes a similar point when he writes that "the definition of self" used by critics of Bradstreet "has "assumed . . . precisely what needs to be examined." See "Gender, Genre, and Subjectivity in Bradstreet's Early Elegies," *Early American Literature* 23 (1988): 152–74, 154. Whereas Sweet identifies the category of the author as the term that needs to be interrogated, I would add the very terms by which gender is understood also call for analysis and historical investigation.

8. Janice Knight, *Orthodoxies in Massachusetts: Rereading American Puritanism* (Cambridge, Mass.: Harvard University Press, 1994), 22–23.

9. For discussions of this change in Puritanism as it became institutionalized in New England, see Knight, *Orthodoxies in Massachusetts*; Andrew Delbanco, *The Puritan Ordeal* (Cambridge, Mass.: Harvard University Press, 1989); and Michael G. Ditmore, "Preparation and Confession: Reconsidering Edmund S. Morgan's Visible Saints," *New England Quarterly* 67 (1994): 298–319.

10. I am by no means the first to see Bradstreet and Hutchinson as intellectual allies. Indeed, the link has been made quite often by scholars. Delbanco, for instance, contends that "the two Annes . . . differed more in the mode of their address than in their convictions" (*Puritan Ordeal*, 154).

11. Knight provides an excellent discussion in *Orthodoxies in Massachusetts* of the differences in the positions I have referred to as Preparationist and Antinomian. She labels the followers of Preparationism as the "Intellectual Fathers" and the Antinomians as the "Spiritual Brethren" (3). Knight places Thomas Hooker, Thomas Shepard, Peter Bulkeley, and John Winthrop in the first group, while John Cotton, John Davenport, and Henry Vane are classified as the major advocates of the second set of views. For earlier treatments of Preparationism, see Perry Miller, *The New England Mind: From Colony to Province* (Cambridge, Mass.: Harvard University Press, 1953), esp. 53–67; Norman Pettit, *The Heart Prepared: Grace and Conversion in Puritan Spiritual Life*, 2nd ed. (Middletown, Conn.: Wesleyan University Press, 1989), esp. 48–124; Perry Miller, "Preparation for Salvation in Seventeenth-Century New England," in *Nature's Nation* (Cambridge, Mass.: Harvard University Press, 1967), 50–77; William Stoever, *"A Faire and Easie Way to Heaven": Covenant Theology and Antinomianism in Early Massachusetts* (Middletown, Conn.: Wesleyan University Press, 1978); Sacvan Bercovitch, *The American Jeremiad* (Madison: University of Wisconsin Press, 1978), esp. 31–92; and Delbanco, *Puritan Ordeal*.

12. Wendy Martin argues the reverse. She claims that Preparationism "restrained" what she terms "Bradstreet's rebellious inclinations" (*American Triptych*, 57). While I find Martin's readings of Bradstreet's poems and her discus-

sion of the role of women in seventeenth-century Massachusetts Bay illuminating and insightful, I think my examination of experience will show that Bradstreet cannot be labeled a Preparationist.

13. For a discussion of the "narrative quality" of Preparationist doctrine, see Sargent Bush's analysis of Thomas Hooker, who has long been considered the preeminent spokesperson for the Preparationist cause in early America (Bush, *The Writings of Thomas Hooker: Spiritual Adventure in Two Worlds* [Madison: University of Wisconsin Press, 1980], 164). Perry Miller, in fact, labeled his work "the most coherent and sustained expression of the essential religious experience ever attained by New England divines." See *The Puritans: A Sourcebook of Their Writings*, vol. 1, rev. ed., edited by Perry Miller and Thomas H. Johnson (New York: Harper & Row, 1963), xlix.

14. Nancy E. Wright, "Epitaphic Conventions and the Reception of Anne Bradstreet's Public Voice," *Early American Literature* 31 (1996): 243–63, 256.

15. The question of an "authoritative text" raises special problems in the case of Bradstreet's writings. Only one edition of her poems appeared during her lifetime, *The Tenth Muse Lately Sprung Up in America* (London, 1650), but precisely how much oversight she had over this edition is unclear. In an epistle to the reader, Bradstreet's brother-in-law, John Woodbridge, writes that the poems were published without the author's "knowledge, and contrary to her expectation." See *The Complete Works of Anne Bradstreet*, edited by Joseph R. McElrath Jr. and Allan P. Robb (Boston: Twayne, 1981), 526.

A second edition of Bradstreet's poems appeared posthumously. In addition to revisions of the poems from *The Tenth Muse*, *Several Poems* (1678) also included a number of works that had not yet been published. Again, the evidence for Bradstreet's role in the revision of these poems is sketchy. The title page claims that the edition was "Corrected by the Author," and one of the new poems, "The Author to Her Book," seems to indicate that the author had made revisions of her previously published work. Ivy Schweitzer argues that the Twayne's editors' choice of the earlier edition as a copy-text represents "a conservative choice" in that it privileges poems "which we know to have been published without her supervision, over versions of poems that we have some evidence to indicate she revised to some extent" (*The Work of Self-Representation: Lyric Poetry in Colonial New England* [Chapel Hill: University of North Carolina Press, 1991], 261). In Schweitzer's view, *The Complete Works of Anne Bradstreet* "serves . . . as a convenient record of Bradstreet's poetry as it was authorized for publication by a male relative who usurped her authority" (261).

Caldwell, on the other hand, prefers the Twayne edition because it "adheres most faithfully to the texts in the order and form in which they were originally published" (30). She contends that the Twayne editors "argue persuasively that the numerous changes in [some] poems by the time of the posthumous second edition cannot be established as having been made solely and entirely by Bradstreet herself" (30). See Caldwell, "Why Our First Poet."

For a history of editions of Bradstreet's work, see Pattie Cowell, "Introduction: Anne Bradstreet 'In Criticks Hands,'" in *Critical Essays on Anne Bradstreet*, edited by Pattie Cowell and Ann Stanford (Boston: G. K. Hall, 1983), ix–xi, and McElrath and Robb, "Introduction," xxiv–xxvii.

I have chosen to use the first published version of a poem for the purposes of my analysis of Bradstreet's writing. All line numbers noted in the text are from the first published version of a poem. In those instances where a poem was not published during Bradstreet's lifetime, I have used the manuscript transcription from *The Complete Works*.

16. Wright, "Epitaphic Conventions," 258.

17. Elizabeth herself implied as much when she used the language of love as the language of policy. See Arthur Marotti, " 'Love Is Not Love': Elizabethan Sonnet Sequences and the Social Order," *English Literary History* 49 (1982): 396–428.

18. For an analysis of the concluding sections of the poem, "Her Epitaph" and "Another," see Wright, "Epitaphic Conventions."

19. James Schramer and Timothy Sweet offer a slightly different reading of the body in Bradstreet's poetry than the one I make here. Whereas I argue that the poem can only represent the spiritual body as disembodied, they contend that "the body in 'The Flesh and the Spirit' persists by defining the terms of the experience of heaven" ("Violence and the Body Politic in Seventeenth-Century New England," *Arizona Quarterly* 48, no. 2 [1992]: 112).

20. In the manuscript version of this poem, no title is given. I will use the title by which the poem has generally been labeled in critical discourse on Bradstreet, "As Weary Pilgrim." For a discussion of the significance of the figure of the pilgrimage in "As Weary Pilgrim" and in New England Puritan writing in general, see Charles Hambrick-Stowe, *The Practice of Piety: Puritan Devotional Disciplines in Seventeenth-Century New England* (Chapel Hill: University of North Carolina Press, 1982), 17, 58–59.

21. *Complete Works*, 215.

22. Ibid., 216.

23. Ibid., 217.

24. In the manuscript version of this poem, no title is given. I will use the title by which the poem has generally been labeled in critical discourse on Bradstreet, "Upon the Burning of Her House."

25. Rosamond R. Rosenmeier argues that the burning of the house would have special significance for New England Puritans. The destruction of the house could have been understood as a "special portent, the record of which might be used to ascertain the design of God's." In the poem, the fire functions as both "an agent of destruction and transmutation" (*Anne Bradstreet Revisited* [Boston: Twayne, 1991], 138–39).

26. See, for instance, Jeffrey Hammond, *Sinful Self, Saintly Self: The Puritan Experience of Poetry* (Athens: University of Georgia Press, 1993), 88–91; Martin, *American Triptych*, 68–69; and Rosenmeier, *Anne Bradstreet Revisited*, 113–28.

27. Kenneth A. Requa, for instance, argues that this line represents a new understanding of the situation by Bradstreet, rather than a recognition of her own powerlessness. He writes that, in the concluding lines, the "poet finds that the house-fire has emblematic significance: from it she can learn that only one home should have meaning for her—the heavenly mansion promised to a saintly Puritan" ("Anne Bradstreet's Poetic Voices," in *Critical Essays on Anne Brad-*

street, edited by Pattie Cowell and Ann Stanford [Boston: G. K. Hall, 1983], 163). I would only argue that this represents no "new" understanding on the part of the speaker, since the speaker voices the same message as she is watching her house burn down early in the poem.

28. Paula Kopacz argues that the very act of "[w]riting a poem . . . was a form of prayer" for Bradstreet (183). See Kopacz, " 'To Finish What's Begun': Anne Bradstreet's Last Words," *Early American Literature* 23 (1988): 175–87.

29. In contrast, Walter Hughes argues that the "ultimate reorientation of desire" is the subject of Bradstreet's "greatest" poems (105). He contends that the "sensual" experiences about which Bradstreet writes "are transitional, leading her through earthly pleasure to a knowledge of the divine" (107). It is such knowledge, I am arguing, that Bradstreet claims is impossible to achieve through purely earthly experience. See Hughes, " 'Meat Out of the Eater': Panic and Desire in American Puritan Poetry," in *Engendering Men: The Question of Male Feminist Criticism*, edited by Joseph A. Boone and Michael Cadden (New York: Routledge, 1990), 102–21.

30. Jeffrey Hammond makes a similar point when he argues that "Bradstreet emphasizes that neither she nor her reader can grasp the spiritual significance of the loss without perceptions renovated by grace" (*Sinful Self, Saintly Self*, 134).

31. In *The Design of the Present,* John Lynen discusses the poem in relation to later American writers, placing it at the forefront of what might be called the "pragmatic tradition" (76). He calls the poem "a study of the experiential process," and argues that the poem indicates how Bradstreet "understood with remarkable prescience the kind of poetry American experience would require" (83). See Lynen, *The Design of the Present: Essays on Time and Form in American Literature* (New Haven, Conn.: Yale University Press, 1969).

32. The reference is to Revelation 2:17, "To him that overcometh, will I give to eat of the Manna that is hid, and will give him a white stone, and in the stone a new name written, which no man knoweth saving hee that receiveth it." Alvin H. Rosenfeld claims that the final stanza also suggests Shakespeare's influence on Bradstreet. Shakespeare, Rosenfeld claims, "was one of Anne Bradstreet's favorite authors" (135). Thus, he argues, the poem "ends . . . on both a religious and an aesthetic note" (135). See Rosenfeld, "Anne Bradstreet's 'Contemplations': Patterns of Form and Meaning," in *Critical Essays on Anne Bradstreet*, edited by Pattie Cowell and Ann Stanford (Boston: G. K. Hall, 1983), 123–36.

33. I do not take up the question here of how "Contemplations" relates to the tradition of meditative poetry. As Anne Stanford points out, "Contemplations" follows the form found in other seventeenth-century meditative poems, and it can be understood in relation to the many commentaries on meditation written by seventeenth-century Puritans. Indeed, the terms "meditation" and "contemplation" were virtually synonymous in seventeenth-century Puritan discourse. See Stanford, "Anne Bradstreet as a Meditative Writer," in *Critical Essays on Anne Bradstreet*, edited by Pattie Cowell and Ann Stanford (Boston: G. K. Hall, 1983), 89–96. Charles Hambrick-Stowe analyzes early New England meditative poetry. See Hambrick-Stowe, *Practice of Piety*, 13–19, 236–40. Barbara Lewalski looks at Bradstreet's poetry in relation to English models of meditative poetry. See Lewalski, *Protestant Poetics and the Seventeenth-Cen-*

tury Religious Lyric (Princeton, N.J.: Princeton University Press, 1979), 179–212. For a discussion of seventeenth-century meditative poetry as a genre, see Louis Martz, *The Poetry of Meditation: A Study in English Religious Literature of the Seventeenth Century* (New Haven, Conn.: Harvard University Press, 1954).

34. Stanford, "Anne Bradstreet as a Meditative Writer," 94. For a discussion of Bradstreet's work in relation to what Stanford calls "the emblem tradition," see Stanford, "Anne Bradstreet's Emblematic Garden," in *Critical Essays on Anne Bradstreet*, edited by Pattie Cowell and Ann Stanford (Boston: G. K. Hall, 1983), 238–53. Reading Bradstreet in relation to this tradition allows Stanford to analyze Bradstreet's work in relation to English discursive systems.

35. Several scholars have argued that "Contemplations" is an attempt to represent the stages of a conversion experience. William Irwin writes that the "poem as a whole presents a version of the Puritan conversion experience, complete with a false conversion and the steps of humiliation leading to the true one" (187). The "new experience of metaphorical perception" (183) that accompanies the speaker's conversion begins with stanza 21. See Irwin, "Allegory and Typology 'Imbrace and Greet': Anne Bradstreet's 'Contemplations,'" in *Critical Essays on Anne Bradstreet*, edited by Pattie Cowell and Ann Stanford (Boston: G. K. Hall, 1983), 174–83. Helen Saltman has argued that "Contemplations" "approaches the ideal conversion" (226). See Saltman, "'Contemplations': Anne Bradstreet's Spiritual Autobiography," in *Critical Essays on Anne Bradstreet*, edited by Pattie Cowell and Ann Stanford (Boston: G. K. Hall, 1983), 226–37.

36. As Rosenmeier points out, "[a]lthough different readers have described these changes differently, there is some agreement that the speaker grows and changes" (*Anne Bradstreet Revisited*, 146). To cite only four examples: Irwin divides the poem in half, with the turning point occurring at stanza 20; see Irwin, "Allegory and Typology," 184; Stanford argues for three sections of stanzas, moving through description, commentary, and apostrophe; see Stanford, "Anne Bradstreet as a Meditative Writer," 93–94; Anne Hildebrand argues that the stanzas can be grouped into four seasons, and these seasons can be related to the four elements, humours, and ages that Bradstreet relied on for structure in her earlier long poems; see Hildebrand, "Anne Bradstreet's Quarternions and 'Contemplations,'" in *Critical Essays on Anne Bradstreet*, edited by Pattie Cowell and Ann Stanford (Boston: G. K. Hall, 1983), 137–44; William Scheick's position is closest to my own. He writes that the poem "fractures in several places, falls into distinctive gaps or lacunae." Scheick divides the poem into four movements and argues that "[b]y fragmenting her poem into four movements Bradstreet distorts the vertical linearity of her poem." See Scheick, *Design in Puritan American Literature* (Lexington: University Press of Kentucky, 1992), 35–45.

37. One of the continuing debates in Bradstreet scholarship has to do with the relationship of "Contemplations" to Romantic poetry. The debate centers on whether one should read the poem as a product of sixteenth-century Calvinism or as a precursor to Romanticism in the speaker's relationship to nature. Both of these positions seem important to me: "Contemplations" utilizes residual cultural formations while simultaneously pointing us toward emergent ones.

See Irwin, "Allegory and Typology," 187–88; Rosenfeld, "Anne Bradstreet's 'Contemplations,'" 125–27; Josephine K. Piercy, *Anne Bradstreet* (Boston: Twayne, 1965), 96–99; and Elizabeth Wade White, *Anne Bradstreet: The Tenth Muse* (New York: Oxford University Press, 1971), 337–38.

38. As Robert Daly has pointed out, "the poem records contemplations rather than structured argument" (121). See Daly, *God's Altar: The World and the Flesh in Puritan Poetry* (Berkeley: University of California Press, 1978).

39. Hammond provides a discussion of this tendency in Bradstreet criticism. Hammond argues that critics can be split into two camps, those who see her poetry as "working well within the expected limits of Puritan art and belief" and those who read her work as "reveal[ing] an ambitious Renaissance poet who achieved at best an uneasy peace with her religion and society" (*Sinful Self, Saintly Self*, 83).

40. Originally published in *The Tenth Muse* (1650), "A Dialogue" was revised for *Several Poems* (1678). As Joseph R. McElrath has noted, "there are considerable substantive differences between the two versions" (62). These "substantive differences" involve altering or deleting criticism of events of the 1640s. Because there remains some doubt about the extent of Bradstreet's involvement in the revisions made for *Several Poems*, just which of these changes are Bradstreet's and which are those of editors or friends is a matter of debate. See McElrath, "The Text of Anne Bradstreet: Biographical and Critical Consequences," *Seventeenth-Century News* 34 (1976): 61–63.

41. White reads "David's Lamentation for Saul" (1650) "as an elegy in scriptural disguise for the king" and thus is "eligible for inclusion in the curious and touching medley, known to exist but usually hidden away in the old country mansions of England, of symbolic testimonials to the martyred king" (*Anne Bradstreet*, 246, 250). Jane Eberwein argues that "[t]o the extent that we can trace the political behavior of persons close to Anne Bradstreet at this turbulent time, her circle seems to have favored a compromise solution that would have promoted church reform and heightened parliamentary power without sacrificing the monarchy" (123–24). Indeed, Eberwein goes on to argue that "Bradstreet's 'Dialogue' shows her . . . enthusiastic support for Parliament's actions in favor of church reform" (124). She further contends that "The Four Monarchies" should be read as Bradstreet's "working out her own response to the threatened collapse of monarchy" (124). See Eberwein, "Bradstreet's Monarchies," *Early American Literature* 21 (1991): 119–44.

42. I do not analyze in detail here the, in Stephanie Jed's words, "crucial role played by cultural commodities [such as *The Tenth Muse*] in the formation of political ties" (203) only because it lies outside the scope of my argument in this chapter. Jed provides an informative if brief discussion of this issue. See Jed, "The Tenth Muse: Gender, Rationality, and the Marketing of Knowledge," in *Women, "Race," and Writing in the Early Modern Period*, edited by Margo Hendricks and Patricia Parker (London: Routledge, 1994), 195–208. For a discussion of the early publication and promotion of *The Tenth Muse* that would be useful to any attempt to understand how New English poetry helped produce an English national self-image that includes colonial New England, see Cowell, "The Early Distribution of Anne Bradstreet's Poems," in *Critical Essays on Anne*

Bradstreet, edited by Pattie Cowell and Ann Stanford (Boston: G. K. Hall, 1983), 270–79.

43. Michel Foucault, *Discipline and Punish: The Birth of the Prison*, translated by Alan Sheridan (New York: Pantheon, 1977), 187.

44. Kathryn Zabelle Derounian also argues that Saffin's love poetry "recalls . . . lines from . . . Anne Bradstreet." However, she comes to the opposite conclusion that I do here about the interchangeable nature of the two sets of love poems. It is important to note that Zabelle Derounian arrives at her conclusions not by a careful comparison of the two, but rather by invoking "[p]revious scholarship on seventeenth-century American Puritan settlements" that she claims "suggests that . . . a man's experience was much different from a woman's." Tellingly, I think, she concludes by remarking that "the poetry of Bradstreet and Saffin shows that such experience could be complementary," and in so doing, she subtly calls into question the very claims of the scholarship she has used to establish the fundamental difference between men's and women's experience during the period. See Zabelle Derounian, "'Mutuall Sweet Content': The Love Poetry of John Saffin," in *Puritan Poets and Poetics: Seventeenth-Century American Poetry in Theory and Practice*, edited by Peter White (University Park, Pa., and London: Pennsylvania State University Press, 1985), 175–84, 176, 183.

45. Harrison T. Meserole's comments are instructive here. He claims that "some of Saffin's tenderest elegies" are written in response to the deaths of his eight sons, and he goes on to contrast Saffin's poems with most of the verse of the period by claiming that Saffin's "voice [is] engagingly personal." These are, of course, precisely the terms used to describe Bradstreet's work and the kind of poems most often cited as her most successful. See Meserole, *American Poetry of the Seventeenth Century* (University Park, Pa., and London: Pennsylvania State University Press, 1985), 193–95, 194, 195.

46. John Saffin, *John Saffin: His Book*, edited by Caroline Hazard (New York: Harbor, 1928), 183, 226.

47. Ibid., 184.

48. For a discussion of how this process took place in English literature, see Nancy Armstrong, *Desire and Domestic Fiction: A Political History of the Novel* (New York: Oxford University Press, 1987). The link between gender and certain narrative patterns has been demonstrated by Nina Baym in "Melodramas of Beset Manhood: How Theories of American Fiction Exclude Women Authors," in *Feminism and American Literary History* (New Brunswick, N.J.: Rutgers University Press, 1992). For a discussion of how sentiment has been linked with femininity in American culture, see Jane Tompkins, *Sensational Designs: The Cultural Work of American Fiction, 1790–1860* (New York: Oxford University Press, 1985).

CHAPTER SIX
A NATIONAL EXPERIENCE

1. Aside from the scholars I have discussed in this chapter, I would also cite Wesley Frank Craven, *The Colonies in Transition, 1660–1713* (New York:

Harper & Row, 1968); Richard R. Johnson, *Adjustment to Empire: The New England Colonies, 1675–1715* (New Brunswick, N.J.: Rutgers University Press, 1981); David S. Lovejoy, *The Glorious Revolution in America* (New York: Harper & Row, 1972); Richard Dunn, *Puritans and Yankees: The Winthrop Dynasty of New England* (Princeton, N.J.: Princeton University Press, 1962); Richard Bushman, *From Puritan to Yankee: Character and the Social Order in Connecticut, 1690–1765* (Cambridge, Mass.: Harvard University Press, 1967).

2. *So Dreadfull a Judgement: Puritan Responses to King Phillip's War, 1676–1677*, edited by Richard Slotkin and James K. Folsom (Middletown, Conn.: Wesleyan University Press, 1978), 11.

3. Quoted in Stephen Saunders Webb, *1676: The End of American Independence* (New York: Knopf, 1984), 222. For a history of relations between the Crown and the New England colonies during this period, see ibid., 221–44 and 409–16. For an overview of the impact of English politics on all the colonies in the empire, including those in New England, see T. O. Lloyd, *The British Empire: 1558–1983* (London: Oxford University Press, 1984). Immanuel Wallerstein examines the significance of European colonization more broadly in *The Modern World-System II: Mercantilism and the Consolidation of the European World-Economy, 1600–1750* (New York: Academic, 1980).

4. See Webb, *1676*, 221–29.

5. For histories of the war, see Francis Jennings, *The Invasion of America: Indians, Colonialism, and the Cant of Conquest* (New York: Norton, 1976); Douglass Leach, *Flintlock and Tomahawk: New England in King Phillip's War* (New York: Macmillan, 1958); Slotkin and Folsom, eds., *So Dreadfull a Judgement*, 3–45; Alden T. Vaughan, *New England Frontier: Puritans and Indians, 1620–1675*, 3rd ed. (Norman: University of Oklahoma Press, 1995); and Webb, *1676*, 355–404. For a discussion of the assumptions that guide this historiographic tradition, see Jane Tompkins, "'Indians': Textualism, Morality, and the Problem of History," in *'Race,' Writing, and Difference*, edited by Henry Louis Gates Jr. (Chicago: University of Chicago Press, 1986).

6. Slotkin and Folsom, eds., *So Dreadfull a Judgement*, 8.

7. Perry Miller, *Errand Into the Wilderness* (Cambridge, Mass.: The Belknap Press of Harvard University Press, 1956), 9.

8. Richard Slotkin, *Regeneration Through Violence: The Mythology of the American Frontier, 1600–1860* (Middletown, Conn.: Wesleyan University Press, 1973), 179.

9. Sacvan Bercovitch, *The American Jeremiad* (Madison: University of Wisconsin Press, 1978), 62.

10. Miller, *Errand Into the Wilderness*, 15; Slotkin, *Regeneration Through Violence*; Bercovitch, *American Jeremiad*.

11. Benedict Anderson, *Imagined Communities: Reflections on the Origin and Spread of Nationalism*, rev. ed. (London: Verso, 1991), 36.

12. Ibid., 7. In Michael Warner's words, this "community of readership is a corporate body realized only metonymically," an "imaginary community" that constitutes the "elemental form of the nation." See, Michael Warner, *The Letters of the Republic: Publication and the Public Sphere in Eighteenth-Century America* (Cambridge, Mass.: Harvard University Press, 1990), 63.

13. David D. Hall, *Worlds of Wonder, Days of Judgment: Popular Religious Belief in Early New England* (Cambridge, Mass.: Harvard University Press, 1990), 106.

14. Ibid., 107.

15. Schramer and Sweet argue that the New England Puritan body politic was—from the very first years of Plymouth colony—"conceived of . . . as an autonomous entity that could sustain itself without the aid of monarchy or episcopacy" (5). They go on to argue that "the threat to the Puritan body politic was perceived to be greater during King Philip's War" (14). While I find their discussion of narratives from King Philip's war illuminating, I will argue in this chapter that the autonomous colonial body politic begins to appear only when self-government becomes an issue in the later years of the century. See Schramer and Sweet, "Violence and the Body Politic in Seventeenth-Century New England," *Arizona Quarterly* 48, no. 2 (1992): 1–32.

16. Of the two, Hubbard has drawn considerably more attention. Notable recent studies of Hubbard's writings include Stephen Arch, *Authorizing the Past: The Rhetoric of History in Seventeenth-Century New England* (DeKalb: Northern Illinois University Press, 1994), 120–23; John Canup, *The Emergence of an American Identity in Colonial New England* (Middletown, Conn.: Wesleyan University Press, 1990), 174–93; Emory Elliot, "New England Puritan Literature," in *The Cambridge History of American Literature*, vol. 1, *1590–1820*, edited by Sacvan Bercovitch (Cambridge: Cambridge University Press, 1994), 223–24; Jennings, *Invasion of America*, 183–85; Dennis R. Perry, "'Novelties and Stile Which All Out-Do': William Hubbard's Historiography Reconsidered," *Early American Literature* 29 (1994): 166–82; and Slotkin, *Regeneration Through Violence*, 164–71. Analyses of Tompson's work are fewer still. See Jane Eberwein, "'*Harvardine* quil': Benjamin Tompson's Poems on King Phillip's War," *Early American Literature* 28 (1993): 1–21; Wayne Franklin, "The Harangue of King Philip in *New-Englands Crisis* (1676)," *American Literature* 51 (1980): 536–40; David S. Shields, *Oracles of Empire: Poetry, Politics, and Commerce in British America, 1690–1750* (Chicago: University of Chicago Press, 1990), 1–2; Slotkin, *Regeneration Through Violence*, 88–91; Schramer and Sweet, "Violence and the Body Politic"; and Peter White, *Benjamin Tompson: Colonial Bard, A Critical Edition* (University Park, Pa., and London: Pennsylvania State University Press, 1980) and "Cannibals and Turks: Benjamin Tompson's Image of the Native American," in *Puritan Poets and Poetics: Seventeenth-Century American Poetry in Theory and Practice*, edited by Peter White (University Park: Pennsylvania State University Press, 1985), 198–209.

17. Biographical sketches of Hubbard are available in Samuel G. Drake, ed., *The History of the Indian Wars in New England* (Roxbury, Mass., 1865); Alasdair Macphail, "William Hubbard," in *The Dictionary of Literary Biography 24: American Colonial Writers, 1606–1734*, edited by Emory Elliott (Detroit: Gale, 1984), 164–72; and Cecelia Tichi, "Introduction," in *The Present State of New England, Being a Narrative of the Troubles with the Indians, 1677* (Facsimile Reprod., Bainbridge, N.Y.: York Mail-Print, 1972).

18. Elliott, "New England Puritan Literature," 224.

19. Anne Kusener Nelsen claims that the choice of Hubbard to deliver the sermon prompted Mather to begin writing a rebuttal to what he thought would be Hubbard's position on the war. See Anne Kusener Nelsen, "King Philip's War and the Hubbard-Mather Rivalry" *William and Mary Quarterly* 3rd ser., 27 (1970): 619–20. Elliott speculates that Hubbard's differences with Mather over the war's significance ultimately led to the "suppression" of Hubbard's *General History of New England* ("New England Puritan Literature," 224).

20. For a thorough biography of Tompson, see White, *Benjamin Tompson*, 16–36.

21. Elliott, "New England Puritan Literature," 224; Perry, "Novelties and Stile," 171. For further discussion of the differences between Mather's and Hubbard's history of the war, see Arch, *Authorizing the Past*; Elliott, "New England Puritan Literature"; Kenneth Murdock, "William Hubbard and the Providential Interpretation of History," *American Antiquarian Society Proceedings* 52 (1942): 15–37; Kusener Nelsen, "King Philip's War"; and Perry, "Novelties and Stile." Some critics find the differences between Mather and Hubbard insignificant. Jennings, for instance, argues that "the same assumptions inform Hubbard's work, but his prose is less nakedly passionate" (*Invasion of America*, 184). Slotkin contrasts Mather not with Hubbard but with Benjamin Church; indeed, Slotkin treats Mather's and Hubbard's texts as products of the same philosophy. What distinguishes Church's book from Mather's and Hubbard's, he claims, is "the concept of the experience of the wilderness that structures each of the works" (*Regeneration Through Violence*, 169). For Slotkin, experience exists as a category whose authority is unchanging throughout history; certain types of experience are preferred over others at different points, but the category itself is always already granted a privileged rhetorical status.

22. Perry, "Novelties and Stile," 170.

23. Ibid., 170–71.

24. Elliott, Perry, and Nelsen, among others, all argue that Hubbard's history represents a step in the direction of modern historiographical methods, that is, in Elliott's words, "objective" and "scientific" ("New England Puritan Literature," 224). Peter Gay, in his study of "the writing of history in colonial America," seems to concur with this assessment of Hubbard. His only mention of Hubbard is to argue that the "theological independence" of Hubbard's *General History of New England* failed to provide "an adequate answer to New England's need for a reliable past" (57). See Gay, *A Loss of Mastery: Puritan Historians in Colonial America* (Berkeley: University of California Press, 1966).

25. For a discussion of English criticism of colonial land claims in the latter half of the seventeenth century, see Webb, *1676*, 221–44.

26. Increase Mather, *A Brief History of the Warr with the Indians*, in *So Dreadfull a Judgement*, 86.

27. William Hubbard, *The Present State of New England, Being A Narrative Of the Troubles with the Indians*, in *The History of the Indian Wars in New England*, vol. 1, edited by Samuel G. Drake (Roxbury, Mass., 1865), 29. All further citations to this volume will be made parenthetically in the body of the chapter.

28. Benjamin Tompson, "*New Englands Crisis*," 86. All citations are to *Benjamin Tompson: Colonial Bard* and will hereafter be made parenthetically in the body of the chapter.

29. Slotkin interprets the same passage in precisely the opposite way. He writes that "[i]n Philip's death all of the anxieties that were embodied in the captivity mythology are projected onto the Indian king and exorcized in his slaughter" (*Regeneration Through Violence*, 170).

30. Alden T. Vaughan argues that after the war, "[r]eferences to the Indians, never especially flattering, now became almost universally disparaging" (*Roots of American Racism: Essays on the Colonial Experience* [New York: Oxford University Press, 1995], 23). Canup contends that "King Philip's War provoked exaggerated, virulent expressions of the old habit of viewing the Indians as beasts or devils" and, as a result, led the colonists to adopt a policy of genocide, believing that " just as the literal wolves and their forest cover would have to be eliminated before the colonists could create a truly new England . . . , so these human wolves . . . would also have to be driven from the land" (*The Emergence of an American Identity in Colonial New England* [Middletown, Conn.: Wesleyan University Press, 1990], 184).

31. Vaughan, *New England Frontier*, 23.

32. The issue of when modern racialist attitudes emerge in the colonies has been the source of considerable debate. For instance, Theodore W. Allen provides a very useful summary of this debate in *The Invention of the White Race*, vol. 1 (London: Verso, 1994), 3–22. See also Kwame Anthony Appiah, "The Uncompleted Argument: Du Bois and the Illusion of Race," in *'Race,' Writing, and Difference*, edited by Henry Louis Gates Jr. (Chicago: University of Chicago Press, 1985); Barbara Fields, "Slavery, Race, and Ideology in the United States of America," *New Left Review* 181 (1990): 95–117; Winthrop Jordan, *White over Black: American Attitudes Toward the Negro, 1550–1812* (Chapel Hill: University of North Carolina Press, 1968); Karen Ordahl Kupperman, *Settling with the Indians: The Meeting of English and Indian Cultures in America, 1580–1640* (Totowa, N.J.: Rowman & Littlefield, 1980), 107–40; Edmund Morgan, *American Slavery, American Freedom: The Ordeal of Colonial Virginia* (New York: Norton, 1975); Michael Omi and Howard Winant, "On the Theoretical Status of the Concept of Race," in *Race, Identity, and Representation in Education*, edited by Cameron McCarthy and Warren Crihlow (New York: Routledge, 1993); Audrey Smedley, *Race in North America: Origin and Evolution of a Worldview* (Boulder, Colo.: Westview, 1993); Vaughan, *Roots of American Racism*, esp. 136–74.

33. Kupperman, *Settling with the Indians*, 140.

34. In contrast to my position, Wayne Franklin has argued that Tompson's language makes the natives, and Philip in particular, "mildly sympathetic figures" and demonstrates how Tompson had "a subtle insight into the native viewpoint" (Franklin, "*Harangue of King Philip*," 538). In a different way, Peter White argues that the image of Indians in Tompson's writings should not be taken as a sign of the writer's attitude toward native peoples. White contends that "Tompson's New England primitives bear little resemblance to his immediate reality" (*Benjamin Tompson*, 201). He argues that, far from attempting to

represent real Indians, Tompson is adapting European sources in an attempt to "visualize myth" (207).

35. Kupperman, *Settling with the Indians,* 108.

36. Schramer and Sweet argue that "Tompson uses an image of a human fetus to represent the concerns of the body politic" ("Violence and the Body Politic," 18). They go on to read the passage I cite here as an instance of Tompson's "fears that the Indian's goal is to usurp New England's position as privileged body, to penetrate and replace the Puritans in the womb of the continent: abortion and rape are represented as a single act of power" (19).

37. Warner, *Letters of the Republic,* xi.

38. Jennings, *Invasion of America,* 183.

39. Randolph G. Adams argues that the number of variants in both the London and Boston editions of Hubbard's *Narrative* make it impossible to establish "any intelligent or intelligible, chronological order" for the appearance of the variant editions. Indeed, for the Boston edition alone, the variants are so numerous that Adams claims that "if a customer had gone into John Foster's bookstore in Boston in 1677 . . he might have picked up not two or four . . . variant printings [of Hubbard's book], but any one of twenty-five" (28). See Adams, "William Hubbard's 'Narrative,' 1677," *Bibliographical Society of America* 33 (1939): 25–39.

The lack of concern for the many "unique" editions of Hubbard's text leads one to speculate on the different notions of textuality that might have been operating at the time. For a discussion of how such issues might be understood in texts from early modern England, see Margreta De Grazia and Peter Stallybrass, "The Materiality of the Shakespearean Text," *Shakespeare Quarterly* (Fall 1993): 255–83.

40. For a detailed discussion of the differences between the two texts, see White, *Benjamin Tompson,* 115–16. Indeed, as White points out, the differences are so great that one commentator, Howard Judson Hall, argues that "*New-Englands Tears* cannot be considered a reprint of *New Englands Crisis*" (115) at all. Eberwein, in fact, treats the poems as separate entities rather than as part of a larger whole. See Eberwein, "'*Harvardine* quil.'"

41. Ibid., 6, 12.

42. Ibid., 2.

43. Ibid., 4.

44. Tichi, "Introduction," xviii, xx.

45. Ibid., xviii. These critics are not alone in their lack of regard for the aesthetic qualities of either Hubbard's or Tompson's writings. Arch, for instance, also finds Hubbard's *Narrative* deficient, arguing that the narrative "lack[s] . . . an organizing principle" and "ends with many loose ends left untied" (*Authorizing the Past,* 120, 121).

46. Eberwein, "'*Harvardine* quil,'" 11.

47. Ibid.

48. The invocations are so common as to be too numerous to list here. For an analysis of the significance of this rhetorical strategy, see Miller, *Errand Into the Wilderness,* and Bercovitch, *American Jeremiad* and *The Puritan Origins of the American Self* (New Haven, Conn.: Yale University Press, 1975). As far as I

have been able to determine, however, this is the only instance where a seventeenth-century New England writer claims that the various generations will be brought together through the experience of reading.

49. Perry claims that the collective community posited in Hubbard's *Narrative* extends well beyond New England. He argues that Hubbard "seems to envision a larger collective self that includes regions outside of New England, moving toward the idea of a new-world self" ("Novelties and Stile," 179). While I find this interpretation very provocative, it is my contention that before such a "new-world self" can be imagined, a more limited national self must first be established.

50. Kusener Nelsen, "King Philip's War," 628.

51. I am greatly indebted in my discussion of maps to the work of J. B. Harley. See Harley, "Silences and Secrecy: The Hidden Agenda of Cartography in Early Modern Europe," *Imago Mundi* 40 (1988): 57–76; "Meaning and Ambiguity in Tudor Cartography," in *English Mapmaking, 1500–1650*, edited by Sarah Tyache (London: British Library, 1983), 22–45; "Maps, Knowledge, and Power," in *The Iconography of Landscape*, edited by Denis Cosgrove and Stephen Daniels (Cambridge: Cambridge University Press, 1988), 277–312; and "Deconstructing the Map," *Cartographia* 26 (1989): 1–20.

52. Michel de Certeau, *The Writing of History*, translated by Tom Conley (New York: Columbia University Press, 1988), 36.

53. Ibid.

54. Howard Marchitello, "Political Maps: The Production of Cartography and Chorography in Early Modern England," in *Cultural Artifacts and the Production of Meaning: The Page, the Image, and the Body* (Ann Arbor: University of Michigan Press, 1994), 13–40.

55. Ibid., 18.

56. Ibid., 24, 22. For a different reading of the relationship between early modern chorography and cartography, see Richard Helgerson, *Forms of Nationhood: The Elizabethan Writing of England* (Chicago: University of Chicago Press, 1992). While Helgerson's objective is to demonstrate how early modern English maps come to "rival the authority of the crown," much of what he says has interesting applications to Hubbard's map (139). For instance, it seems to me that Hubbard's map allows the colonists (and his countrymen in England) to, as Helgerson quotes J. R. Hale, "'visualize the country to which he belonged" in a radically new way, a way of visualizing the colonies that helps the colonists claim an authority to rival that of the Crown's (108).

57. de Certeau, *Writing of History*, 36.

58. For a discussion of Mather's use of Biblical passages as opposed to Hubbard's, see Arch, Perry, and Kusener Nelsen.

BIBLIOGRAPHY

Adair, Douglass G. "'Experience Must Be Our Only Guide': History, Democratic Theory, and the United States Constitution." In *The Reinterpretation of the American Revolution*, edited by Jack P. Greene, 397–416. New York: Harper & Row, 1968.

Adams, Randolph G. "William Hubbard's 'Narrative,' 1677." *Bibliographical Society of America* 33 (1939): 25–39.

Alexander, Sir William. *An Encouragement to Colonies*. London, 1624.

Allen, Theodore W. *The Invention of the White Race*. Vol. 1. London: Verso, 1994.

Anderson, Benedict. *Imagined Communities: Reflections on the Origin and Spread of Nationalism*. Rev. ed. London: Verso, 1991.

Andrews, Kenneth. *Trade, Plunder, and Settlement: Maritime Enterprise and the Genesis of the British Empire, 1480–1630*. Cambridge: Cambridge University Press, 1984.

Appiah, Kwame Anthony. "The Uncompleted Argument: Du Bois and the Illusion of Race." In *'Race,' Writing, and Difference*, edited by Henry Louis Gates Jr., 21–37. Chicago: University of Chicago Press, 1985.

Arch, Stephen. *Authorizing the Past: The Rhetoric of History in Seventeenth-Century New England*. DeKalb: Northern Illinois University Press, 1994.

Armstrong, Nancy. *Desire and Domestic Fiction: A Political History of the Novel*. New York: Oxford University Press, 1987.

Armstrong, Nancy, and Leonard Tennenhouse. *The Imaginary Puritan: Literature, Intellectual Labor, and the Origins of Personal Life*. Berkeley: University of California Press, 1992.

Arneil, Barbara. *John Locke and America: The Defence of English Colonialism*. Oxford: Clarendon, 1996.

Ashcroft, Bill, Gareth Griffiths, and Helen Tiffin. *The Empire Writes Back: Theory and Practice in Post-Colonial Literatures*. London: Routledge, 1989.

Axtell, James. *The Invasion Within: The Contest of Cultures in Colonial North America*. New York: Oxford University Press, 1985.

Axton, Marie. *The Queen's Two Bodies: Drama and the Elizabethan Succession*. London: Royal Historical Society, 1977.

Baker, Houston. "Archaeology, Ideology, and African American Discourse." In *Redefining American Literary History*, edited by Jerry W. Ward and A. LaVonne Brown Ruoff, 157–95. New York: The Modern Language Association of America, 1990.

Bakhtin, Mikhail. *Rabelais and His World*. Translated by Helene Iswolsky. Cambridge, Mass.: MIT, 1968.

Barbour, Philip L. *The Three Worlds of Captain John Smith*. London: Macmillan, 1964.

Barkan, Leonard. *Nature's Work of Art: The Human Body as Image of the World*. New Haven, Conn.: Yale University Press, 1975.

Barker, Francis. *The Tremulous Private Body: Essays on Subjection.* 2nd ed. Ann Arbor: University of Michigan Press, 1995.

Battis, Emery. *Saints and Sectaries: Anne Hutchinson and the Antinomian Controversy in the Massachusetts Bay Colony.* Chapel Hill: University of North Carolina Press, 1962.

Baum, Rosalie Murphy. "John Williams's Captivity Narrative: A Consideration of Normative Ethnicity." In *A Mixed Race: Ethnicity in Early America,* edited by Frank Shuffelton, 56–76. New York: Oxford University Press, 1993.

Baym, Nina. "Melodramas of Beset Manhood: How Theories of American Fiction Exclude Women Authors." In *Feminism and American Literary History.* New Brunswick, N.J.: Rutgers University Press, 1992.

Bellamy, Elizabeth J., and Artemis Leontis. "A Genealogy of Experience: From Epistemology to Politics." *Yale Journal of Criticism* 6 (1993): 163–84.

Bercovitch, Sacvan. "Introduction." In *The Cambridge History of American Literature,* vol. 1, *1590–1820,* edited by Sacvan Bercovitch. Cambridge: Cambridge University Press, 1994.

———. "Afterword." In *Ideology and Classic American Literature,* edited by Sacvan Bercovitch and Myra Jehlen, 418–43. Cambridge: Cambridge University Press, 1986.

———. "The Problem of Ideology in American Literary History." *Critical Inquiry* 12 (1986): 631–53.

———. *The American Jeremiad.* Madison: University of Wisconsin Press, 1978.

———. *The Puritan Origins of the American Self.* New Haven, Conn.: Yale University Press, 1975.

Best, George. "Experiences and Reasons of the Sphere." 1578. *The Principal Navigations, Voyages, Traffiques and Discoveries of the English Nation.* Glasgow: James Machehorse, 1903–5.

Boorstein, Daniel. *The Americans: The Colonial Experience.* New York: Vintage, 1958.

Bozeman, T. Dwight. *To Live Ancient Lives: The Primitivist Dimension in Puritanism.* Chapel Hill: University of North Carolina Press, 1988.

Bradstreet, Anne. *The Tenth Muse, Several Poems.* Boston, 1678.

———. *The Tenth Muse Lately Sprung Up in America.* London, 1650.

Breen, Timothy H. *The Character of the Good Ruler: A Study of Puritan Political Ideas in New England, 1630–1730.* New Haven, Conn.: Yale University Press, 1970.

Breen, Timothy H., and Stephen Innes. *"Myne Owne Ground": Race and Freedom on Virginia's Eastern Shore, 1640–1676.* New York: Oxford University Press, 1980.

Breitwieser, Mitchell Robert. *American Puritanism and the Defense of Mourning: Religion, Grief, and Ethnology in Mary White Rowlandson's Captivity Narrative.* Madison: University of Wisconsin Press, 1990.

Bremer, Francis J. *The Puritan Experiment: New England Society from Bradford to Edwards.* Rev. ed. Hanover, N.H.: University Press of New England, 1995.

———. *Puritan Crisis: New England and the English Civil War, 1630–1670.* Westport, Conn.: Greenwood, 1989.

Brereton, John. *A Briefe and True Relation of the Discoverie of the North Part of Virginia* (1602). In *The English New England Voyages, 1602–1608*, edited by David B. Quinn and Alison M. Quinn. London: The Hakluyt Society, 1983.

Bush, Sargent. "John Wheelwright's Forgotten Apology: The Last Word in the Antinomian Controversy." *New England Quarterly* 64 (1991): 22–45.

———. *The Writings of Thomas Hooker: Spiritual Adventure in Two Worlds*. Madison: University of Wisconsin Press, 1980.

Bushman, Richard. *The Refinement of America: Persons, Houses, Cities*. New York: Vintage, 1992.

———. *From Puritan to Yankee: Character and the Social Order in Connecticut, 1690–1765*. Cambridge, Mass.: Harvard University Press, 1967.

Butler, Judith. *Gender Trouble: Feminism and the Subversion of Identity*. New York: Routledge, 1990.

Butts, Francis T. "The Myth of Perry Miller." *American Historical Review* 87 (1982): 665–94.

Caldwell, Patricia. "Why Our First Poet Was a Woman: Bradstreet and the Birth of an American Poetic Voice." *Prospects* 13 (1988): 1–35.

———. *The Puritan Conversion Narrative: The Beginnings of American Expression*. New York: Cambridge University Press, 1983.

———. "The Antinomian Language Controversy." *Harvard Theological Review* 69 (1976): 345–67.

Campbell, Mary. "The Illustrated Travel Book and the Birth of Ethnography: Part I of De Bry's America." In *The Work of Dissimilitude: Essays from the Sixth Citadel Conference on Medieval and Renaissance Literature*, edited by David G. Allen and Robert A. White, 177–95. Newark, N.J.: University of Delaware Press, 1992.

———. *The Witness and the Other World: Exotic European Travel Writing, 400–1600*. Ithaca, N.Y.: Cornell University Press, 1988.

Canny, Nicholas. "Identity Formation in Ireland: The Emergence of the Anglo-Irish." In *Colonial Identity in the Atlantic World, 1500–1800*, edited by Nicholas Canny and Anthony Pagden, 159–212. Princeton, N.J.: Princeton University Press, 1987.

Canup, John. *Out of the Wilderness: The Emergence of an American Identity in Colonial New England*. Middletown, Conn.: Wesleyan University Press, 1990.

———. "Cotton Mather and 'Criolian Degeneracy.'" *Early American Literature* 24 (1989): 20–34.

Cave, Alfred A. *The Pequot War*. Amherst: University of Massachusetts Press, 1996.

———. "Who Killed John Stone? A Note on the Origins of the Pequot War." *William and Mary Quarterly* 3rd ser., 49 (1992): 509–21.

Chaplin, Joyce E. "Natural Philosophy and an Early Racial Idiom in North America: Comparing English and Indian Bodies." *William and Mary Quarterly* 3rd ser., 54 (1997): 229–52.

Chartier, Roger. *The Cultural Origins of the French Revolution*. Translated by Lydia G. Cochrane. Durham, N.C.: Duke University Press, 1991.

Chay, Deborah G. "Rereading Barbara Smith: Black Feminist Criticism and the Category of Experience." *New Literary History* 24 (1993): 635–52.

Cohen, Charles Lloyd. *God's Caress: The Psychology of Puritan Religious Experience.* New York: Oxford University Press, 1986.

Colbourn, H. Trevor. *The Lamp of Experience: Whig History and the Intellectual Origins of the American Revolution.* New York: Norton, 1965.

Collinson, Patrick. *The Elizabethan Puritan Movement.* Berkeley: University of California Press, 1967.

Cowell, Pattie. "Anne Bradstreet." In *Heath Anthology of American Literature*, vol. 1, edited by Paul Lauter. 2nd ed. Lexington, Mass.: D. C. Heath, 1990.

———. "The Early Distribution of Anne Bradstreet's Poems." In *Critical Essays on Anne Bradstreet*, edited by Pattie Cowell and Ann Stanford, 270–79. Boston: G. K. Hall, 1983.

———. "Introduction: Anne Bradstreet 'In Criticks Hands.'" In *Critical Essays on Anne Bradstreet*, edited by Pattie Cowell and Ann Stanford, ix–xi. Boston: G. K. Hall, 1983.

Craven, Wesley Frank. *The Colonies in Transition, 1660–1713.* New York: Harper & Row, 1968.

Cressy, David. *Coming Over: Migration and Communication Between England and New England in the Seventeenth Century.* Cambridge: Cambridge University Press, 1987.

Crews, Frederick. "Whose American Renaissance?" *New York Review of Books*, 27 October 1988, 68–81.

Cronon, William. *Changes in the Land: Indians, Colonists, and the Ecology of New England.* New York: Hill & Wang, 1983.

Crosby, Alfred W., Jr. *Ecological Imperialism: The Biological Expansion of Europe 900–1900.* Cambridge: Cambridge University Press, 1986.

———. "Virgin Soil Epidemics as a Factor in Aboriginal Depopulation in America." *William and Mary Quarterly* 3rd ser., 33 (1976): 289–99.

———. *The Columbian Exchange: Biological and Cultural Consequences of 1492.* Westport, Conn.: Greenwood, 1972.

D'Emilio, John, and Estelle B. Freedman. *Intimate Matters: A History of Sexuality in America.* New York: Harper & Row, 1988.

Daly, Robert. *God's Altar: The World and the Flesh in Puritan Poetry.* Berkeley: University of California Press, 1978.

De Grazia, Margreta, and Peter Stallybrass. "The Materiality of the Shakespearean Text." *Shakespeare Quarterly* (Fall 1993): 255–83.

de Certeau, Michel. *The Writing of History.* Translated by Tom Conley. New York: Columbia University Press, 1988.

Dear, Peter. *Discipline and Experience: The Mathematical Way in the Scientific Revolution.* Chicago: University of Chicago Press, 1995.

———. "Narratives, Anecdotes, and Experiments: Turning Experience into Science in the Seventeenth Century." In *The Literary Structure of Scientific Argument: Historical Studies*, edited by Peter Dear. Philadelphia: University of Pennsylvania Press, 1991.

———. "Miracles, Experiments, and the Ordinary Course of Nature." *Isis* 81 (1990): 663–83.

———. "Jesuit Mathematical Science and the Reconstitution of Experience in the Early Seventeenth Century." *Studies in History and Philosophy of Science* 18 (1987): 133–75.

Delbanco, Andrew. *The Puritan Ordeal.* Cambridge, Mass.: Harvard University Press, 1989.

Demos, John. *A Little Commonwealth: Family Life in Plymouth Colony.* London: Oxford University Press, 1970.

Ditmore, Michael G. "Preparation and Confession: Reconsidering Edmund S. Morgan's Visible Saints." *New England Quarterly* 67 (1994): 298–319.

Douglas, Mary. *Purity and Danger: An Analysis of Concepts of Pollution and Taboo.* London: Routledge & Kegan Paul, 1966.

Drake, Samuel G., ed. *The History of the Indian Wars in New England.* Roxbury, Mass., 1865.

Dunn, Richard. *Puritans and Yankees: The Winthrop Dynasty of New England.* Princeton, N.J.: Princeton University Press, 1962.

Eberwein, Jane. "'*Harvardine* quil': Benjamin Tompson's Poems on King Phillip's War." *Early American Literature* 28 (1993): 1–21.

———. "Bradstreet's Monarchies." *Early American Literature* 26 (1991): 119–44.

Eburne, Richard. *A Plain Pathway to Plantations.* 1624. Edited by Louis B. Wright. Ithaca, N.Y.: Cornell University Press, 1962.

Elliott, Emory. "New England Puritan Literature." In *The Cambridge History of American Literature*, vol. 1, *1590–1820*, edited by Sacvan Bercovitch. Cambridge: Cambridge University Press, 1994.

Emerson, Everett H. *Captain John Smith.* Boston: Twayne, 1971.

Fields, Barbara. "Slavery, Race, and Ideology in the United States of America." *New Left Review* 181 (1990): 95–117.

Foster, Stephen. *The Long Argument: English Puritanism and the Shaping of New England Culture, 1570–1700.* Chapel Hill: University of North Carolina Press, 1991.

Foucault, Michel. *Discipline and Punish: The Birth of the Prison.* Translated by Alan Sheridan. New York: Pantheon, 1977.

———. "Nietzsche, Genealogy, History." In *Language, Counter-Memory, Practice: Selected Essays and Interviews by Michel Foucault*, edited by Donald F. Bouchard; translated by Donald F. Bouchard and Sherry Simon. Ithaca, N.Y.: Cornell University Press, 1977.

———. *The Order of Things: An Archaeology of Human Sciences.* New York: Vintage, 1970.

Franklin, Wayne. "*The Harangue of King Philip* in *New-Englands Crisis* (1676)." *American Literature* 51 (1980): 536–40.

———. *Discoverers, Explorers, Settlers: The Diligent Writers of Early America.* Chicago: University of Chicago Press, 1979.

Fuller, Mary. *Voyages in Print: English Travel to America, 1576–1624.* Cambridge: Cambridge University Press, 1995.

Fuss, Diane. *Essentially Speaking: Feminism, Nature, and Difference.* New York: Routledge, 1989.

Gallop, Jane. "Quand no levres s'ecrivent: Irigaray's Body Politic." *Romantic Review* 74 (1983): 77–83.

Gay, Peter. *A Loss of Mastery: Puritan Historians in Colonial America.* Berkeley: University of California Press, 1966.

Gent, Lucy, and Nigel Llewellyn, eds. *Renaissance Bodies: The Human Figure in English Culture, c. 1540–1660.* London: Reaktion, 1990.

Glacken, Clarence J. *Traces on the Rhodian Shore: Nature and Culture in Western Thought from Ancient Times to the End of the Eighteenth Century.* Berkeley: University of California Press, 1967.

Goldberg, Jonathan. *James I and the Politics of Literature: Jonson, Shakespeare, Donne, and Their Contemporaries.* Baltimore: Johns Hopkins University Press, 1983.

Gorges, Sir Ferdinando. *A Briefe Relation of the Discovery and Plantations of New England* (1622). In *Publications of the Prince Society*, vol. 18, *Sir Ferdinando Gorges and His Province of Maine*, edited by James Phinney Baxter. Boston: The Prince Society, 1890.

Greenblatt, Stephen. *Marvelous Possessions: The Wonder of the New World.* Chicago: University of Chicago Press, 1991.

———. "Introduction." *Genre* 14 (1981): 3–6.

———. *Renaissance Self-Fashioning: From More to Shakespeare.* Chicago: University of Chicago Press, 1980.

Greenblatt, Stephen, ed. *New World Encounters.* Berkeley: University of California Press, 1993.

Greene, Jack P. *The Intellectual Construction of America: Exceptionalism and Identity from 1492–1800.* Chapel Hill: University of North Carolina Press, 1993.

———. *Imperatives, Behaviors, and Identities: Essays in Early American Cultural History.* Charlottesville: University Press of Virginia, 1992.

———. *Pursuits of Happiness: The Social Development of Early Modern British Colonies and the Formation of American Culture.* Chapel Hill: University of North Carolina Press, 1988.

Greene, Jack P., and J. R. Pole, eds. *Colonial British America: Essays in the New History of the Early Modern Era.* Baltimore: Johns Hopkins University Press, 1984.

Guard, Theodore de la. *The Simple Cobbler of Aggawam in America.* London, 1647.

Gura, Philip F. "Turning Our World Upside Down: Reconceiving Early American Literature." *American Literature* 63 (1991): 104–12.

———. "The Study of Colonial American Literature, 1966–1987: A Vade Mecum." *William and Mary Quarterly* 3rd ser., 45 (1988): 305–42.

———. *A Glimpse of Sion's Glory: Puritan Radicalism in New England, 1620–1660.* Middletown, Conn.: Wesleyan University Press, 1984.

Hakluyt, Richard. *The Principal Navigations.* 12 vols. Glasgow: J. MacLehose & Sons, 1903–5.

Hale, David George. *The Body Politic: A Political Metaphor in Renaissance English Literature.* The Hague: Mouton, 1971.

Hall, David D. *Worlds of Wonder, Days of Judgment: Popular Religious Belief in Early New England.* Cambridge, Mass.: Harvard University Press, 1990.

Hall, David D., ed. *The Antinomian Controversy, 1636–1638: A Documentary History.* Durham, N.C.: Duke University Press, 1990.

Hambrick-Stowe, Charles. *The Practice of Piety: Puritan Devotional Disciplines in Seventeenth-Century New England.* Chapel Hill: University of North Carolina Press, 1982.

Hammond, Jeffrey. *Sinful Self, Saintly Self: The Puritan Experience of Poetry.* Athens: University of Georgia Press, 1993.

Harley, J. B. "Deconstructing the Map." *Cartographia* 26 (1989): 1–20.

———. "Maps, Knowledge, and Power." In *The Iconography of Landscape,* edited by Denis Cosgrove and Stephen Daniels, 277–312. Cambridge: Cambridge University Press, 1988.

———. "Silences and Secrecy: The Hidden Agenda of Cartography in Early Modern Europe." *Imago Mundi* 40 (1988): 57–76.

———. "Meaning and Ambiguity in Tudor Cartography." In *English Mapmaking, 1500–1650,* edited by Sarah Tyache, 22–45. London: British Library, 1983.

Harriot, Thomas. *A Briefe and True Report of the New Found Land of Virginia.* 1588. New York: Dover, 1972.

Helgerson, Richard. *Forms of Nationhood: The Elizabethan Writing of England.* Chicago: University of Chicago Press, 1992.

Hensley, Jeannine, ed. *The Works of Anne Bradstreet.* Cambridge, Mass.: The Belknap Press of Harvard University Press, 1967.

Higginson, Francis. *New Englands Plantation.* London, 1630.

Hildebrand, Anne. "Anne Bradstreet's Quaternions and 'Contemplations.'" In *Critical Essays on Anne Bradstreet,* edited by Pattie Cowell and Ann Stanford, 137–44. Boston: G. K. Hall, 1983.

Hill, Christopher. *The World Turned Upside Down: Radical Ideas During the English Revolution.* London: Penguin, 1975.

———. *Intellectual Origins of the English Revolution.* Oxford: Clarendon, 1965.

———. *The Century of Revolution, 1603–1714.* London: Nelson, 1961.

Hillman, David, and Carla Mazzio, eds. *The Body in Parts: Fantasies of Corporeality in Early Modern Europe.* New York: Routledge, 1997.

Hodgen, Margaret T. *Early Anthropology in the Sixteenth and Seventeenth Centuries.* Philadelphia: University of Pennsylvania Press, 1964.

Holt, Thomas C. "Experience and the Politics of Intellectual Inquiry." In *Questions of Evidence: Proof, Practice, and Persuasion across the Disciplines,* edited by Arnold I. Davidson, James Chandler, and Harry Harootunian, 386–96. Chicago: University of Chicago Press, 1991.

hooks, bell. "Essentialism and Experience." *American Literary History* 3 (1991): 172–83.

Hubbard, William. *The Present State of New England, Being A Narrative Of the Troubles with the Indians.* 1677. *The History of the Indian Wars in New England.* Vol 1. Edited by Samuel G. Drake. Roxbury, Mass., 1865.

Hughes, Walter. "'Meat Out of the Eater': Panic and Desire in American Puritan Poetry." In *Engendering Men: The Question of Male Feminist Criticism,* edited by Joseph A. Boone and Michael Cadden, 102–21. New York and London: Routledge, 1990.

Irwin, William. "Allegory and Typology 'Imbrace and Greet': Anne Bradstreet's 'Contemplations.'" In *Critical Essays on Anne Bradstreet,* edited by Pattie Cowell and Ann Stanford, 174–83. Boston: G. K. Hall, 1983.

Jardine, Alice. *Gynesis: Configurations of Woman and Modernity.* Ithaca, N.Y.: Cornell University Press, 1985.

Jed, Stephanie. "The Tenth Muse: Gender, Rationality, and the Marketing of Knowledge." In *Women, "Race," and Writing in the Early Modern Period,* edited by Margo Hendricks and Patricia Parker, 195–208. London: Routledge, 1994.

Jehlen, Myra. "The Papers of Empire." In *The Cambridge History of American Literature,* vol. 1, *1590–1820,* edited by Sacvan Bercovitch, 13–168. Cambridge: Cambridge University Press, 1994.

———. "History before Fact; or, Captain John Smith's Unfinished Symphony." *Critical Inquiry* 19 (1993): 677–92.

Jennings, Francis. *The Invasion of America: Indians, Colonialism, and the Cant of Conquest.* New York: Norton, 1976.

Johnson, Edward. *Johnson's Wonder-working Providence, 1628–1651.* Edited by J. Franklin Jameson. New York: C. Scribner's Sons, 1910.

———. *A History of New-England From the English planting in the Yeere 1628 untill the Yeere 1652.* London, 1653.

Johnson, Richard R. *Adjustment to Empire: The New England Colonies, 1675–1715.* New Brunswick, N.J.: Rutgers University Press, 1981.

Jones, Ann R., and Peter Stallybrass. "Dismantling Irena: The Sexualizing of Ireland in Early Modern England." In *Nationalisms and Sexualities,* edited by Andrew Parker, Mary Ruso, Doris Sommer, and Patricia Yaeger, 157–71. New York: Routledge, 1992.

Jones, Howard Mumford. *O Strange New World: American Culture: The Formative Years.* New York: Viking, 1964.

———. "The Colonial Impulse: An Analysis of the 'Promotion' Literature of Colonization." *Proceedings of the American Philosophical Society* 90, no. 2 (1946): 131–61.

———. "The European Background." In *The Reinterpretation of American Literature: Some Contributions Toward the Understanding of Its Historical Development,* edited by Norman Foerster, 62–82. New York: Harcourt, Brace, 1928.

Jordan, Winthrop. *White over Black: American Attitudes Toward the Negro, 1550–1812.* Chapel Hill: University of North Carolina Press, 1968.

Kahn, Coppélia. *Roman Shakespeare: Warriors, Wounds, and Women.* London: Routledge, 1997.

Kantorowicz, Ernst. *The King's Two Bodies.* Princeton, N.J.: Princeton University Press, 1957.

Kaplan, Amy. "'Left Alone with America': The Absence of Empire in the Study of American Culture." In *Cultures of United States Imperialism,* edited by Amy Kaplan and Donald E. Pease. Durham, N.C.: Duke University Press, 1993.

Karlsen, Carol. *The Devil in the Shape of a Woman: Witchcraft in Colonial New England.* New York: Norton, 1987.

Kibbey, Ann. *The Interpretation of Material Shapes in Puritanism: A Study of Rhetoric, Prejudice, and Violence.* Cambridge: Cambridge University Press, 1986.

Knapp, Jeffrey. *An Empire Nowhere: England, America, and Literature from Utopia to The Tempest.* Berkeley: University of California Press, 1992.

Knight, Janice. *Orthodoxies in Massachusetts: Rereading American Puritanism.* Cambridge, Mass.: Harvard University Press, 1994.

Kolodny, Annette. "Letting Go Our Grand Obsessions: Notes toward a New Literary History of the American Frontiers." *American Literature* 64 (1992): 1–18.

Kopacz, Paula. "'To Finish What's Begun': Anne Bradstreet's Last Words." *Early American Literature* 23 (1988): 175–87.

Kupperman, Karen Ordahl. *Providence Island, 1630–1641: The Other Puritan Colony.* New York: Cambridge University Press, 1993.

———. "Fear of Hot Climates in the Anglo-American Colonial Experience." *William and Mary Quarterly* 3rd ser., 41 (1984): 213–40.

———. "The Puzzle of the American Climate in the Early Colonial Period." *American Historical Review* 87 (1982): 1262–89.

———. *Settling with the Indians: The Meeting of English and Indian Cultures in America, 1580–1640.* Totowa, N.J.: Rowman & Littlefield, 1980.

Lake, Peter. "Defining Puritanism—Again?" In *Transatlantic Perspectives on a Seventeenth-Century Anglo-American Faith,* edited by Francis J. Bremer, 3–29. Boston: Massachusetts Historical Society, 1993.

Lang, Amy Schrager. *Prophetic Woman: Anne Hutchinson and the Problem of Dissent in the Literature of New England.* Berkeley: University of California Press, 1987.

Laqueur, Thomas. *Making Sex: Body and Gender from the Greeks to Freud.* Cambridge, Mass.: Harvard University Press, 1990.

Lauter, Paul. *Canons and Contexts.* New York: Oxford University Press, 1991.

Lauter, Paul, ed. *The Heath Anthology of American Literature.* Vol. 1. 2nd ed. Lexington, Mass.: D. C. Heath, 1990.

Leach, Douglass. *Flintlock and Tomahawk: New England in King Phillip's War.* New York: Macmillan, 1958.

Lechford, Thomas. *Plain Dealing; or, Newes from New-England.* 1642. Rpt. New York: Johnson Reprint Corporation, 1969.

Lemay, J. A. Leo. *The American Dream of Captain John Smith.* Charlottesville: University Press of Virginia, 1991.

Leverenz, David. *The Language of Puritan Feeling: An Exploration in Literature, Psychology, and Social History.* New Brunswick, N.J.: Rutgers University Press, 1980.

Levin, David. "A Survivor's Tale." *William and Mary Quarterly* 3rd ser., 45 (1988): 345–47.

Lewalski, Barbara. *Protestant Poetics and the Seventeenth-Century Religious Lyric.* Princeton, N.J.: Princeton University Press, 1979.

Lindholdt, Paul J. "The Significance of the Colonial Promotion Tract." In *Early American Literature and Culture: Essays Honoring Harrison T. Messerole,* edited by Kathryn Zabelle Derounian-Stodola, 57–72. Newark, N.J.: University of Delaware Press, 1992.

Lloyd, T. O. *The British Empire: 1558–1983.* London: Oxford University Press, 1984.

Locke, John. *Two Treatises of Government.* 1698. Edited by Peter Laslett. Cambridge: Cambridge University Press, 1988.

Lovejoy, David S. *The Glorious Revolution in America.* New York: Harper & Row, 1972.

Lynen, John. *The Design of the Present: Essays on Time and Form in American Literature.* New Haven, Conn.: Yale University Press, 1969.

Mack, Phyllis. *Visionary Women: Ecstatic Prophecy in Seventeenth-Century England.* Berkeley: University of California Press, 1992.

MacLear, J. F. "Anne Hutchinson and the Mortalist Heresy." *New England Quarterly* 54 (1981): 77–91.

Macphail, Alasdair. "William Hubbard." In *The Dictionary of Literary Biography 24: American Colonial Writers, 1606–1734,* edited by Emory Elliott, 164–72. Detroit: Gale, 1984.

Madison, James. *Notes of Debates in the Federal Convention of 1787 Reported by James Madison.* New York: Norton, 1987.

Marchitello, Howard. "Political Maps: The Production of Cartography and Chorography in Early Modern England." In *Cultural Artifacts and the Production of Meaning: The Page, the Image, and the Body,* edited by Margaret J. M. Ezell and Katherine O'Brien O'Keefe, 13–40. Ann Arbor: University of Michigan Press, 1994.

Mariscal, George. *Contradictory Subjects: Quevedo, Cervantes, and Seventeenth-Century Spanish Culture.* Ithaca, N.Y.: Cornell University Press, 1991.

Marotti, Arthur. "'Love Is Not Love': Elizabethan Sonnet Sequences and the Social Order." *English Literary History* 49 (1982): 396–428.

Martin, Wendy. *An American Triptych: Anne Bradstreet, Emily Dickinson, Adrienne Rich.* Chapel Hill: University of North Carolina Press, 1984.

Martz, Louis. *The Poetry of Meditation: A Study in English Religious Literature of the Seventeenth Century.* New Haven, Conn.: Yale University Press, 1954.

Mather, Cotton. *Magnalia Christi Americana.* 2 vols. New York: Russell & Russell, 1977.

Mather, Increase. *A Brief History of the Warr with the Indians.* 1676. In *So Dreadfull a Judgement: Puritan Responses to King Phillip's War, 1676–1677,* edited by Richard Slotkin and James K. Folsom, 81–163. Middletown, Conn: Wesleyan University Press, 1978.

McEachern, Claire. *The Poetics of English Nationhood, 1590–1612*. Cambridge: Cambridge University Press, 1996.

McElrath, Joseph R., Jr. "The Text of Anne Bradstreet: Biographical and Critical Consequences." *Seventeenth-Century News* 34 (1976): 61–63.

McElrath, Joseph R., Jr., and Allan P. Robb, eds. *The Complete Works of Anne Bradstreet*. Boston: Twayne, 1981.

McKeon, Michael. *The Origins of the English Novel, 1600–1740*. Baltimore: Johns Hopkins University Press, 1987.

Meserole, Harrison T., ed. *American Poetry of the Seventeenth Century*. University Park, Pa., and London: Pennsylvania State University Press, 1985.

Michaelson, Scott. "John Winthrop's 'Modell' Covenant and the Company Way." *Early American Literature* 27 (1992): 85–100.

Middlekauff, Robert. *The Mathers: Three Generations of Puritan Intellectuals, 1596–1728*. New York: Oxford University Press, 1971.

Miller, David Lee. *The Poem's Two Bodies: The Poetics of the 1590 Farie Queen*. Princeton, N.J.: Princeton University Press, 1988.

Miller, Perry. "Preparation for Salvation' in Seventeenth-Century New England." In *Nature's Nation*, 50–77. Cambridge, Mass.: Harvard University Press, 1967.

———. *Errand Into the Wilderness*. Cambridge, Mass.: The Belknap Press of Harvard University Press, 1956.

———. *The New England Mind: From Colony to Province*. Cambridge, Mass.: Harvard University Press, 1953.

———. *Jonathan Edwards*. Amherst: University of Massachusetts Press, 1981. Rpt. 1949.

———. *The New England Mind: The Seventeenth Century*. Cambridge, Mass.: Harvard University Press, 1939.

Miller, Perry, and Thomas H. Johnson, eds. *The Puritans: A Sourcebook of Their Writings*. Vol. 1. Rev. ed. New York: Harper & Row, 1963.

Morgan, Edmund. *American Slavery, American Freedom: The Ordeal of Colonial Virginia*. New York: Norton, 1975.

———. *The Puritan Family: Religion and Domestic Relations in Seventeenth-Century New England*. Rev. ed. New York: Harper & Row, 1966.

———. *Visible Saints: The History of a Puritan Idea*. New York: New York University Press, 1963.

———. *The Puritan Dilemma: The Story of John Winthrop*. Boston: Little, Brown, 1958.

Morton, Thomas. *New English Canaan*. Amsterdam, 1637.

Mourts Relation: A Journal of the Pilgrims at Plymouth. 1622. Edited by Dwight B. Heath. Chester, Conn.: Applewood, 1963.

Muldoon, James. "The Indian as Irishman." *Essex Institute Historical Collections* 111 (1975): 267–89.

Mulford, Carla. "What *Is* the Early American Canon, and Who Said It Needed Expanding?" "Special Issue: Expanding the Early American Canon." *Resources for American Literary Study* 19 (1993): 165–73.

Murdock, Kenneth. "William Hubbard and the Providential Interpretation of History." *American Antiquarian Society Proceedings* 52 (1942): 15–37.

Nelsen, Anne Kusener. "King Philip's War and the Hubbard-Mather Rivalry." *William and Mary Quarterly* 3rd ser., 27 (1970): 615–27.

Oberholzer, Emil. *Delinquent Saints: Disciplinary Action in the Early Congregational Churches of Massachusetts.* New York: Columbia University Press, 1956.

Omi, Michael, and Howard Winant. "On the Theoretical Status of the Concept of Race." In *Race, Identity, and Representation in Education*, edited by Cameron McCarthy and Warren Crihlow. New York: Routledge, 1993.

Pacheco, Anita. "Royalism and Honor in Aphra Behn's Oroonoko." *Studies in English Literature, 1500–1900* 34 (1994): 491–506.

Parker, Patricia. "Fantasies of 'Race' and 'Gender': Africa, *Othello* and Bringing to Light." In *Women, "Race," and Writing in the Early Modern Period*, edited by Margo Hendricks and Patricia Parker, 84–100. London: Routledge, 1994.

Pearce, Roy Harvey. *The Savages of America: A Study of the Indian and the Idea of Civilization.* Rev. ed. Baltimore: Johns Hopkins University Press, 1965.

———. "The Significance of the Captivity Narrative." *American Literature* 29 (1947): 1–20.

Pease, Donald. "New Americanists: Revisionist Interventions into the Canon." *boundary* 2, no. 17 (1990): 1–37.

Perry, Dennis R. "'Novelties and Stile Which All Out-Do': William Hubbard's Historiography Reconsidered." *Early American Literature* 29 (1994): 166–82.

Pettit, Norman. *The Heart Prepared: Grace and Conversion in Puritan Spiritual Life.* 2nd ed. New Haven, Conn.: Yale University Press, 1989.

Piercy, Josephine K. *Anne Bradstreet.* Boston: Twayne, 1965.

Porter, Roy. "History of the Body." In *New Perspectives on Historical Writing*, edited by Peter Burke, 206–32. University Park: Pennsylvania State University Press, 1991.

Porterfield, Amanda. *Female Piety in Puritan New England: The Emergence of Religious Humanism.* New York: Oxford University Press, 1992.

Prospo, R. C. de. *Theism in the Discourse of Jonathan Edwards.* Newark, N.J.: University of Delaware Press, 1985.

Pudaloff, Ross. "Sign and Subject: Antinomianism in Massachusetts Bay." *Semiotica* 54 (1985): 147–63.

Purchas, Samuel. *Purchas his pilgrimage; Or relations of the world and the religions obserued in all ages and places discouered, from the Creation vnto this present.* London, 1613.

Rabb, Theodore. *Enterprise and Empire: Merchant and Gentry Investment in the Expansion of England, 1575–1630.* Cambridge, Mass.: Harvard University Press, 1967.

Raleigh, Walter. *The Discoverie of the Large, Rich, and Bewtifvl Empyre of Gviana, with a Relation of the Great and Golden City of Manoa (which the Spanyards call El Dorado) and of the prouinces of Emeria, Arromaia, Amapaia, and other Countries, with their riuers, adioyning.* London, 1596.

Ramenofsky, Ann F. *Vectors of Death: The Archaeology of European Contact.* Albuquerque: University of New Mexico Press, 1987.

Reising, Russell. *The Unusable Past: Theory and the Study of American Literature*. New York: Methuen, 1986.

A Relation of Maryland. 1635. In *Narratives of Early Maryland: Original Narratives of Early American History 10*, edited by Clayton Colman Hall. New York: Charles Scribner's Sons, 1910.

A Relation or Journal of the beginning and proceedings of the English Plantation settled in Plimouth in New England. London, 1622.

Requa, Kenneth. "Anne Bradstreet's Poetic Voices." In *Critical Essays on Anne Bradstreet*, edited by Pattie Cowell and Ann Stanford, 150–65. Boston: G. K. Hall, 1983.

Rich, Adrienne. "Anne Bradstreet and Her Poetry" and "Postscript." In *The Works of Anne Bradstreet*, edited by Jeannine Hensley. Cambridge, Mass.: The Belknap Press of Harvard University Press, 1967.

Rosenfeld, Alvin H. "Anne Bradstreet's 'Contemplations': Patterns of Form and Meaning." In *Critical Essays on Anne Bradstreet*, edited by Pattie Cowell and Ann Stanford, 123–36. Boston: G. K. Hall, 1983.

Rosenmeier, Rosamond. *Anne Bradstreet Revisited*. Boston: Twayne, 1991.

Rosier, James. *True Relation of the Most Prosperous Voyage*. Ann Arbor: University Microfilms, 1966.

Saffin, John. *John Saffin: His Book*. Edited by Caroline Hazard. New York: Harbor, 1928.

Said, Edward. *Orientalism*. New York: Vintage, 1979.

Salisbury, Neal. *Manitou and Providence: Indians, Europeans, and the Making of New England, 1500–1643*. New York: Oxford University Press, 1982.

Saltman, Helen. "'Contemplations': Anne Bradstreet's Spiritual Autobiography." In *Critical Essays on Anne Bradstreet*, edited by Pattie Cowell and Ann Stanford, 226–37. Boston: G. K. Hall, 1983.

Sargent, Rose-Mary. "Scientific Experiment and Legal Expertise: The Way of Experience in Seventeenth-Century England." *Studies in History of Philosophy of Science* 20 (1989): 19–45.

Sawday, Jonathan. *The Body Emblazoned: Dissection and the Human Body in Renaissance Culture*. London: Routledge, 1995.

Scheick, William. *Design in Puritan American Literature*. Lexington: University Press of Kentucky, 1992.

Schmitt, Charles B. "Experience and Experiment: A Comparison of Zabarella's View with Galileo's in *De motu*." *Studies in the Renaissance* 16 (1969): 80–138.

Schramer, James, and Timothy Sweet. "Violence and the Body Politic in Seventeenth-Century New England." *Arizona Quarterly* 48, no. 2 (1992): 1–32.

Schutte, Anne Jacobson. "'Such Monstrous Births': A Neglected Aspect of the Antinomian Controversy." *Renaissance Quarterly* 38 (1985): 85–106.

Schweitzer, Ivy. *The Work of Self-Representation: Lyric Poetry in Colonial New England*. Chapel Hill: University of North Carolina Press, 1991.

———. "Anne Bradstreet Wrestles with the Renaissance." *Early American Literature* 23 (1988): 291–312.

Scott, Joan W. "The Evidence of Experience." In *Question of Evidence: Proof, Practice, and Persuasion across the Disciplines,* edited by James Chandler, Arnold I. Davidson, and Harry Harootunian, 363–87. Chicago: University of Chicago Press, 1994.

———. "A Rejoinder to Thomas C. Holt." In *Question of Evidence: Proof, Practice and Persuasion across the Disciplines,* edited by James Chandler, Arnold I. Davidson, and Harry Harootunian, 397–400. Chicago: University of Chicago Press, 1994.

Seelye, John. *Prophetic Waters: The River in Early American Life and Literature.* New York: Oxford University Press, 1977.

Shapin, Steven. *A Social History of Truth: Civility and Science in Seventeenth-Century England.* Chicago: University of Chicago Press, 1994.

Shapiro, Barbara J. *Probability and Certainty in Seventeenth-Century England: A Study of the Relationships between Natural Science, Religion, History, Law, and Literature.* Princeton, N.J.: Princeton University Press, 1983.

Shepard, Thomas. *God's Plot: The Paradoxes of Puritan Piety, Being the Autobiography and Journal of Thomas Shepard.* Edited by Michael McGiffert. Amherst: University of Massachusetts Press, 1972.

Shields, David S. "Literature of the Colonial South." *Resources for American Literary Study* 19 (1993): 174–222.

———. *Oracles of Empire: Poetry, Politics, and Commerce in British America, 1690–1750.* Chicago: University of Chicago Press, 1990.

Shuffelton, Frank. "Introduction." In *A Mixed Race: Ethnicity in Early America,* edited by Frank Shuffelton, 3–16. New York: Oxford University Press, 1993.

———. "Privation and Fulfillment: The Ordering of Early New England." *Early American Literature* 25, no. 2 (1990): 200–207.

Shurtleff, Nathaniel B., ed. *Records of the Governor and Company of the Massachusetts Bay in New England (1628–86).* 5 vols. Boston, 1853–54.

Simpson, Alan. *Puritanism in Old and New England.* Chicago: University of Chicago Press, 1955.

Slotkin, Richard. *Regeneration Through Violence: The Mythology of the American Frontier, 1600–1860.* Middletown, Conn.: Wesleyan University Press, 1973.

Slotkin, Richard, and James K. Folsom, eds. *So Dreadfull a Judgement: Puritan Responses to King Phillip's War, 1676–1677.* Middletown, Conn.: Wesleyan University Press, 1978.

Smedley, Audrey. *Race in North America: Origin and Evolution of a Worldview.* Boulder, Colo.: Westview, 1993.

Smith, Barbara. "Reply to Deborah Chay." *New Literary History* 24 (1993): 653–56.

Smith, Henry Nash. *Virgin Land: The American West as Symbol and Myth.* Cambridge, Mass.: Harvard University Press, 1950.

Smith, John. *The Complete Works of Captain John Smith.* 3 vols. Edited by Philip Barbour. Chapel Hill: University Press of North Carolina, 1986.

———. *The General Historie of Virginia, New-England, and the Summer Isles.* London, 1624.

Smits, David D. " "We Are Not to Grow Wild": Seventeenth-Century New England's Repudiation of Anglo-Indian Intermarriage." *American Indian Culture and Research Journal* 11 (1987): 1–32.

Snow, Dean R., and Kim M. Lamphear. "European Contact and Indian Depopulation in the Northeast: The Timing of the First Epidemics." *Ethnohistory* 35 (1988): 16–38.

Spengemann, William C. *A New World of Words: Redefining Early American Literature.* New Haven, Conn.: Yale University Press, 1994.

———. *A Mirror for Americanists: Reflections on the Idea of American Literature.* Hanover, N.H.: University Press of New England, 1989.

Stallybrass, Peter. "Shakespeare, the Individual, and the Text." In *Cultural Studies*, edited by Lawrence Grossberg, Cary Nelson, and Paula Treichler, 593–612. New York: Routledge, 1992.

———. "Patriarchal Territories: The Body Enclosed." In *Rewriting the Renaissance: The Discourses of Sexual Difference in Early Modern Europe*, edited by Margaret Ferguson, Maureen Quilligan, and Nancy J. Vickers, 123–42. Chicago: University of Chicago Press, 1986.

Stallybrass, Peter, and Allon White. *The Politics and Poetics of Transgression.* Ithaca, N.Y.: Cornell University Press, 1986.

Stanford, Ann. "Anne Bradstreet as a Meditative Writer." In *Critical Essays on Anne Bradstreet*, edited by Pattie Cowell and Ann Stanford, 89–96. Boston: G. K. Hall, 1983.

———. "Anne Bradstreet's Emblematic Garden." In *Critical Essays on Anne Bradstreet*, edited by Pattie Cowell and Ann Stanford, 238–53. Boston: G. K. Hall, 1983.

———. *Anne Bradstreet: The Worldly Puritan.* New York: Burt Franklin, 1974.

Steele, Ian. *Warpaths: Invasions of North America.* New York: Oxford University Press, 1994.

Stoever, William. *'A Faire and Easie Way to Heaven': Covenant Theology and Antinomianism in Early Massachusetts.* Middletown, Conn.: Wesleyan University Press, 1978.

Stout, Harry S. *The New England Soul: Preaching and Religious Culture in Colonial New England.* New York: Oxford University Press, 1987.

Strong, Roy C. *The Cult of Elizabeth: Elizabethan Portraiture and Pageantry.* London : Thames & Hudson, 1977.

Sullivan, Garrett. "Staging Space: The Theatre and Social Relations in Early Modern England." Ph.D. diss., Brown University, 1995.

Sweet, Timothy. "Gender, Genre, and Subjectivity in Bradstreet's Early Elegies." *Early American Literature* 23 (1988): 152–74.

Tawney, R. H. *Religion and the Rise of Capitalism: A Historical Study.* New York: Harcourt, Brace, 1926.

Tennenhouse, Leonard. *Power on Display: The Politics of Shakespeare's Genres.* New York: Methuen, 1986.

Thornton, Russell. *American Indian Holocaust and Survival: A Population History since 1492.* Norman: University of Oklahoma Press, 1987.

Tichi, Cecelia. "Introduction." In *The Present State of New England, Being a Narrative of the Troubles with the Indians, 1677.* Facsimile Reprod., Bainbridge, New York: York Mail-Print, 1972.

Tobin, Lad. "A Radically Different Voice: Gender and Language in the Trials of Anne Hutchinson." *Early American Literature* 25 (1990): 253–70.

Tompkins, Jane. "'Indians': Textualism, Morality, and the Problem of History." In *'Race,' Writing, and Difference*, edited by Henry Louis Gates Jr., 59–77. Chicago: University of Chicago Press, 1986.

———. *Sensational Designs: The Cultural Work of American Fiction, 1790–1860*. New York: Oxford University Press, 1985.

Turner, Bryan S. *The Body and Society: Explorations in Social Theory*. 2nd ed. London: Sage, 1996.

Turner, Frederick Jackson. *The Frontier in American History*. New York: Holt, 1920.

Ulrich, Laurel Thatcher. *Good Wives: Image and Reality in the Lives of Women in Northern New England, 1650–1750*. New York: Oxford University Press, 1982.

Underhill, John. *Newes from America; or, A New and Experimental Discoverie of New England*. London, 1638.

Vane, Henry. *A Brief Answer to a Certain Declaration*. London, 1637.

Vaughan, Alden T. *New England Frontier: Puritans and Indians, 1620–1675*. 3rd ed. Norman: University of Oklahoma Press, 1995.

———. *Roots of American Racism: Essays on the Colonial Experience*. New York: Oxford University Press, 1995.

———. "Introduction." In *New Englands Prospect*, edited by Alden T. Vaughan. Amherst: University of Massachusetts Press, 1993.

———. *American Genesis: Captain John Smith and the Founding of Virginia*. Boston: Little, Brown, 1975.

Vincent, Philip B. "A True Relation of The late Battell fought in New-England, between the English and the Pequet Salvages." In *Underhill, Vincent, Gardener and Mason's Pequot War*. Boston: Massachusetts Historical Society, 1837.

Walker, Cheryl. *The Nightingale's Burden: Women Poets and American Culture before 1900*. Bloomington: Indiana University Press, 1982.

Wallerstein, Immanuel. *The Modern World-System II: Mercantilism and the Consolidation of the European World-Economy, 1600–1750*. New York: Academic, 1980.

Warner, Michael. *The Letters of the Republic: Publication and the Public Sphere in Eighteenth-Century America*. Cambridge, Mass.: Harvard University Press, 1990.

Watts, Emily Stripe. *The Poetry of American Women from 1632–1945*. Austin: University of Texas Press, 1977.

Webb, Stephen Saunders. *1676: The End of American Independence*. New York: Knopf, 1984.

Weber, David J. *The Spanish Frontier in North America*. New Haven, Conn.: Yale University Press, 1992.

Weber, Donald. "Historicizing the Errand." *American Literary History* 2 (1990): 101–18.

Wheelwright, John. *The Writings of John Wheelwright*. 1876. Rpt. New York: Burt Franklin, 1968.

White, Elizabeth Wade. *Anne Bradstreet: The Tenth Muse*. New York: Oxford University Press, 1971.

White, John. *The Planters Plea or The Grounds of Plantations Examined, And usual Objections answered*. London: William Jones, 1630.

White, Peter. "Cannibals and Turks: Benjamin Tompson's Image of the Native American." In *Puritan Poets and Poetics: Seventeenth-Century American Poetry in Theory and Practice*, edited by Peter White, 198–209. University Park: Pennsylvania State University Press, 1985.

White, Peter, ed. *Puritan Poets and Poetics: Seventeenth-Century American Poetry in Theory and Practice*. University Park: Pennsylvania State University Press, 1985.

———. *Benjamin Tompson: Colonial Bard, A Critical Edition*. University Park, Pa., and London: Pennsylvania State University Press, 1980.

Wigglesworth, Michael. *The Diary of Michael Wigglesworth, 1653–1657: The Conscience of a Puritan*. Edited by Edmund Morgan. New York: Harper & Row, 1965.

Winslow, Edward. *Good Newes from New England*. 1624. In *Chronicles of the Pilgrim Fathers of the Colony of Plymouth from 1602–1625*, edited by Alexander Young. Boston: Charles C. Little & James Brown, 1841.

Winthrop, John. "A Modell of Christian Charity." 1630. *Old South Leaflets* No. 207, edited by Samuel Eliot Morrison. Boston: Old South Association, n.d.

———. "John Winthrop's Relation of His Religious Experience." In *Winthrop Papers*. Vol. 3. Boston: Massachusetts Historical Society, 1929–47.

———. *Winthrop's Journal: "History of New England," 1630–1649. Original Narratives of Early American History Series*, edited by James Kendall Hosmer. 2 vols. New York: Charles Scribner's Sons, 1908.

———. *A Short Story of the Rise, reign, and ruine of the Antinomians, Familists and Libertines*. London, 1644.

Wood, Gordon. "Struggle Over the Puritans." *New York Review of Books*, 9 November 1989, 26–34.

Wood, William. *New Englands Prospect*. 1634. Edited by Alden T. Vaughan. Amherst: University of Massachusetts Press, 1993.

———. *New Englands Prospect. A true, lively, and experimentall description of that part of America, commonly called New England: discovering the state of that Country, both as it stands to our new-come English Planters; and to the old Native inhabitants*. London, 1634.

Woodbridge, Linda. "Palisading the Elizabethan Body Politic." *Texas Studies in Literature and Language* 33 (1991): 327–54.

Wright, Nancy E. "Epitaphic Conventions and the Reception of Anne Bradstreet's Public Voice." *Early American Literature* 31 (1996): 243–63.

Wroth, Lawrence C. "Introduction." In *The Simple Cobbler of Aggawam of America*, i–vii. By Theodore de la Guard. New York: Scholars' Facsimiles & Reprints, 1937.

Zabelle Derounian, Kathryn. "'Mutuall Sweet Content': The Love Poetry of John Saffin." In *Puritan Poets and Poetics: Seventeenth-Century American Poetry in Theory and Practice*, edited by Peter White, 175–84. University Park, Pa., and London: Pennsylvania State University Press, 1985.

Ziff, Larzer. "Text and Context." *William and Mary Quarterly* 3rd ser., 45 (1988): 348–49.

———. *Puritanism in America: New Culture in a New World*. New York: Viking, 1973.

INDEX